#23

THE
EIGHTH
PROMISE

THE EIGHTH PROMISE

AN AMERICAN SON'S TRIBUTE
TO HIS TOISANESE MOTHER

WILLIAM POY LEE

RODALE

Rodale books may be purchased for business or promotional use or for special sales. For information, please write to: Special Markets Department, Rodale Inc., 733 Third Avenue, New York, NY 10017.

Printed in the United States of America
Rodale Inc. makes every effort to use acid-free ∞, recycled paper ♻.

Cover calligraphy by Master Er Cai Feng
Mother and child cover photograph courtesy of the Lee family

Book design by Chris Rhoads

Library of Congress Cataloging-in-Publication Data

Lee, William Poy, date
   The eighth promise : an American son's tribute to his Toisanese mother / by William Poy Lee.
       p.   cm.
   ISBN-13 978–1–59486–456–8 hardcover
   ISBN-10 1–59486–456–X hardcover
   1. Lee, William Poy, date   2. Lee, William Poy, date—Family.   3. Chinese Americans—Biography.   4. Mothers—United States—Biography.   5. Mothers and sons—Case studies.   6. Chinese Americans—Ethnic identity.   7. Taishan Shi (Guangdong Sheng, China)—Biography.   8. Taishan Shi (Guangdong Sheng, China)—Social life and customs.   I. Title.
   E184.C5L538 2007
   973'.049510092—dc22   2006029369
   [B]

Distributed to the trade by Holtzbrinck Publishers

2   4   6   8   10   9   7   5   3   1   hardcover

RODALE
LIVE YOUR WHOLE LIFE™

We inspire and enable people to improve their lives and the world around them
For more of our products visit rodalestore.com or call 800-848-4735

CONTENTS

Part IV
CHAOS UNDER HEAVEN (1972–1978)

Part V
RENEWAL (1979–1983)

EPILOGUE

ACKNOWLEDGMENTS

**To all my ancestors,
who lived well and wisely so we may be born**

To Alice Walker,
who mentored me in the art of writing . . . and of patience

To my editor, Leigh Haber,
for her prescience and wholehearted support

To my agent, Marly Rusoff,
for her energy and faith in this new writer

To my brother, Richard,
for allowing me to share part of his story

To my mother,
who loves her sons and all the children of the world

May you be happy, may you have endless joy, may you be free.

Ten Thousand Thanks

A RETURN TO THE VILLAGE

Suey Wan Chuen (水灣村) is the name of my ancestral village, a small, unchanged place in the Pearl River delta in China's semi-tropical southeast corner. Well, actually it's my ancestral village on Mother's side. Father's own village is quite nearby, but I don't ascribe ancestral village status to it, by far not. For as I look back on more than fifty years of living, I source my essence, for better, back to Mother's village. I have come to see and accept that it was my mother's earthbound spirituality, that of the Toisan (台山) Chinese people, that kept me safe, sound, and sane, especially through those tumultuous American decades of the 1960s and 1970s.

The journey back home was twisting, long, and almost never made. But oh, when I reached it, how invaluable it turned out to be.

Like so many Americans, I wittingly pushed my way forward in our restless, mobile, attention-scattering, and energy-zapping culture. All too many decisions were finance driven—the "right" college, mate, work, friends, place to live, and clothes to wear. It wasn't always so, but certainly during my midthirties to mid-forties, I was racing this marathon in overdrive. Perhaps not so surprisingly, after several decades of hitting the American marks of university and several professional milestones, I was pounding out that last lap toward the finish line to snatch the prize of financial freedom. This was my final burst of a frenzied, strategically focused workaholism that would pull it all together, a time I dubbed the "the brain sweat" decade.

And then I paused.

The year was 1995.

Actually, I came to a complete stop, a paralyzing, crackling, debris-filled breakout, as I departed business, home, and a fading love. I stayed stopped for more than a year as I considered whether there was more to my journey. I knew there was more, of course, and I knew I had previously lived with more dimensions of being and values, in ways that had been more personal, immeasurable, and profoundly enriching. Oh, how had I lost touch with those deeper places, spending an entire decade burying them with the shining, expensive, attention-getting, and excessive material marks of success?

Carefully, I took back my time, spending days walking beaches and state park trails, haunting bookstores, bicycling along San Francisco Bay to beneath the Golden Gate Bridge, and basically rethinking life. I made new friends, people like me, who, by choice or circumstance, were not only questioning but were ahead of me, redesigning meaning back into their lives.

And that's when I completely opened up to my ancient past in another land and culture, China, a place then still considered a struggling third-world economy recovering from the excesses of Mao's Cultural Revolution. This was not a Luddite romanticization of some pastoral, agricultural Shangri-la of self-sufficiency. If anything, it turned out to be a rediscovery of old ways, values, and, yes, tried-and-true wisdom of immense value to my modern American life. Having now integrated those lessons into my metropolitan lifestyle, what once was a daily, pulse-pounding, thigh-burning leg race to the finish line has morphed into a rhythmic glide—in the Zone, as it were—where I not only can smell the roses but also have time to plant a few, observe their stages of coming to blossom . . . and still complete the Tour d'Amerique race in the winner's circle.

I would suggest making this kind of internal journey to all Americans. It may well reward you with a level of wholeness and happiness still too elusive for far too many.

I slowly realized that I came from a wonderful beginning, even before I was born in San Francisco, from a people in an old, unmapped village located in the southeast corner of China. I rediscovered that I was born of ancestors who were farmers and lived not as individuals or the mobile nuclear family unit, not even just as an extended family, but as a Clan composed of many extended families in one village and of hundreds of people. They have lived and loved in one locale and harvested the same fields for a millennium or more. I had forgotten that place and the tried-and-true wisdom of that Clan culture. I reached back there, ever so slowly and carefully, for resuscitation, revival, and a critically transformed fresh start.

So where and what is Suey Wan, and how did I almost miss getting there? It is an innocuous farmers' village nestled among remote hills in the backwater heart of the fertile Pearl River delta of Guangdong Province, a village that is one of many within the six counties collectively known as Toisan (or *Taishan*, as it's pronounced in Mandarin, the official dialect of China). Toisan's origins are more legendary than historically established, but unquestionably, the first Chinese settlers arrived there around 1000 AD, fleeing the chaos of the declining decades of the once-expansive, culturally rich, and cosmopolitan T'ang Dynasty, hoping to find peace in this then-far-off corner of the Chinese empire.

And for a millennium, my forebears lived relatively unperturbed, rarely traveling farther than twenty miles away from their village. These farmers developed their own cuisine, honed their own farming methods, learned to resolve community problems without government interference, and eventually evolved their own version of the Cantonese dialect, the rustic, rough-sounding, and salty tongue of Toisanese.

In 1983, I was the first of my family to visit Suey Wan since 1949, when Chairman Mao Tse-tung's Communist armies prevailed over Generalissimo Chiang Kai-shek's Nationalist armies. The new government's quick imposition of a "bamboo curtain" around China terminated emigration abroad and access to returning migrants alike. That was why it was some thirty-four years after my mother fled to America before I, a Chinese American, was the first of my family to return. I did not expect much from this little village, which did not even have electricity or running water in the early 1980s, as I was soon to discover.

Even so, the Suey Wan visit was more an afterthought than the purpose of the trip, pinned on, so to speak, to the end of a five-week grand tour of China's width and breadth: hiking crumbling portions of the Great Walls, climbing verdant holy Buddhist Mount Emei to overnight in a still-practicing Buddhist monastery, and measuring myself against Xian's life-size terracotta warriors, to name just a few of the splendors. Standing transfixed before China's wonders, I questioned visiting Suey Wan, just another peasant village and one of millions dotting China. What did Suey Wan have to offer me beyond the obligation to pay my respects to unknown relatives, a vague promise I made to my mother before I left San Francisco that summer?

If I believed in signs, I might never have made it—and would have missed the most meaningful and richest part of my trip.

The first contrary sign was Mother herself, as she was against my going. Her family had fled Communist China when newly arrived cadres drove her older brother, a Western-educated man—just like me—to commit suicide by leaping off the family home's roof. She feared the same fate for me, but from my perch as an international banker and lawyer with Bank of America, I assured her that those times had changed.

During those final few days of my grand tour, I became concerned that for the first time in a month, I would be completely on my own. Mr. Wong, the senior China Travel Services (CTS) official who had smoothed all our travels throughout China, would not be there to solve travel glitches. Still he provided me with letters of introduction to my hotel (he had personally booked the reservation) and to the local CTS manager to ensure that I got to Suey Wan. But disturbingly, Mr. Wong's first letter of introduction proved ineffective, for after a great show of opening and slamming drawers, looking for my "lost" reservation, the night manager booked me into a poorly lit, humid dormitory for male travelers that was composed of several rows of wooden beds, each covered with a mosquito net and a high-school-gym-style common shower area that coughed up tepid water, too warm to relieve the humidity. I considered heading straight to Hong Kong at the crack of dawn to rejoin my traveling companions, more kin now than accidental colleagues, and dig into a T-bone steak laden with grilled onions and crisscrossed with ketchup, with a side of crispy *pommes frites*—inside an air-conditioned Sheraton Hotel.

Then, during my late-night stroll along the Pearl River, with radios secreted in the inky dark booming Hong Kong pop songs—a weird parody of Top 40 tunes eroding any chance of nocturnal tranquility—another bad sign reared up in the form of a young Cantonese couple who emerged out of nowhere and roundly cursed me out for nearly bumping into them. We hadn't even been that close to collision and a polite "Excuse us" would have warned me away. My traveling companions had warned me to expect harsh rudeness from Southerners.

All this brought back to mind the horror they had predicted, with their emphatic warnings of opportunistic Toisanese villagers fleecing returning American-born Chinese searching for their roots like me: relatives demanding gifts of TV sets, refrigerators, expensive watches, and stylish clothing; of vastly "extended" families running up large banquet bills, night after night, to celebrate the return of one of Toisan's own; and finally, playing off the guilt of having done well, of living free and easy in America while the home folks had suffered during Communist China's reconstruction into a modern nation, indelicately demanding hundreds, if not thousands of dollars, on the eve of their departure.

Even on the eve of this leg of the trip, the omens kept warning me away. But I stuck it out in true Toisan style when confronted with adversity. In the early morning, Mr. Wong's second letter of introduction proved effective. The young and amiable local manager, eyes wide open, recognizing Mr. Wong as the national second-in-command of CTS, immediately secured me a chauffeured private car at a good rate, one that would depart in an hour for Suey Wan. He then returned to the hotel with me, investigated the previous night's mishap with the day manager, and made sure that I would have my private, air-conditioned room with bath upon my return in three days (I did!).

So, I was finally on my way—sort of. An obstacle course blocked our transit—the scores of construction sites and traffic jams of a miserably smoggy and dusty industrial metropolis that was clumsily enduring a curse of endless redevelopment projects. Eventually, we reached the clean countryside and cruised along a two-lane tarmacadam road, past green landscapes filled with men and women farmers, faces brown from the sun, some working their fields while others bicycled to market, precariously balancing baskets of vegetables, trussed pigs, or caged chickens across their handlebars and rear tires. There was also, of course, the occasional child ubiquitously and delicately astride the back of a muscular, horned water buffalo.

All very charming, but in previous weeks, I had come to tolerate these farmscapes—to be sure, quite picturesque—as time-consuming but necessary passages to the world-class cultural treasures of China, that is, the China worth seeing. Only today I wasn't heading toward any place arising to the level of a destination. While not exactly heading into the heart of darkness by any means, I was certainly struggling upstream toward an unmapped, tangential backwater of the nondescript and wondering about my sanity the whole way.

In truth, it took many more hours and much patience to get to Toisan, even if there was no "there" there. Without air-conditioning in the car, the heat and humidity increased as the morning turned into noon. My hired driver and I stood in the sun for long stretches while waiting for the slow flatbed ferries to transport us across each of three rivers blocking my path to Suey Wan. With the not-so-subtle gesture of brushing his waxed car with a handkerchief, he warned curious passengers away from touching this rarity—a private automobile. The only other sign of modernity was a beat-up, light-blue Mitsubishi tractor, more the size of a well-off child's battery-run toy than a full-size John Deere, a machine that could run on practically any fuel, including, my driver informed me, the peanut oil my mother cooked with. At some point, the driver decided it was time for lunch (a mini banquet for two that I paid for, of course) and selected a restaurant that was unexpectedly nicely appointed and air-conditioned, given our location in China's countryside. But fine cuisine is a first and foremost necessity for Cantonese, and of course a three-star establishment could be found even on the way to Toisan.

Late in the afternoon, we reached my first destination, the small town of Hoisin (台 城), the only town in this region of rice paddies, vegetable fields, low hills, and farming villages.

Auntie Kow Woon lived here. With my mother's handwritten address in hand, my driver easily found her quite modern, apartment-style, two-story home with a balcony.

Auntie Kow Woon came out and immediately broke into a never-ending smile. She touched my arms and shoulders, pinched me again and again as if to convince herself that I was really in front of her. In no time at all, she began chatting merrily, then introduced me to an old childhood friend of my mother's, Hung Yick, the town postman. To my surprise, Hung Yick was loud, boisterous, and opinionated, far different from the mostly quiet and reserved Chinese I knew in America. Within minutes, he and Auntie Kow Woon were laughing out loud, moving and gesturing as if they owned the streets. Well, they did own the streets in a way that Chinese Americans of my father's generation and generations before did not, grimly and quietly knowing that other Americans—white Americans—owned the streets of San Francisco. In the America of my father's youth, Chinese Americans walked with terror, their eyes averted, stealthy like shadows, and quickly scampered around white Americans to avoid the glares, cussing, and inevitable violence of the everyday enforcers of America's racial caste system of the time.

But here I was deep in the homeland of my own people, marveling at my relatives' free and easy body language, as natural as that of any free people and so unlike the reserved, contracted bodies of many Chinese Americans, and, now that I could compare, a constriction obviously inflicted by our harsh historical experience.

And everyone spoke Toisanese as if it were the universal language of the world, the only language. Here, it felt that, by contrast, only those with a limited education were stuck with Big City Cantonese. As for those Mandarin speakers, well, they must be foreigners, official dialect of China or not.

Auntie Kow Woon and Hung Yick remarked on the purity of my tones, surprised not only that an American-born Chinese was able to speak any Chinese at all—as many did not—but also saying that I spoke like a native who had never left. It was because of Mother, I said, and that, to this day, that's the dialect we converse in.

Auntie Kow Woon and Hung Yick booked my driver and me into a local inn—small, clean, and quiet. Compared to the dormitory, my room was a welcome, cool comfort. In fact, compared to Guangzhou, the town of Hoisin resembled the old-time, pastoral Chinese villages in the Hong Kong movies of my youth: whitewashed, low-slung homes trimmed with reds and blues; long, tiled garden walls between portals; uncrowded streets whose townfolk frequently stopped to chat as they made their way through their day; naturalistically trimmed trees and blossoming flowerpots splashing their colors against earthen streets; and, oh, such a pacific quiet, free of speeding, honking traffic, radios blaring Hong Kong pop music, and unsolicited, rude Cantonese put-downs.

In this idyllic antiquity, I would not have been surprised to pass two young lovers bedecked in flowing silk gowns and elaborate royal headgear singing a high-pitched duet to the lyrical strumming of the two-stringed violinlike erhu in the background, or to have to duck down for a score of martial arts fighters cartwheeling from rooftops over our heads, fists slashing and legs whirling in an honorable duel to the death.

Over dinner at the inn's restaurant—simple, traditional dishes just like Mother's cooking—I explained to Auntie Kow Woon and Hung that I wanted to visit my mother's childhood house in Suey Wan, abandoned when everyone left for Hong Kong but maintained since by Hung Yick. I wanted to visit Father's village, his childhood house and a home now occupied by his childhood schoolteacher. I didn't even know the name of Father's village, but, of course, Auntie Kow Woon knew it and its exact location. Hung Yick had his postal rounds and couldn't join us, but he arranged a time to give Auntie Kow Woon the keys to my mother's childhood home.

Then, unexpectedly, Auntie Kow Woon picked up the check over my protests. I noted that they had ordered only a few dishes, not a lavish banquet. Amazingly, no large crowds of unknown extended family members had spontaneously appeared to "celebrate" my return. Nor had anyone hinted that they could use a new refrigerator or television.

So far, so good. Contrary to my traveling companions' well-meaning warnings, perhaps my relatives were different.

Early the next morning, after a night's rest so deep it made up for my restless night in Guangzhou, my driver drove Auntie and me to Suey Wan. I felt like an overseas Chinese tourist intruding into the daily movement of this ancient village, for I had not been able to announce my homecoming because telephone lines did not reach here. So I was happy when we had to park our car at a narrow pedestrian footbridge for a much more low-key hike in. My dapper driver declined our invitation to accompany us; ostensibly it was too "country" for a Big City Cantonese like him. Even Auntie Kow Woon said, "I never come here anymore, only for you," and then suddenly pressed a handkerchief against her nose as we rounded a bend into the uncompromising fragrance of an outhouse.

"I am definitely in the furthest realms of backcountry China now," I thought to myself, for the outhouse struck me as symbolic of a different sensibility. Not only was it the largest I'd seen in China, but it was shamelessly placed at the official footpath entrance as if to suggest that a toilet was the happiest welcome a village could offer a rustic traveler after such a long journey. Huge and freshly painted red characters screamed the location of the women's entrance at one end and the men's at the opposite end. "No shame about natural bodily processes here," I thought.

We then passed a simple temple, perhaps a pastoral traveler's second-most-desired facility, a place to give thanks for a safe journey. "Was this the temple of my parents' wedding?" I wondered. As we continued along the earthen footpath, the sun burned hot on my face, but here it was pleasant, not sticky, and I enjoyed the walk across clear fields of rice paddies crisscrossed by red-hued mud retaining walls. The green semitropical plants and the rich brown earth were suffused in iridescence, as in a French pointillist painting. The pristine air refreshed me. On three sides, forested hills cradled the distant, dusky-gray stone buildings of the village.

As we came closer, I saw a long row of houses, their doors facing south in order to catch the sun. A young girl carrying a bundle of reed grass walked to one house, then placed her bundle by the hearth fire visible on the other side of the open door. She started cooking the midday meal, alternately pushing the reed grass into the flames and tending the pots. She was dressed in wide black trousers and a traditional flowered blouse buttoned off her right shoulder.

At the end of this row of homes was a simple, unmarked open area that served as an informal village square. Adults squatted there in silence as children chased chickens and ducks pecked the ground for food. Auntie Kow Woon announced me to them by my Chinese name, Poy Jom, the son of Poy Jen, invoking my mother's maiden name.

No one had known I was coming. No one there had seen my mother in thirty-four years.

An elderly man looked up into my face, gazing briefly but directly into my eyes. "Yes," he announced. "You look exactly like your mother. Welcome home."

This man had not seen my mother in three and a half decades, yet he spoke as if he had seen her only yesterday. His words stripped away my outsider conceit. No longer the tourist, I began to pay attention, the kind of attention that shakes itself free of the broader but shallower passage through a typical day, that narrows and focuses like a laser beam, homing in on and then affixing itself to a clue that has just loudly announced itself—a vital, significant clue to a lifelong mystery, one that may have been unconsciously puzzling—until this moment.

After greeting me, this elder returned to his silence as the children continued their play and the ducks and chickens their running around. The other adults smiled, uttered short phrases of welcome, and then returned to their quiet and mysterious communion.

No one asked me how my mother and father or my mother's sisters and brother were doing. No one asked about opportunities in America or whether I was rich. No one asked what I did for a living or whether I had come seeking a wife. The conversational politeness of Northern Chinese was absent, as was the town chatter of Auntie Kow Woon and Hung Yick, for on this day, she too sank into this reverie of silence. Yet the villagers' silence was not rude, nor were they uninterested in me, for their smiles were genuine and their welcomes sincere. They reminded me of monks, cruising silent in deepest meditation behind temple walls. But instead of being removed from the world, these Toisanese villagers were sitting smack-dab in the midst of their real lives.

So there we all were, with the ducks and chickens, caring not whether we were in China, America, or Burkina Faso. Everyone and everything appeared so changeless, so present. Sitting in the warm sun. Connected in silent companionship.

Life could be that simple.

Suddenly, my toes, my feet, and then all of my skin began tingling with some extraordinary energy. I started to effervesce, as if I were showering in bubbling champagne. Then I felt the energy move deeply inside me, like an underground stream surging through my chest, up my neck, and finally shooting out the top of my head. I felt like I would explode with joy, the deep, hearty joy of coming home. This was the joy of belonging, of being recognized and accepted fully, even though they hadn't met me before that day and hadn't known I was coming.

My state of mind snapped into a state of joyousness, a hilarious joy as my body bubbled like fresh-popped champagne, and I chuckled and laughed at every little thing. Then I sensed a living presence, some sort of power underneath the soil of the village, like a gargantuan mother-root bulb, thriving and streaming Toisan Ch'i essence into me, so that wherever I may call home, I am still just one of her many shoots, and she will always replenish me.

Was this a spiritual or mystical experience? I don't remember any traces of religiosity to any of this, just that my two legs were firmly planted upon my Clan's homeland—the tuning fork of my being and spirit—and I was feeling just so completely right.

PART I

SOURCE

(1930–1950)

CHAPTER 1

ONE STORY, TWO VOICES

That first visit to Toisan in 1983 turned out to be the keystone of a slow reintegration of self. Until that day, I had always felt as if I had been dropped out of the sky, birthed one perplexing day in America, focused exclusively on an American future that was unconnected to my parents' past. That was the first moment I realized that, even before my birth, I had a complete past and came from a complete people. Since then, like a sailing vessel retrofitted with a deep keel, I no longer feel so vulnerable to the shifting winds and the ebbing and rising of the currents of life.

Within the sensibility of America's mobile lifestyle, I think that few of us appreciate the power of place or how place molds a people's character. So many questions have jumped out from that day: What creates the resonance of a place and its people? What makes Toisan people so, well, so Toisanese? I know that Hawaiians speak of the *mana*, their individual soul force that is so inextricably connected to and dependent on their *aina*, or homeland, that when deprived of their own land, their mana suffers. I had read that for countless millennia, Australian aborigines have trekked the mysterious song lines of their own ancient land in rites of initiation into adulthood, of stepping fully into their way of life. Had the demands and bounty of Toisan similarly forged something so unique, a *terroir* of personality and character?

But it was nearly two decades after that 1983 visit before I recognized my mother was the connecting link to Toisan. Responding then to an inner call to write—first short stories, then reflective essays, and finally this memoir—I eventually asked Mother whether I could interview her and audiotape our conversations. Mother was initially hesitant, genuinely self-deprecating even. "What does a simple woman like me have to say?" she asked.

"Probably a lot, but why don't we try it and find out?" I responded, and she agreed to at least a couple of sessions. The first one took place in my writing studio in my Berkeley home, when she and Father slept over one weekend. It went well, and eventually we recorded thirty-plus hours of her remembrances of her Toisanese upbringing—a way of life relatively unchanged for a millennium—and how and why she sought to preserve this sensibility in America. That's when I began to discern the quiet but key role she had played in my upbringing, for as children, my brother Richard, younger by two years, and I had resisted her. She had succeeded after all in keeping us rooted in the Toisanese ways.

Over the course of these interviews, I came to understand that this connection to the land and ways of Toisan was the source of power that helped my brother Richard and me to retain our strength of character, the moral compass that kept us both on track. This is why we were able, during our bleakest hours through the social upheavals of the 1960s and 1970s and in our roles in a desperate power struggle in our community of Chinatown, San Francisco, to ultimately eschew the violence of retribution as an instrument of change and justice.

Realizing this, I finally understood that when my mother had admonished me to "stay Chinese," she wasn't telling me to learn the facts of Chinese history or the lineage of the outrageous emperors whose Great Walls can be seen from the moon. In any case, my peasant-farmer mother wasn't that well versed in Chinese history and culture. Except for her free Chinatown bank calendars, my mother's own home was entirely devoid of art. Nor was Mother asking me to subscribe to an ethnic or nationalistic sense of superiority, for she never taught us to consider ourselves superior or to look down on any other race.

In truth, my mother didn't know much about any of those things; she was a simple daughter of the earth. For her, to "stay Chinese" meant to retain, nurture, and pass on the virtues of intuitive cooperation and recognition of the humanity of others that are embodied in the ways of the Toisanese people. She meant for me to internalize the strength, flexibility, and pragmatism of a people who lived within the cycles, embracing both the abundance and the fickleness of nature. She wanted me to recognize myself as a child of Toisan.

I know now that Mother's story leads into my story and, in fact, preordained many of my life choices. So I share this memoir with her. That is why alternating chapters are her own, in her voice, translated from those audio recordings. Mother's chapters are italicized to clearly mark her voice—of how she lived her life, loved her two men, and raised her three sons—even though, because Toisanese is her lifelong exclusive tongue, I am entrusted, as son and author, to capture that voice and project her personality onto these pages.

My own chapters remain in plain text. While my narrations of many of the key conversations and scenes of her upbringing in Toisan and early life in America are mostly based on our taped conversations, her story is complemented and confirmed by interviews with her two younger sisters and a brother who now live in America and with those village Clan Sisters among whom I was raised in San Francisco. I also interviewed her Clan Sisters in Toisan, first in 1983 and then again in 2001.

This is the story of how my mother transmitted Toisanese ways to me even as I occupied myself with becoming completely American. Of how those Toisanese ways helped us to navigate the personal tragedy that tore through our family in the early 1970s.

This is the story of my mother as my greatest wisdom teacher, who ensured that I received the best of my Toisanese heritage, the story of how my mother's Eighth Promise kept the ways of Toisan strong within us through life's ten thousand joys and ten thousand sorrows.

CHAPTER 2

ANCESTRAL HOME

I was born on May 26, 1928. My parents named me Poy Jen (陳 佩 貞). *My name means "one who deflects negative events and generates positive outcomes." It means that when misfortune dislodges our family, I am the one who returns us to the center and keeps us centered.*

I am a direct descendant of the first families who settled in our village one thousand years ago. Suey Wan is the name of our village, and it is a thriving village to this day. We still have a house there. It has sat empty for fifty years, awaiting our family's return. We are a Chun Clan village, and so my maiden name is Chun. Your father was born and raised in a nearby Lee Clan village, before he left for America at the age of thirteen. Years later, he came back to marry me.

We were farmers, and we came from somewhere else in Northern China about one thousand years ago. We are people of the T'ang Dynasty. That's why we still call ourselves T'ang Ren *or, as we say it in Toisanese,* H'ong Ngeen—*people of the T'ang. Our soil was* how sek—*rich and wet, for Toisan is in the Pearl River delta. Water so shiny you have to squint to see it. Our village faced a large paddy where we grew rice and other crops for market. All of us helped with farming, even the kids. Together, we prepared the fields, fixed the mud walls, planted, fertilized, and harvested. Every family raised their own vegetables in their private garden patch. Cabbage, scallions, bok choy, mustard greens, lettuce—so many vegetables. Fruit trees grew in yards throughout the village, for the weather was hot and moist for most of the year. Oh, so many kinds* of fruit trees—red apples, bananas, plums, peaches, and many, many more.

Our hills were full of trees that we used for building houses, wheelbarrows, plows, and furniture. Our water came from a village well. Deliciously cold, clean, and sweet water. When I was old enough, the first thing I did every morning was to fill two pails and carry them home. This kind of life makes you strong. Even today, I am strong. Until a few years ago, I still could carry a twenty-five-pound bag of rice several blocks from the store to our home.

Chickens and ducks ran freely through the village. "Gop, gop, gop," pecking away at this and that. We ate them or sold them. Many families raised pigs for market. We didn't raise pigs—uggghh—too stinky and messy.

Instead, we raised fish in the village fishpond for eating and for market. As kids, we played in the fishpond. We weren't supposed to because none of us could swim. But we liked catching tiny fishes. With my younger sisters, Tien and Yoong, and our girlfriends, like Kow Woon, we would sit on our heels and, with tiny nets, catch baby fish. Hslout, hslout, hslout was the sound of the fishes squirming in our hands and flapping on the ground. "Ha, ha, ha," we laughed so much. We always got a little wet, but the sun dried us off before we got in trouble with Mother. Then we put the fish into a bowl and played with them for days.

Every few months, village men dropped nets in the water to catch fish for market. We chased after the fishes that flipped free, flopping all over the ground. We'd grab one or two for dinner. The men scolded us, "Eating money instead of putting it in your pocket!" as we ran off, half-closing our eyes as the fish thrashed, splashing water all over our faces. But no one really minded a few fish being taken. Especially for Chinese New Year or a wedding.

Life was not easy in the village like it is in America. Farmers worked constantly. Sweating and breathing hard. Worried all the time about enough rain and sun, daily checking for insects and rats that ate our crops. Our clothes were patched over and used until *they fell completely apart. But still, we had lots more time to relax, to chat with one another, and to play. Once everything was done, it was done. You can't make the crops grow any faster by acting busy.*

Life was simpler in the village in that way and safer—that is, until the Japanese army attacked us.

CHAPTER 3

THE BUTTERFLIES OF DEATH

It was 1938, and I wish my mother could tell you herself about that tragic first day and then of the near-fatal events of the second day, recounted at the end of this chapter. But my mother does not believe in revealing the sorrows in her life. She says it kills the spirit to recite bad times. Brings the bad times back. She says I should focus on the positive, look ahead, think good thoughts no matter what happens, and the future will be happy. I've pressed Mother, but except for a few grunts of acknowledgment that "yes, something like that happened," she goes no further. I've used my best trial lawyer's techniques to corner her, including relentless "yes or no" cross-examinations. But Mother waves her hand like a judge, easily vanquishing this irrelevant line of inquiry.

So I must fill in the gaps for her and tell the stories of the sorrows in her life. I do so in order to understand her and the nature of her gifts to me. To uncover this particular story, I have interviewed my father, who is more Americanized and thus more forthcoming. I have also spoken with several Clan Sisters who live in San Francisco and with relatives in the village who knew Mother as a child. Her two sisters and brother, San Franciscans too, are like her—they haven't been very helpful. Besides, they don't understand me, and, because of that, they don't think particularly well of me. To them, I am the lawyer who irresponsibly decided to become a struggling writer. I am the successful businessman who thinks that while making money is okay, it is not the primary reason for living.

I should explain that my mother is not afraid of hearing bad news or of facing hard times. Nor is she afraid of tackling the sorrows of life on their own terms. Quite the contrary. She speaks her mind clearly, loudly, and emotionally when she is unhappy. She wraps her arms around unhappiness in a bear hug. Then slowly, steadily, and with great care, she turns misfortune around, one problem at a time, one day at a time. Perhaps it was this first near-death experience as a girl that taught her that tragedy could be averted or, if unavoidable, turned around.

That morning in 1938 was the first time a Japanese Zero fighter plane attacked Mother's village. No one had actually seen an airplane before, so no Toisanese warning shout was issued.

That first plane flew low over the old village—a clutch of cottages of no strategic importance. It was the *woo-woo-woo* sound of the plane that caught the children's attention. Curious, they rushed out of their classrooms, jumping up and down and scanning the skies. Parents soon joined them outside their homes, shading their eyes with their hands as they too looked into the sky in the direction of the *woo-woo-woo* sound.

The Zero's pilot discharged its machine guns, raking the ground toward the schoolchildren. The bullets were red and orange, arcing down through the air, bouncing along the play fields. The children thought the red and orange bullets were butterflies. They ran closer to catch them. "Butterflies, butterflies," they gleefully shouted. Suddenly their laughter twisted into screams of agony. Children fell everywhere, shrieking. Blood spread and gathered in pools. Then the bombs fell into the crowds of confused adults and onto the row of houses.

Thereafter, whenever the sound of *woo-woo-woo* was heard, the villagers would cry, "Run and hide. The butterflies of death. The butterflies of death are coming."

Kow Woon's family was killed that day. In the way of the village Clan system, there were no orphans. Grandmother Chun adopted Kow Woon as her own child, simply declaring that she was now Kow Woon's mother. Compassion meant that no child was ever homeless, and if Grandmother Chun was known for anything, it was for her compassion.

Years later, on a singularly stormy day in 1942, at the height of the Japanese invasion of China, the specter of death came again. In expanding their occupation of China, the Japanese war machine persisted in indiscriminately slaughtering the unarmed peasants of China. It was part of a brutal, inhumane strategy of genocide designed to break the will of the people and enslave them. All too well known were the tales of captured young teenage girls and young women, raped, tortured, and murdered. Or worse, to be programmatically raped to death as sex slaves by entire units of men, euphemistically designated as "comfort women."

After the first few raids of the mid-1930s, the villagers devised a verbal alert system, and everyone would flee into the hills and hide until danger passed. They learned that for soldiers on foot, searching for the villagers was just too much work for a day's ration of rice and vegetables or even for the thrill of capturing fresh young girls.

This day, however, some villagers did not make it to the safety of the hills in time. The stranded included my grandmother, my mother, her two younger sisters, Yoong and Tien, and their adopted sister, Kow Woon. Perhaps the loud, hard rains had muffled earlier warnings, for not even the harsh sounds of hollered Toisanese syllables could pierce the deluge's clatter. Only too late had they heard the cries, "Japanese soldiers! Japanese soldiers! Run! Hide!" Grandmother Chun quickly hustled the girls outside, but then she realized they could not cross the rice paddies to reach the safety of the hills because the water was rapidly rising in the paddies.

Grandmother knew their only hope was to hide in an abandoned house situated on the outskirts of the village. The obviously fallen structure was far enough off the main footpath that maybe the soldiers might skip it. They'd see that the roof had fallen through, that the windows were broken and the wind and rain could blow through freely, and conclude that any food inside would be ruined. They'd notice that the inside was too cobwebbed and dirty for a hiding place. Yes, perhaps the Japanese soldiers would ignore it. That was their only hope.

My grandmother scooted the girls toward the house. Once inside, she found a hiding place amid a large pile of reeds used for cooking fires that was stored in a shadowy corner. She pulled aside the tied bundles of long reed grass, shooed her four girls onto the floor, and piled the reeds on top, making a womblike cave that was big enough to hide all of them, including herself. She carefully tucked in their little feet and hands, crawled in, and then spread her arms over the girls, two on each side, like a mother hen.

Through the sound of the pouring rain, they heard the soldiers' advance. Their boots beat toward them—*bawk, bawk, bawk*. Yelling loudly in Japanese, they kicked down the partially rotted front door, yanking open doors to bedrooms, closets, and cupboards. They shouted what sounded like angry curses.

The girls and Grandmother huddled, frozen together, swallowing their terror.

A soldier trampled in their direction, reaching close to the stack of reeds. Soon, it would all be over. Maybe they would at least be spared bayonet practice. But just then someone outside shouted, and miraculously, the soldier stopped, muttered, and turned around. The soldiers stomped outside. Their voices died down, then the *bawk, bawk* rhythm faded into the cadence of the falling rain.

"Be quiet. Don't move. It could be a trick," Grandmother whispered carefully, keeping her arms over the four girls. They remained still for a long, long time. But the Japanese soldiers had indeed left, and they were safe.

Grandmother's quick thinking had saved them all; they would live another season. "Ten thousand joys and ten thousand sorrows—this is the promise of life," she undoubtedly muttered to herself as she thanked Kuan Yin, the bodhisattva of compassion who aids all beings who are suffering.

CHAPTER 4

THE CLAN SISTERHOOD

The most important thing a Toisanese girl learns is this: that all the females of our village are hung dee moy, *Clan Sisters. It doesn't matter if you were born in another village, like a Lee- or Wong-surnamed village, and married a Chun man. A wife automatically becomes a Chun Clan Sister once she moves into her husband's house and is treated by the Sisterhood as if she had been born in the village. It also doesn't matter if you marry and move to another village—you remain a Chun Clan Sister.*

The Clan Sisterhood is like your best friend for life. We're a family that will always welcome you no matter what. We're a huge women's club, so you always have friends to drink tea with, share gossip with, and babysit for you. A Clan Sister will always help you no matter where you are, no matter what you do. We raise each other's children as our own and teach them the good things, which are to know right from wrong, study hard, respect everyone, save money, and help take care of the family. The Clan Sisterhood has been a big part of my life. Perhaps you've noticed that my Clan Sisters have always been involved in your life?

That's why when someone I have never met is introduced to me as hung dee moy—*Clan Sister—I immediately give her the same respect, assistance, and affection I would to a hung dee moy I was raised with. I would help a new sister in any way I can.*

In Toisanese, hung dee moy *collectively means all sisters together, or in its singular form, a sister of our village Clan, as in "she is hung dee moy." Hung dee moy can also be a title, like aunt or niece or grandmother. That's why, when you sometimes ask me who was that lady we just met, I say "She is hung dee moy" instead of "my aunt" or "elder" or "friend." The younger sisters call the adults "yee-yee," or Auntie. Aunties call the younger ones "moy-moy," or Little Sister.*

To understand the workings of the Clan Sisterhood, you have to understand a few things about our village, like our customs, our daily life, and how we were organized. There was a lot to do every day because we were on our own. There was no government to provide social assistance, regulations, or emergency services. But we got things done—all of it, without repair shops to call to fix broken things, like in America. But broken tools got fixed, leaking roofs replaced, and aging levees repaired. We even built our own grammar school.

There were no college-educated experts telling us how to farm or build canals and levees, like in America. Yet we fed ourselves and made money by selling vegetables, rice, chickens, pigs, beef, and even fish to the towns. And hundreds of years ago, we built a canal that connected us to Guangzhou. We built levee walls for each village all along the way. Over the centuries, the widest boats traveled to Guangzhou, Hong Kong, and back. That's why Toisan people are all over the world—the canal took us to the sea. The canal is there today, still being used. When you drive from Hoisin to the village, you can still see it along the road.

To get it all done, men and women had separate jobs. That's how the village was divided, by our jobs. This has been so for many centuries, and so the Clan Sisterhood started to meet and talk, to do things better and better each year. The men had a Clan Brotherhood, but you'll have to talk to your father about that. Better yet, talk to my younger brother, your uncle Wah. I can only talk about the Clan Sisterhood.

I am telling you all this so you can see that even though we were farmers in a village that's not even on a map, we were smart people and good to each other. You think we could have lasted one thousand years if we weren't smart people? Famine, flood, sickness, bandits, and the Japanese war? You think we could go through all those hard times together if we didn't treat each other well, no matter how bitter life was?

The Clan Sisterhood had special knowledge that men did not. Elder Clan Sisters cooked herbal medicinal soups to heal illnesses. Mothers cooked season-change herbal soups to adjust their children's Ch'i levels so they wouldn't catch cold when the chilly north wind swept far south into our village. Aunties spent hours preparing the Ch'i energy soups for a new mother during her postpartum rejuvenation.

Each generation of younger Clan Sisters learned the older generations' knowledge and then added on. So you see, the Clan Sisterhood was like a college for women. We taught one another what we had to know, passing on women's expertise and wisdom, generation after generation.

Women had to know how to plant different types of crops, how much to water each plant and when. Men were not the only ones farming! Szooon, szooon, szooon—plant by plant, we checked the stalks in the mud and water. Women knew how to harvest the crop, how to separate the grain from the husks. Women tended the vegetable gardens, protected them against insects and rats, and picked the vegetables at the best time to eat. Green, sweet, and crunchy! Tawk-tawk-tuie—that's the noise vegetables should make when you eat them. Women preserved food, like salted fish, fatback pork, sun-dried oily duck, sausages, dried vegetables, and dried fruits. Women even raised chickens, pigs, and fish for market.

At the age of six, I was raising the chickens for our family, and I was good at it. Every morning, I fed them rice husks and vegetable leaves. "Gawk, gawk, gawk, gawk," they said as they ran down from the chicken coop. That's the best food to feed them so that they grow sweet to the taste. These were real chickens, not like the US kind with chemical injections to make them look tasty. Even my hens tasted good after they stopped laying eggs. My chickens ran around all day and at night jumped back into the coop all by themselves. I counted them to be sure, and if any didn't make it home, I went out in the dark, held my thumb and index finger over my lips,

and called to them, "Ject, ject, ject." Wherever they were sleeping,
like leaning against a corner or lying under a bush, they'd recog-
nize my voice and wobble out to me, very sleepy-headed. Easy to
carry, about a foot tall when full grown. Always found them—
nobody stole anyone else's chicken.

And women ran the household for the entire family. Cooked
everyone's favorite foods all the time and all the special dishes of
Chinese New Year and the Harvest Moon Festival. Women raised
the children. Toisanese believe that mothers must raise their own
children; that's what mothers have to do if you want happy children.
Yes, no matter how busy we were in the fields, we saw them several
times each day, even if we had to walk fast back and forth, back and
forth. Kept them healthy and taught them manners. Tutored them in
Chinese, history, math, and the Three Principles of Democracy. I
mean, it seems sometimes that women did everything.

I was already working when I was five years old. Started early
every morning. Got two pails of water from the well. Cut reeds for
the cooking fire. Checked plants in the paddies to make sure there
were no snails. Sometimes it was so cold my hands would be numb
from sticking them into the paddies, and my breath would blow out
like smoke. Phoo, phoo, phoo—*I blew into my hands to keep them*
warm. Bum, bum, bum—*I jumped up and down to warm up.*

I tended the vegetables in our garden plot and carried them
home to cook. As I got older, I learned when a chicken was best for
eating and when it was too old, how to defeather and cut the
chicken, and how to cook it so the skin was chewy, the meat juicy,
and the inside of the bones still red.

The Clan Sisterhood—that's teaching by working together, not
through books. Oh, girls went to school too, for about six years.
But that was to learn how to read and write Chinese, add and sub-
tract, and learn a little Chinese history. We studied Sun Yat-sen,
because he was Cantonese like us. We celebrated his democratic
revolution of 1911, which ended the imperial system, every year on
October 10, or "Ten-Ten Day." We memorized his Three Principles

of Democracy, ideas he got from America. But only some really smart men kept going to school. Like my oldest brother who became a schoolteacher.

Over the centuries, the Clan Sisterhood developed a special way of making decisions, the speaking-round-and-round. This speaking-round-and-round is not like gossiping or socializing. That's more like "ji-ji-ja-ja . . . ji-ji-ja-ja . . . "—everyone talking at the same time. But when a speaking began, everyone quieted down. Each person could speak, and no one would interrupt until she was finished. This was part of everything we did. Before we planted the new crop, we gathered in a speaking-round-and-round. Before we built a new house, we met in a speaking-round-and-round. Before we helped a mother give birth, we assessed any health dangers and assigned duties in a speaking-round-and-round.

Actually, in Toisanese, we call it "Gong loi, gong huie," or "speech coming and speech going." But I think you American-born would understand it better as speaking-round-and-round because it's not like arguing back and forth like how lawyers do it. You know what I mean; you're a lawyer. We stand in a circle and take turns listening until we understand the situation.

The Clan Sisterhood solved many village disputes using this way. There were no courts to settle matters and no sheriffs to enforce the right thing to do. Everyone who wanted to could get involved. This had to be done without taking sides, even if one party was a stinky, rotten rind. The solution had to be fair for each party to accept the solution. You see, we couldn't have someone so unhappy they wouldn't work with someone else. There was always some task that needed everyone's help—flood repair, seeding, harvest time, or fixing a roof. In this way, the speaking-round-and-round kept us united and cooperating as one village.

So this was how I was raised and taught, surrounded by women of all ages from many villages. Watching and learning from their deliberations. Knowing what to do by helping out with my own hands. Self-reliance, acting for the common good over one's own *needs. Finding common ground and crafting solutions when there were problems.*

From them, I not only learned to cook meals, but the recipes for the medicinal Ch'i soups and how to gather herbs and heat them up for poultices to cure sprained ankles and wrists and bruised muscles.

Finally, one of the most important jobs left to the Clan Sisterhood was to ensure the future of the village by finding a husband for each Little Sister—hopefully, a kind man. Every Sister wanted a say, but you wouldn't bring everyone to the first meeting between the prospective bride and groom and their families. Only the elder Aunties went, the ones who were good at sizing up a man. The Little Sisters could meet him later, if he was acceptable to the Aunties.

Like with your father, the first time we met, before we became engaged.

CHAPTER 5

GO-BETWEEN MAN

In 1948, a go-between arranged a marriage between Poy Jen and a young Toisanese American man named Fook Toon Lee. Traditionally, China had never subscribed to the romantic ideal of marriage. Marriage was a group decision, decided upon by the families of the prospective bride and groom and, in the case of Toisanese villagers, with the communal consent of their respective village Clan Sisterhoods. Within their cloistered farmers' lives, Toisanese families were typically oblivious of the identities of young men and women coming of age even in nearby villages. Many hired professional marriage brokers to scout out the best marriage prospects. Others entrusted discerning villagers who were lifelong friends of the family or who worked in professions or trades that exposed them to the children of many villages. These individuals were not full-time marriage brokers, but more like skilled go-betweens with successful track records of matches. So Fook Toon's mother, who was still in Toisan, hired his childhood grammar school teacher, a member of the Lee Clan village who knew him well, as a go-between to identify a suitable bride.

Fook Toon was born in the Lee Clan village, mere miles from Suey Wan, on November 14, 1922. He was summoned to America at the age of thirteen by his father, a US citizen who lived in Chinatown, San Francisco. In 1948, when the go-between reported that he had identified three bridal prospects—Poy Jen being one of them—Fook Toon was twenty-six and Poy Jen was twenty. Fook Toon and Poy Jen had never met each other.

The go-between's biographical sketch of Fook Toon's life

gave Poy Jen's mother assurance that he could be a good match for her first and favorite daughter. He told her that he had taught him as a child, Fook Toon had been a good student, bright and eager to learn, that Fook Toon loved writing poetry. Even at that young age, he had achieved a level in classical poetry equal to that of scholars from wealthy families.

The go-between recited Fook Toon's intentions: He wanted to marry and raise a family, but they would be raised in America, not China. Having emigrated to America as a boy, he returned as a successful adult only to seek his bride. Fook Toon must be well off, for how else could he afford to travel back and forth across the Pacific to find a bride instead of doing what poorer men did, exchanging photos and letters?

What a go-between really knows versus what he chooses to portray is often a more idealized version of the starker truth. So, in this way, even arranged marriages don't seem so different from the romantic process in that each party puts her or his best foot forward during the mating dance, and, similarly, one often sees what one needs to see, with the harsher traits oftentimes diminished in significance and left to be worked out later.

In truth, Fook Toon's father had summarily ordered Fook Toon to join him in San Francisco in 1935. He had not sentimentally requested his presence because he missed him, out of fatherly love, or wanted to successfully wean him into American society. But at the age of thirteen, Fook Toon did not question this summons. He was not only an obedient son, he was also alert enough to notice that there just weren't enough inheritable hectares of farmland for both him and his younger brother to each support a family. So he gladly left Toisan for America, or *Geem San*, the Gold Mountain, the whispered promise of boundless wealth that lingered long after the California Gold Rush of 1849, when Chinese first arrived in California in large numbers. America was a new and strange land with a language that Fook Toon did not speak. But he trusted that his father, whom he had not seen in years, had paved the way.

So, culturally and linguistically unprepared, the dutiful son unhesitatingly left on a huge ocean he had never seen before for a voyage of many weeks belowdecks in steerage class on a rusting ship that stopped en route only in Honolulu for fresh provisions.

Fook Toon, like most Chinese emigrants to America via the West Coast, was initially detained on Angel Island in San Francisco Bay, a West Coast Ellis Island that processed thousands of Chinese immigrants. This quarantine did not apply to non-Chinese immigrants, many of whom sailed directly into the port of San Francisco to be promptly dispatched by the Immigration and Naturalization Service (INS) onto the streets of San Francisco.

But the documents of many Chinese males claiming to be sons of US citizens, a priority preference for immigration and citizenship, were presumptively suspect as fraudulently obtained, and the INS devised very detailed tests to separate genuine claims from false ones. Depending upon your performance during the oral examination, detention on Angel Island could be as short as a week, up to several months, and occasionally eighteen months or longer.

Why this draconian test? For decades, the era's anti-Chinese exclusion legislation severely limited the number of Chinese migrants, and the few who were admitted had to be related by birth to American citizens. So, when San Francisco's great earthquake and fire of 1906 destroyed City Hall and all its birth records, the Chinatown community seized the opportunity to claim mythical sons and reregister their apocryphal births at the new City Hall. These newly minted fathers then sold these false birth certificates for huge profits throughout the Pearl River delta. Their numerous counterfeit sons came to be known as *mai jee loi*, or "paper sons."

In response, the INS devised tests to determine the authenticity of a son and, in some cases, of a daughter. In order to do so, they obtained maps of the main Toisan villages, the names of neighboring families, several generations of relationships by name, and other detailed information that only a genuine offspring could know. A male who did not know the layout of the village of origin of his father was deemed a paper son and could be deported, as could any male who did not know relatives by name for several generations. Thus, the test had unintended and cruel consequences: Often even legitimate children could fail, for the questions were frequently based on information that was old or poorly reconstructed, mistranslated, or misunderstood by the interrogator, to the horror of the genuine offspring.

Every Chinese immigrant had to pass this very detailed and tricky test. Fook Toon knew from Toisanese who had been deported back to the village that the consequences of giving even one wrong answer could be devastating. On that first day on the island, he read bitterly worded calligraphy, carved on the barrack walls, that recited detentions of months on end, testing and testing until each test became a torture session. The result was devastating deportation back home without ever setting foot in San Francisco. Fook Toon encountered the broken spirits of several about to be sent back. He heard rumors of others who had thrown themselves overboard into the sea, preferring death to returning home in failure and shame.

For these reasons, Fook Toon had spent weeks studying the layout of his village's streets, memorizing everyone's complete formal name, and diagramming charts of everyone's relatives for three generations. He even obtained lists of questions and answers compiled from the memories of those who made it into America. He walked every lane of his village, memorized who lived next door to whom, when a particular building had been torn down, and when a new one replaced it. He drilled himself on even the most mundane details of his village's life and history, for any detail could end up meaning the difference between admission and deportation. The sinister reputation of the tests was so great that Father had sequestered crib sheets in an inside coat pocket to study in a secretive daily review in quiet corners of the ship. When he was less than three days out from San Francisco, he tore them up, tossing them into the wind so they could not be used against him in any way by the suspicious authorities, perhaps as evidence to accuse him of only memorizing the village layout, never having lived there in fact.

On his test day at Angel Island, Fook Toon passed completely. A few days later, he ferried over to San Francisco.

The go-between related all this to Poy Jen's mother to impress her with Fook Toon's persistence and planning. The chillier truth was that, within days of his arrival, instead of giving him a loving, fatherly welcome, Fook Toon's father immediately delivered him to a job as a live-in domestic, a houseboy, in the home of a well-to-do physician in wealthy Marin County, which was, within the racial caste system of the time, a completely white enclave just north of San Francisco. In his time, employing a live-in Chinese male domestic, or houseboy as they were then called regardless of age, was as common as having a Latino gardener is to our time. Despite Fook Toon's vulnerability as a thirteen-year-old who spoke only Toisanese, literally fresh off the farm and clueless about American society, his father treated him like an indentured servant and contracted him out into an alien suburb far from Chinese Americans. Moreover, for the first year, Fook Toon was unable to save any money because his father came knocking once a month, on payday, and took his cash. Eventually, he knew to hide a few dollars before the hour of that knock on the door.

The go-between continued, saying that Fook Toon diligently attended American school and learned to speak and write the American language. Truly, Fook Toon soon earned very good grades at the local middle school—his test scores often were higher than those of his American-born classmates, as one history teacher opined several times in an attempt to shame his native-born fellow students to do better. Yet, given the racial climate of the times, Fook Toon knew that prospects for a Chinese American immigrant in Marin were severely curtailed, if not downright nonexistent. Too, he grew tired of the endless cleaning up required to maintain a certain household immaculateness. It was often not until 10 p.m., when all his chores were finally done, that Fook Toon could study, and then he was often berated for using up the lightbulb and running up the electric bill. And the family's frequent Saturday night soirees kept him on duty for entire weekends: all day Saturday in preparation, all evening serving food and drinks, preliminary cleaning up into the wee hours, and a complete cleanup all day Sunday to make it look as if there had never been a party.

So Fook Toon departed, giving up his chance at the superior high school education offered by Marin, one of the finest public school districts in the Bay Area, whose graduates typically matriculated into America's best universities. When he informed his employer of this decision, the physician sardonically responded, "I knew you would quit," which Fook Toon construed as revealing a not-so-hidden agenda. The doctor had intentionally worked him hard so as to discourage him from staying on in Marin and to close the doors that might have opened for him had he finished high school there.

Whatever the factors, Fook Toon had decided to move on, so he headed for Southern California with its demand for migrant farmworkers and its location too far away for his father to take his cash. He worked the bountiful Central Valley, and when the harvest season was over, he headed to Los Angeles and finally returned to San Francisco's Chinatown, only to find himself exploited by his own people, the Chinese restaurateurs. Double shifts, six and sometimes seven days a week. Low wages, and the owners kept the tips. He discovered that the Chinatown powers-that-be were completely complicit with this exploitation. In fact, they enforced it by busting unionization efforts, so he turned his back on Chinatown society. This system repulsed him because he had been raised in the communal sensibility of mutual fairness and cooperation. He understood now why his own father had so coldly exploited him—that was the way things were in China-town, and his father had lived there too long. Still, Fook Toon refused to work any other Chinatown jobs.

But diligent student Fook Toon, childhood classical poet, the one who had passed his Angel Island test on the first interroga-tion, had indeed learned to read and write American in his Marin County middle school and had done well enough and with a cer-tain glibness that he could join the restaurant workers' union. Equally important, he had not been culturally overwhelmed and isolated despite his hostile household load, but instead had learned invaluable social skills, especially how to get along with main-stream Americans. So Fook Toon found jobs with white-owned restaurants serving white customers, and the owners loved his uncomplaining diligence, clockwork attendance, and good-humored optimism. The union guaranteed him steady wages with paid vacations and a health plan; and with its grievance pro-cedure, it protected him from overtly unfair treatment and arbi-trary firings.

But the union also kept Chinese American men in second-tier jobs—as busboys, dishwashers, and backroom supply men. Typi-cally, union busboys eventually moved on to become waiters, but Chinese union men were not afforded this opportunity. As a union man, Fook Toon was safely employed, got his biweekly paycheck, and upon retirement would receive a nominal monthly pension and Social Security payments; but he would remain stuck in a lower-income bracket, unlikely ever to break into the middle class.

The go-between simply assured my grandmother that Fook Toon had a steady job with a regular paycheck—this was accurate as far as it went.

Grandmother Chun then asked whether Fook Toon sent remittances home to his mother. The go-between assured her he did so regularly. Besides, only those with cash and a future could return to Toisan to find a bride to take back to America. The go-between continued idealizing Fook Toon's attributes.

Grandmother Chun knew there were tens of thousands of unmarried Toisan men in America and very few eligible Toisan women. She fully understood the value of her first daughter as a bride for any Chinese American man. America had historically kept out Chinese women, granting visas only to Chinese men in order to exploit their cheap labor, then expecting them to return to China when they were old and physically spent. She knew of the antimiscegenation laws and customs against a Chinese American man marrying an American woman of another race.

Yes, she could afford to be selective, for there were a lot of lonely Toisan men in America, but not too selective, for Toisanese men coming home for a bride also became a way out of China for Toisan women, and many families now wanted their children out. Chinese society had been disintegrating for decades, a breakdown accelerated by the decade-long Japanese invasion. Now, in the fourth year of the civil war following the Japanese defeat, China was surly in its final stage of collapse. Who knew who would win—the Communists or the democratic Nationalists—but especially, who knew how the new China would turn out? Would this ancient sleeping dragon of a civilization continue to thrash about in death throes for several more decades? Or would it, like the other favored Chinese mythical creature with whom the dragon is often symbolically portrayed, the phoenix, arise from its ashes, reborn whole, singing life's song, and soaring into the new day?

No one knew. The future was at best uncertain.

My grandmother had proven herself a pragmatic, resilient woman, for after all, it was her quick thinking that had saved her children and Kow Woon on that noisy, stormy day when they were stranded during the Japanese raid. I finally met her in the mid-1960s, when she arrived in America. Then I had a chance to witness her undemanding kindness as she watched over everyone's comfort. She never corrected, only suggested. I can imagine her practical yet loving ruminations for her daughter.

I surmised that my grandmother surely must have thought

more about her daughter's future happiness than her own. Grandmother had survived the Japanese war, but I knew she had lost her husband, who was killed during a Japanese air raid in Burma when a bomb hit the laundry that he had started there to make money to send home. I knew that with her family active in the Nationalist party and her eldest son a Nationalist official, she understood that her immediate family was on the losing side of the civil war.

So in 1948, my pragmatic and flexible grandmother decided that the wisest course was to marry off her favorite daughter, her first-born daughter, Poy Jen, not to a local suitor, but to a Toisanese American, as a way out to America, where she would be safe. Poy Jen would then be a bridge for her family, finding Toisanese American husbands for all her sisters—Yoong, her second daughter, to be followed by Tien, her third daughter, and even Kow Woon, her adopted daughter—to squire them away to the safety of America. After all, they could always return when China modernized, when the village was safe again. I imagine my grandmother hoping that she could join them later in America. But, because she so reflexively put her own needs behind those of others, perhaps she dared not hope too much. In her traditional way of being, life and opportunity should always pass to the younger generation.

There was never a chance that Poy Jen could end up an old maid. She was too pretty, too nice, too skilled—and too much like my revered grandmother. With time, her Sisterhood could explore many marriage options. I believed that was why Grandmother Chun so readily agreed to a so-called "first meeting," for a different desperation drove her now—one of fundamental survival. This first meeting was not really a first encounter between Fook Toon and Poy Jen, but a meeting of the Chun Clan Sisterhood and the Lee Clan Sisterhood, and was intentionally set up to look like an accidental encounter. That way if, despite the hopeful prospects, one party or both decided against it, no one would appear to be rejected, and future prospects would be left unsullied.

At an agreed-upon date, time, and location in the town of Hoisin, both Clan Sisterhoods, along with Poy Jen and Fook Toon, arrived at a busy street and stood on their own corners, though all pretended not to notice each other, as if they were just casually hanging out chatting.

Mother remembers the Chun Clan Sisterhood slyly evaluating Fook Toon, the only young male among the Lee Clan Sisterhood, whispering that Fook Toon was still young, probably in his midtwenties, and seemed healthy. He was around five foot four inches, which was a good height for a Toisan male, and slender with sinewy muscles. Delighted that he wasn't one of those wrinkled, spindly, old-time bachelors in their fifties and sixties who had finally earned enough to come home for a bride, the Chun Clan Sisterhood decisively moved into the important stage of their speaking-round-and-round, assessing Fook Toon's character.

"Certainly, he must work hard," said a Clan Sister.

"Not one to sit around all day eating and gossiping," chimed in another.

"These are good traits for a husband and father," said Grandmother Chun.

"He's not dressed like a dandy but wears practical, clean clothing," noted all the Aunties. Thus, they concluded he didn't waste any money he earned, meaning Poy Jen would have money to send home to her family in China.

"These are good points," concluded all the Clan Sisters.

Seeing the smiles of satisfaction on the Chun Clan Sisters' faces and hearing the rising volume and merry uplifting tone of their speaking-round-and-round, their glances no longer guarded but staring smack-dab at Fook Toon, the go-between moved the encounter to the next stage. He would now bring the two groups together. He casually walked over to the Chun Clan Sisterhood and evenly assured them that Fook Toon always sent money home to his mother. Then he let drop that Fook Toon had substantial savings, not only enough to bring his new wife to America, but also to start a home with new furniture and pots and pans and to dress his bride in the latest American fashions.

"Well, a thrifty man who saves is a good match," said several Clan Sisters.

"Fook Toon's success in America is a point in his favor," concluded all the Clan Sisters.

At this point, the marriage go-between summoned the Lee Clan Sisterhood over and introduced the two groups, naming each female elder. He saved Fook Toon's introduction for last, portraying him as a good son returning from America to visit his mother. He encouraged Fook Toon to say a few words in American.

"Hello. How are you today? Nice to be home," Fook Toon rattled off in his best American.

"Well, he certainly knows how to speak the American language, and he didn't before he went to America. Smart—that's a good point in his favor," whispered an elder Clan Sister as several buzzed in agreement.

Fook Toon then switched to Toisanese and carefully offered the most polite Toisanese greeting: "Mrs. Chun, have you had a chance to eat today?" In the world of the village, asking whether one had eaten was the American version of "Truly an honor to meet you," "Hoping you are in perfect health," and then taking the extra step of letting your visitor know how completely welcomed they are by suggesting you would like nothing better than to serve them a sumptuous meal.

As polite conversation continued, Poy Jen, hiding behind her Clan Sisters, took several careful but full looks at Fook Toon.

"But his Chinese is behind the times and his accent is rough," hissed a Clan Sister. "He's not Chinese enough—too Western," she concluded harshly.

An elder Auntie balanced this defect. "He left many years ago as a child. It's not fair to fault him for speaking poor Chinese if it's in his favor that he speaks American. It's not fair to say he's not Chinese enough if America is where Poy Jen will live," she

29

countered. "It's good that he's American. The more American, the better." She drove her point home.

After some reflection, all the Clan Sisters agreed it would be unfair to hold against him his inadequate Chinese or the impression that he didn't seem Chinese enough anymore.

Although shy, Fook Toon struck everyone as a nice man. "He will probably treat my daughter decently," said Grandmother Chun. "I think he should provide well and Poy Jen will be happy. He sends money to his mother." Grandmother Chun's summation was the stamp of approval of the match, and so the Clan Sisterhood knew they were nearing the end of this speaking.

After a last turn of speaking, the Clan Sisterhood approved of Fook Toon Lee, the overseas Chinese from America, as an acceptable husband for their beloved younger Sister, Poy Jen.

But my canny Grandmother Chun knew that the Sisterhood had left unspoken Fook Toon's main attraction—that he was offering Poy Jen safe passage out, a lifeline that could eventually pull all of her family to America's safe shores. Ultimately, this would have overridden many of Fook Toon's or another man's shortcomings. Others had agreed to marriages to much older, even elderly, men who had turned out to be mean and abusive or otherwise of questionable character just to get their daughters out of war-torn China. Sometimes this was done on the basis of a few letters and outdated photographs of someone now much older. Once married, their letters home often chronicled their growing misery. So my grandmother was deeply grateful that Fook Toon was young, pleasant enough, and a hard worker. By this standard, everything was shaping up quite well.

The accidental meeting now shifted to its final stage. All present declared that the engagement should go forward. Only then did the go-between introduce Mrs. Chun and Mrs. Lee. After exchanging pleasantries and their mutual hopes for the future, the two mothers finally introduced Poy Jen and Fook Toon to each other.

My father, Fook Toon, later told me he liked Poy Jen right away, considering her the best of the three prospects scouted by the marriage go-between. He had met the other two "accidentally" as well, but those encounters had not advanced to an actual introduction. In Fook Toon's mind's eye, Poy Jen was the prettiest and the kindest of the three young women. Fook Toon posed only one question to her: "Are you willing to make your home in America?"

Fook Toon knew that his future family's best prospects were as Americans. Despite his hardships in the States, Fook Toon had no desire to return to China to live. He had to know that his bride could leave China behind completely and for the rest of her life.

Poy Jen replied clearly and unequivocally, "Yes."

The marriage go-between beamed. He had served his prized former student and younger Clan Brother, Fook Toon, well. He had earned his fee. He then closed the deal by arranging a time for the two mothers to work out the details, especially the selection of the astrologically ideal date for the wedding celebration in accordance with the ancient moon calendar.

Both Clan Sisterhoods smiled and merged together as everyone unabashedly chatted away—"*Ji-ji ja-ja, ji-ji ja-ja.*"

Poy Jen and Fook Toon took turns smiling and blushing as they exchanged nervous glances, staring for the first time into each other's eyes.

CHAPTER 6

LUCKY DAY

My marriage celebration lasted five days and five nights. "Ohhhh—
gow-hen, how gow-hen"*—happy time, happy-happy. People came*
from nearby villages and slept over to help with the preparations.
Our village simply opened its doors, and the guests made them-
selves at home.

My mother hand-sewed a red silk dress with matching pants
decorated with dragons and phoenixes for my bridal dress. No, I
didn't wear the traditional heavy red headdress with the tassels in
front hiding my face until I was presented to the groom. That was
out of fashion then. Nor was I carried in a sedan chair, accompa-
nied by a blaring band of musicians, to your father's village. After
all, I was going to America, and that's why the wedding took place
in my village. Your father was dressed in a blue satin scholar's gown
imprinted with medallions of dragons. Over one shoulder, a shiny
red sash hung down to his waist. He wore a scholar's cap with a red
band. Tucked into the red band was a sprig of clover, freshly plucked
out of the ground that morning. This sprig symbolized the start of
our fresh future together.

Weddings were a special time for everyone in the village
because that's when we replaced our old, patched-over clothes we
wore every day until they fell apart. But for a wedding celebration,
everybody bought bolts of cloth to make new clothes, and we spent
days designing, cutting, fitting, and sewing. Weddings—that's the
time everyone got brand-new clothes!

Everyone was busy during the five-day wedding celebration.
Even visitors helped with babysitting, keeping the children out of

our way, and organizing the banquet. Lots to do. Lots and lots. "Ji-ji, ja-ja. Ji-ji, ja-ja." Everyone running around and chirping away like baby chickens.

On the first day, everyone took out their best bowls, plates, chopsticks, and serving spoons. No one family had enough bowls for a big banquet, you see, just enough for their own families, so we pooled everything together. We then decided who would contribute which vegetables or chickens or ducks.

Those who didn't have much helped out with the cleaning. They dusted and wiped down our house, even washed the floors. They cleaned the temple where the wedding banquet was to take place, as well as other houses in the village where relatives would be sleeping over—like a giant slumber party.

On the second day, everyone prepared for the feast, first setting aside the best vegetables from each family's garden plot and then organizing the plates, bowls, pots, and pans. Who would cook, who would serve, who would clean up, and so on. We made sure that enough meat had been ordered from Hoisin and that it would be delivered on time. Hoisin is the nearest town, and that's where you could buy barbecued pig, roast duck, and cuts of beef.

On the third day, the food preparation really got busy. Everyone washed the vegetables, then chopped and sliced them. The Sisters minced the meats for the wedding dumplings and, oh, so much to do. We decided which chickens and ducks to kill for the next day. You see, young birds taste sweeter and are not fatty like old birds. You can't just serve any old chicken or duck at a wedding!

There was plenty of food everywhere. Some of the poorer people pilfered food to eat later. No one said anything, for this was a celebration and there was plenty of food, even if some guests "borrowed" for later.

On the fourth day, there was a private banquet for the families of the bride and the groom. My own Clan Sisterhood cooked, served, and cleaned up afterwards.

At last the fifth day, the wedding day, arrived. More guests arrived from other villages, bringing more cooked chickens, fresh roasted duck, barbecued pork, cuts of beef, homemade dumplings, and so many special treats. There were endless plates of fresh fruits, dried fruits, watermelon seeds, and oh so many, many gifts. Everyone gave us red packages with money.

The banquet itself was held in the temple, which was the only building large enough to fit everyone. Traditionally, men were seated and served first by all the women. After they finished eating, we cleaned up, and then we women had our very own banquet. No, the men didn't serve us—we served ourselves. All dressed up in our wedding clothes, your father and I went from table to table, toasting with strong liquor.

We ate the same kind of food prepared for Chinese New Year. After all, that's positive food, full of hope, good thoughts, and looking forward to a great year. Eight precious ingredients in vegetarian jai, because its long rice noodles symbolized long life for us, and with its luscious black mushrooms, crunchy water chestnuts, chewy flat bean curd noodles, earthy black cloud fungus, salty seaweed hair, thin-sliced lotus root, and very green cabbage, all well cooked and dripping with a stewy soy and sesame oil sauce. Lots of very fresh, very green vegetables. Must have lots of green, for green is a color of life.

Musicians played music the whole time—trumpets and gongs and drums. Very loud the whole time, playing over our own loud gossiping, laughter, and toasts of good fortune. "Doot, doot. Doot, doot," all day long and into the night.

Then there was a special tea ceremony for the parents, your father's parents and my mother, to thank them for all the time, work, and love they had put into raising and protecting us, to say we are adults now and can make our own way and raise our own family. But we would remember them in gratitude. We would take care of them whenever they needed help. Especially when they got older, we would take them into our homes as valued members of our family.

After those five days, your father left. Tradition required that during the new-bride period, I spend an entire month with my family before I could leave with my new husband for his home in America. Your father went to stay with his family. We would reunite at the end of new-bride month and start our journey to America.

I did my daily chores, of course. Drew water from the well. Gathered weeds for the cooking fire. But mainly, I performed new-bride rituals. I burned incense and red paper with blessings before the family altar. I thought only good thoughts for the future. Like Chinese New Year, banish bad thoughts. Think positive affirmations every day about every little thing, especially your husband. About healthy babies. Boys! Prosperity. A good home. Happy, happy, everything happy, happy. Prepare your attitude for a happy future, and the years will turn out well.

This period was also a final time to spend with my sisters and especially my mother, a last opportunity for her to teach me whatever else I would need to know as a woman. Because I was the first daughter, she was even closer to me than to my younger sisters, so this turned out to be a very special time for us.

Even as a child, I had always known my mother was unique. Everyone in the village revered her—like a saint. When my mother was out of earshot, older people often said to me, "Your mother is just the best person. She is so good. Grow up to be like her." They noticed that my mother never said a harsh word or passed rumors behind people's backs. They marveled that she said only good things and helped anyone who needed help without hesitation or to get anything back. They pointed out how she was raising Kow Woon as good as her own daughter after she was orphaned by the Japanese plane attack. Everyone knew my mother always took the initiative to help everyone in the village solve difficulties, always encouraging them to talk things through, work things out—speaking-round-and-round. And whenever she spoke up in a speaking, I noticed that the entire circle always quietly paused for a longer time than usual as everyone mulled over her words before adding their ideas and oftentimes their agreement.

"Ai gah, how pang yu. Hung toon yeet maan nian lah, chah-um-dall (Everyone, please let's not forget we are all kin, one village, one Clan, for close to a thousand years now)," she constantly reminded everyone. Her reputation was as the finest person of the village, the one who reminded us that we have more in common than in dispute, and that if we could remember that, nothing was really worth fighting over for long. We could work anything out.

That was the main thing she reminded me of several times that month: to always try to work out difficulties for the better, not just for yourself or for your own family, but for everyone's good. In this way, I was raised to be very much like her. Even today, people in the village and in America say that of all her daughters, I am the one most like her.

Finally, I had only a few days remaining. Everyone prepared special good-bye dumplings. We gathered the ingredients, chopped them fine, mixed the dough, and put it all together. It was great fun, and we joked and gossiped as we made these dumplings. But for me, I felt sadness. Those were the closing days of my life in my village. Soon I would no longer see my sisters, my Clan Sisters, and especially my mother. I was going to a new land very far away and did not know when we would be reunited. But, of course, I remembered to stay positive, stay focused on a happy future.

The last day of my final month with my mother was called Lucky Day, and soon enough, Lucky Day dawned. During that whole month, I wasn't allowed to wash my hair. But on Lucky Day, my mother trimmed and washed it. The tradition was that she had to do everything herself. Not even my sisters or the elder Clan Sisters could help.

My mother set some water to boil. Then, as we sat in our living room, the sun streaming through the windows, Mother took my long hair into her hands and slowly cut it with scissors, a few inches at a time, then higher and higher. A few days before, she had pur-

chased a special soap for this day, a kind of shampoo. Now she used it to wash my hair, lathering it up with the special soap before washing it out again. Mother slowly toweled my hair and head dry. Finally, she carefully combed out my hair, taking a long time, much longer than usual.

At the end of this last day, I paid my final respects to my mother.

The next day, I left for Guangzhou with my new husband, your father.

CHAPTER 7

POY JEN MAKES
EIGHT PROMISES

They were made during Mother's new-bride time, that precious month of womanly isolation, the chrysalis within which my grandmother transmitted to my mother the final measure of feminine knowledge so that she could reemerge as a woman, a wife, and a soon-to-be mother.

Whatever unshared wisdom—whether personal, practical, emotional, or concerning community dynamics—Grandmother Chun could or would impart to her first daughter, this was the special time, in the Toisan way, to present them to Poy Jen. Whatever unspoken, known, or unknown difficulties had come up for her during her marriage and how she had coped with them, this was the time to teach those lessons.

Then, too, they reviewed the practical, ensuring that Poy Jen knew all the village recipes for favorite Toisanese dishes and especially for the medicinal Ch'i soups that at each change of season would strengthen the family's health. They especially went over which soups she should drink during her own pregnancy and postpartum recovery and of course which ones would build the internal energy field of her newborns. And perchance she should actually have a garden plot in her American life, Mother learned what seeds might sprout best under those new conditions, how to amend the soil with the proper nutrients, and what each plant should look like, from shoot to just before harvesting.

Who knew when they might reunite again, in a few years, not for decades, or perhaps even never again. Who knew what awaited

Poy Jen and her children to come. Because of this greater urgency to their conversation, my grandmother impressed more clearly upon Mother certain obligations that, under normal circumstances, might not have even been broached.

And so Mother described to me the eight promises that evolved during new-bride month, eight promises she swore to her mother to fulfill. My grandmother, a compassionate person by all accounts (a quality I experienced during her brief years later in America), did not sit my mother down, wag her index finger at her, and lay down the law in some stern, edictlike fashion. Instead, Grandmother Chun wove the promises delicately, slowly, and yet clearly into the conversations during their time together. As if casting a loving spell, she guided Poy Jen to envision their flow in the design of her own tapestry of life as a woman.

When Mother described the promises to me, she smiled, as if remembering her happiness at being entrusted with each one. She remembered them with a faraway look in her eyes that suggested that, despite her youth and her lack of exposure to the larger world, my grandmother had asked of her only that which she could fulfill. They were weighty promises, to be sure, but she took them on with a steady daily application in the same manner that she had learned from the Clan Sisterhood's way of passing on new skills, firmed up by the bonds of love of the Clan and feeling her mother's complete lifelong confidence in her—as a child, then as a teenager, and now as a young woman. I could hear in Mother's tone of voice, see in her eyes and in the way her back strengthened even more upright, the quality of the sacredness of these familial vows, her awareness at the time that she had been trained, prepared, and was more than ready—perhaps eager—at this young age not only to assume, but to perform these promises.

Although Mother did not recite them to me in order—nor, do I think, did she and my grandmother ever bother to count them—these are the eight promises she described to me, the ones that emerged and then blossomed forth during her new-bride month, that special cocoon of farewell intimacy between Toisan mother and Toisan daughter:

The first promise was to raise her children to be Chinese by teaching them the language, customs, and history so they could return to their ancestral village when the difficult times had passed.

The second promise was to find suitable Chinese American husbands for her two sisters, Kow Woon, and other Clan Sisters so that they might emigrate to America as soon as possible.

The third promise was to become an American citizen and sponsor the emigration of her mother and two brothers to America.

The fourth promise was to keep alive in her children the dream of a democratic Nationalist China—the dream of Sun Yat-sen, the George Washington of China, who was a Cantonese like them. Later, when her oldest brother was driven to suicide by a Communist investigation in Suey Wan, the fourth promise was expanded to include keeping alive his memory as a teacher and as a Nationalist official of the village.

The fifth promise was to keep her children connected to the village. Mother agreed to write letters describing their progress. She agreed to send back photos so they could be recognized when they returned. The photos would be mounted in her childhood home so her children's life force could join with the ancestral fires.

The sixth promise was to seek out the Clan Sisterhood in America and keep the Sisterhood traditions alive.

The seventh promise was to cook the traditional mind-body balance and Ch'i energy soups for her family to protect their inner Ch'i and their outer energy body.

The eighth promise was to live her life in complete compassion, starting with her own family and Clan, but especially her own birth children; then expanding out to all people regardless of who they were, where they came from, or whatever their livelihoods; and finally, to instill this same compassion in her children.

It is the Eighth Promise, to live with compassion toward all, that I think of as the ever-living promise, the one for all of one's days. And this promise, this way of living—perhaps arising to the level of a moral path even—strikes me as the distillation of all the wisdom of my kin, from a millennium of Toisanese living, in one small locale, self-reliant, with the same families in each house generation after generation, as everyone faced daily life, equally at the mercy of nature as well as the larger foibles of humanity. I think that during those last days before her departure, Grandmother realized that it would be this Toisanese compassion, specifically honed by our Clan experience, that would get her daughter through all her days to come in an unknown land and provide whatever it would take to fulfill the other seven promises.

In coming to embrace this last promise, Mother was clearly guided by the quiet example of my grandmother's life. Even on the eve of this momentous separation, Grandmother Chun carefully put Mother at ease about the promise to pull the rest of her family into the safety of America. Don't worry about me—just get your sisters to America one way or another, she said kindly, assuring Mother she would be fine in Toisan or in Hong Kong, if they managed to get there. She was already too old to start over in a new country anyway, Grandmother said.

Poy Jen knew these words weren't true but that Grandmother Chun said them because she didn't want her simple, farm-girl daughter to feel overwhelmed. In this kind gesture, Mother implicitly recognized that Grandmother Chun was living out the Toisanese way of caring for the emotional and mental balance of the other. Never overburden another with your needs and fears. Stay strong. Endure. Most of all, trust that your children, having been raised right, will be the best people they can be, even in your absence. They will remember you and will help you even if you never ask for it.

From the day she was born, Mother had experienced the Eighth Promise as it was lived by her own mother and by her village Aunties. She learned from them that a mother always gives to her children, first and foremost, the fullest, deepest, greatest, never-ending measure of nurturing, time, sustenance, and, at times, rescue. This promise was not discharged even after one's children grew into adults, when, by the Confucian tradition and its familial ethics, adult children should be caring for their elder parents and never the other way around. Yet at any point in time, the Eighth Promise required a Toisan mother to reflexively charge into any of life's dangerous twists and turns and wrest that child to safety.

I could feel from Mother's descriptive tone that for her the embrace of the Eighth Promise was a deeper commitment than any of the other promises, as burdensome as they all were to a twenty-one-year-old. From the viewpoint of spiritual sensibility, this struck me in retrospect as the deeper intuitive rite of an unspoken Clan Sisterhood initiation. By her birth into the Chun Clan village, she had already qualified for membership in the Chun Clan Sisterhood, and later, her honeymoon lovemaking would elevate her from maidenhood to womanhood. Yet, as new-bride month drew closer to its end, she was no longer a girl, but had become a woman in the eyes of her Clan Sisterhood. She was no longer a Little Sister, but had transformed into a full-fledged Auntie of the Clan Sisterhood. In the moment of the making of that deeper commitment of the Eighth Promise, by some alchemy of our time-tested ways, Mother now had what it took.

She knew that she was not only ready to bear children into this world, but that she would give of herself completely and always to her children, exactly as her own mother had given of herself to her during so many yesterdays.

I think that soul promises such as this are the ones we are most loathe to break, most determined to keep; and in a mysterious way, soul promises do not chain us or deplete us, but rejuvenate us in each turn of their keeping. Such deeper commitments are spiritual in nature, like the adult confirmation of a swaddling baptism or being born again (and again!) in Jesus Christ, or the taking on of lifelong vows to live in accordance with the seamless Eight Point Path of the Buddha, making the hajji to Mecca and Medina, or praying before the Wailing Wall. So, too, the Eighth Promise was paradoxical in this way: It could never be completed, but would always be fulfilled time and again as life presented each of its ten thousand joys and ten thousand sorrows.

Compassion so intrinsic cannot be confined to one's own children, but rather, as Poy Jen knew from her village's daily communalist sensibility, naturally extends itself beyond family to Clan, to other villagers, and even to total strangers—becoming a kind of telltale Toisanese character trait.

I have often wondered how this kind of compassion could have embedded itself so completely into our character. Was its genesis in a coping strategy, arising from the lessons of living in one locale, practically indistinguishable from the land that fed them, and adapting to the four seasons that either blessed the peasant farmers with timely and bountiful rain and sun or destroyed their fields with too much sun or too much rain? Was it that in order to make it year after year, generation after generation, one must always let go of grievances, resentments, and disappointments and so imbue kindness, acceptance, and forgiveness at all times, under all circumstances, into their character? It certainly wasn't because Toisan families were devout Buddhists, Taoists, or Christians guided by formal teachings. Except for an ancestral hearth, most barely gave a nod to religion in their daily lives.

I only began to learn the answers to these questions as I sifted through the fragments of my life and the life of my mother. Just as my mother learned the ways of Toisan from her Clan Sisters, I had to go back and study my own past. Thus, my story also traces the story of Toisanese Americans, as well as of how the Eighth Promise was brought to America.

That final day of new-bride month, Lucky Day, was to be Mother's last day in the village. Her family planned on leaving soon, within a year or two, for Hong Kong to wait for Mother to find grooms for her two sisters and then to attain American citizenship and sponsor her mother's and brothers' emigration to America.

Poy Jen's adopted sister, Kow Woon, decided to stay, staking her future on a new China under the Communists. Many others also decided to stay, and so the village did not become a ghost town, but remained vital, with living roots for the emigrants who might later return. Arrangements were made for Hung Yick, a decorated officer in the People's Liberation Army, to feed the family's ancestral fires. He agreed to open the house once a year, during the lunar New Year celebration. Then he would burn incense and offer food and wine in our names in front of the family altar, in ritual renewal of our unbroken connection to those who came before us. Thus anointed, he was entrusted with the only set of keys to the home.

On the eve of her departure, Mother spent her final hours scrutinizing her home and the village, as if to burn them into her memory. The house was a stand-alone building, constructed of the same uneven, dark stones as all the other homes. Yet it was the only two-story house in the village, paid for by remittances from an uncle in Seattle. Facing the broad paddies, the house received bright, warm sunlight all day long. The entrance was a double door, unusually ornate for this village, letting air and light into the reception hall. Windows all around allowed in even more light, along with cooling breezes and a lovely view of the glistening wet fields and forested hills. The interior walls were painted a wash yellow. Hand-painted vines of multicolored flowers graced the trim of windows and doorways. Ceilings delighted upturned faces with their painted platters of green, honey-yellow, and rust-red floral arrangements. Poy Jen's childhood home had been a happy one in design as well as spirit. She was leaving all this behind.

That night, as Poy Jen completed her final packing, Grandmother asked her to take several Nationalist army uniforms. "Raise your boys to return the Nationalists to power in China. Your eldest brother is a Nationalist official. And remember, Sun Yat-sen, the George Washington of China, was a Cantonese," she admonished. The *Wah Kue*, the Diaspora of over forty million overseas Chinese, had funded the Nationalist Party's overthrow of the last emperor in 1911, the revolution that introduced democratic principles into China. "You are and your family will be Wah Kue—the overseas Chinese, China's bridge with other nations, but Chinese always. You can do the same; you can support the Nationalists from America to retake China once again," she concluded.

"Ah, Mah, how can I ever forget that I am Chinese and Cantonese, like Sun Yat-sen, and that I am of the Toisan people," Poy Jen assured her mother. "And that you are my mother. I will keep my word to you in all things." Even the lifelong vow of the Eighth Promise, she said to herself.

She then left to sleep in her childhood bed, possibly for the last time.

CHAPTER 8

CROSSING THREE RIVERS

Your father's younger brother accompanied us to Guangzhou to register our marriage and start the immigration process.

Was I scared? The only people I was ever scared about were the Japanese army, and they had surrendered. No, I was more excited than anything else. After all, I was going with a good man to a good country, America, our friend in the war with Japan and now in the anti-Communist civil war. Besides, Toisanese sons and daughters had left for foreign countries for hundreds of years—to America, South America, Europe, Southeast Asia, Australia, and even Africa. Some came back and some stayed, but they always remained in touch with the village. This is part of the Toisan way, to go out into the world, learn the ways of the new land, make friends with people of other cultures, and earn money—all without forgetting the ways of Toisan. I was just another Toisan bride joining a Toisan man overseas somewhere far away. Our roots remained in Toisan, but our own lives were to blossom in a new land.

No, I didn't know anything about white people or modern cities. But I was young, excited by the adventure. Still, I was happier to be going to San Francisco, with its own Toisanese-speaking Chinatown, than to a city with few Chinese.

To get to Guangzhou, we boarded these long boats where we sat single file and didn't dare move. The boatman warned us that we could tip over if anyone moved. You could lie down flat or sit up, but whatever you decided, you were stuck and you couldn't change position for the entire trip. Men with long paddles grunted and groaned and through sheer muscle rowed us toward Guangzhou. It was really uncomfortable—hours before we could step off the boat. We changed boats three times over three rivers. Finally we caught a motorboat that took us the rest of the way.

I was very happy to go to Guangzhou. As kids, we dreamed of Guangzhou. You see, this was our big city, and getting married to your father got me there. Otherwise there would have been no chance. I would have lived all my life in my husband's village. Died in the village.

Ahhh, Guangzhou. Those were happy days. It was the first time I spent alone with your father. No daily chores like carrying buckets of water or cutting cooking grass. It was all new and fun— pretty clothes, dinners, and sightseeing. We stayed in a hotel with a mattress bed—and sheets that they changed every day! They brought fresh tea and hot water to our room every morning and whenever we wanted more!

We didn't have a private bathroom. We shared a shower and a squat toilet at the end of the hallway. But a hot-water bathroom and a flush toilet for a country girl who had known only outhouses, run around barefoot all day, and bathed in the river—what an idea anyway! This was already first class! As far as I was concerned, all Guangzhou was first class!

The next few weeks, your father and I filled out so many papers—marriage license, immigration, and medical—just a lot of papers. Doctors and nurses examined me to make sure I was healthy and wouldn't bring any diseases to America. You see, in our village, we were barefoot most of the time, picking up hookworms and who knows what other germs through our feet. I was lucky and had no diseases. Still, they tested me three times before giving me an okay. They x-rayed me too. Others that had diseases were given medicine until they were well. Then tested again. They weren't trying to stop anyone from going to America. They wanted to make sure you were 100 percent "okay-okay."

The first time I saw a Westerner—a white person—was in that clinic where I was tested so many times. The doctors and nurses were all Chinese. I guess the Westerners worked for the American government. Maybe immigration officers. They were taller than Cantonese, with huge, long noses and kind smiles with large, perfect teeth. Sure enough, Americans must be nice people indeed to help make sure we were healthy enough to go to America.

This went on for several months, testing and waiting, more testing and more waiting. After I passed all the medical tests and all the immigration papers were completed, we waited for the visa. Then one day, we were told that it would take "some more time" and they didn't know how long. "Maybe months." Always "maybe"; never "for sure, for sure."

Your father thought it best to return to America to his job. He had spent quite a lot of money for the wedding, the immigration papers, and waiting in Guangzhou. He wanted to earn some more money instead of waiting around day after day, not knowing when the visa would be issued. But before he left, his younger brother agreed to escort me directly from Toisan to Hong Kong once I got my visa. He would make sure I safely boarded the ship to America.

I returned home to wait. It was like a present to spend more time with my family. The visa was eventually issued, of course, and I left Toisan once again. The long, narrow, uncomfortable boat and the hours unable to move—again, I thought! But this time, to my surprise, the boat went only a short distance before we boarded a motorized ferryboat direct to Hong Kong, no stopping in Guangzhou. Boot, boot, boot—you could hear the motors all the way! But what a difference! We could walk around and breathe the air. There were a restaurant, food stands, bathrooms, and comfortable chairs.

In Hong Kong, I boarded a President Ocean Liner to America. I was in steerage class with other Toisan women joining new husbands in America. I slept in a bed in a large dormitory. Others who paid more shared four or even as few as two to a room. Crew members changed our bedsheets every day. That was a luxury!

And they sold us large, fresh, sweet oranges for a quarter per orange. Oranges were a real treat. "Orrr-lan-geee! Orrr-lan-geee!"

Since we didn't speak English, they would raise a finger to show the price—one US quarter—and hold up a big, bright orange in the other hand. Good thing one of the ladies had changed some Chinese money into US coins. They wouldn't take Chinese money. She bought us all oranges. So sweeeeeet!

We all got seasick the first few days. I was okay after two days. By the time we got to Honolulu, everyone was used to the ocean. Most of our time was very relaxed, walking around or sitting on the deck chairs gossiping, wondering about America, and watching the ocean.

The boat stopped in Honolulu for several days for fresh food and new passengers, but we couldn't get off. Hula girls danced and Hawaiian men dove into the water for coins. We saw the green hills and then the nighttime lights of the city. The air was warm and pleasant.

Soon enough, we reached San Francisco. I cleared Immigration and Customs. Your father was waiting for me on the other side.

"How was the voyage? You didn't get too seasick, did you?" he asked. He looked very happy to see me.

"Seasick only the first few days. Voyage was easy, very relaxing," I responded. I, too, was very happy to see him, to be in America.

"Welcome to America. This is your new home," he said.

On January 16, 1951, a little over a year later in the Chinese lunar Year of the Tiger, you, William, were born in Chinese Hospital, San Francisco Chinatown. My first son!

PART II

THE NEW LAND

(1951–1963)

CHAPTER 9

RED EGG DAY

The Clan Sisterhood organized women's business, like giving birth. Men did not get involved. No hospitals and no doctors—it was all up to us. The Clan Sisterhood took care of the mother when she was pregnant. When she was ready, we midwifed the baby into the world. Then we took complete care of her during the first thirty days following birth. We really had to work together then as a Sisterhood, and so we used the speaking-round-and-round to organize everyone.

At least one Auntie was a midwife, but no one had formal training. We learned everything by watching, listening, and doing. We would recognize that Auntie So-and-so was really good during birth. Or we noticed Little Sister Ling-ling really liked helping out with birthing, so we would make sure she always assisted the midwife. Yes, even as young girls, we helped out at births. Not in the room, but cooking, boiling water, cleaning. Like that.

This is how we took care of a pregnant mother all the way. The Clan Sisterhood cooked the special Ch'i soups for the health of the mother and the unborn child during pregnancy. Every day, Little Sisters picked the best vegetables, scooped out the best grains of rice, and slaughtered the tastiest young chickens for the mother. Aunties boiled a big clay pot of herbal soup the whole day, down to a small bowl of broth. Slowly, we fed the mother, saying good things about the baby, always staying positive in intention, feeling, and words.

As the birth time neared, the Aunties talked more and more about who would do what during the birth. All day long, we checked up on the mother. Her facial color, her appetite, what she had been eating, and the size of her stomach. We felt for the kicking of the baby, which way the head was facing, and so on. We made sure her husband left her alone and treated her well if he was a mean man. We helped with her chores.

After the birth, the mother and baby stayed in their own room for thirty days. During this time, Aunties prepared special soups to rebuild her Ch'i energy and her outer energy body. Toisan people know that pregnancy and birth deplete internal Ch'i energy and make holes in the outer energy body. So a new mother had to avoid blowing wind, or chu feng. *If the wind blew through the holes, she lacked Ch'i to fight back. She would get sick in winter. Later in life, she would get arthritis, rheumatism, or bronchitis. Toisan people know that it takes one moon cycle with special care to rejuvenate a new mother's Ch'i.*

How do I know this? I learned as a Little Sister by watching, listening, and doing.

Only a few people could visit during this month. Just close family members and elder Aunties. Everyone else stayed away. The isolation was so important that new mothers stayed in bed even in the middle of harvest. The baby remained inside too.

These were the soups we cooked for this special time. The first-week soup cleans out the system of any leftover blood and membranes that did not come out during birth. We cooked this soup with hok mook ngee *(blackwood ear fungus),* keem jeen *(related to the* Lonicera *flower),* nganh nah *(ginger), and* gai *(chicken). The blackwood ear fungus grows on the bottom of tree trunks. It's shaped like a human ear, is black in color, sometimes dark brown. She drank this soup in the beginning, two or three times only. You see, this soup has a very strong yin quality, enough to bring down her Ch'i fire if we were not careful. So, it's only served once or twice in the first week.*

The second-week soup ensures that the mother's milk is plentiful, nutritious, and sweet so the baby will drink lots of it. This soup's main ingredients include smooth bean curd, ginger, and a little bit of pork for taste. About half a bowl three times that second week.

We served one main soup throughout the month, cooked with our five basic herbs. Always lots of ginger for fire to rebuild the Ch'i inside the mother. Cook ginger in everything. Also, bok kee (Astragalus) sliced to look like a doctor's tongue depressor; hong-ong (Codonopsis), which looks like a dusty brown twig; gee-doo (red lycium berries), which are tiny, soft, and wrinkled like raisins; and of course hung dow (red jujubes), marble-sized wrinkled berries with a pit inside. These five herbs have to be in each pot of this main soup. They add a sweet taste, build fire, and provide every nutrient a mother needs to rejuvenate.

Like a soupy multiple vitamin.

And at every meal, we cooked a fresh pot of herbal chicken soup with liquor stock and boiled it for one hour, down to a small bowl. Then we fed her steamed chicken—the white meat only, no skin—with ginger over rice. Or salted preserved fish with ginger over rice. Salted preserved pork is okay too.

A new mother was so weak after birth that there were foods she could not eat because they would affect her in a bad way, possibly for life. No vegetables, because during this time, vegetables easily cause diarrhea. Why leak away the nutrients we spent so much time cooking! No fresh fish, because the scales weaken the Ch'i body, causing the mother to get sick in the chest every winter. No beef, because it causes incontinence in old age. No duck, because the meat has too many toxins. Oh, no fruit too, because it flushes out all the special foods and will cause the same problem as beef when you're older.

These soups have another purpose: They produce good milk for the baby. Milk is all the baby should have for the entire month. If for some reason the mother was not making enough milk, we boiled up rice broth for the baby. After cooling it, we slowly fed *the rice soup using a tiny, tiny soup spoon. Sometimes we used a finger to spread the rice broth onto the baby's lips. The baby would lick the liquid. This is not like* jook, *the thick rice soup, but much thinner.*

*By the end of the month, both the mother and the baby were strong enough to come out. This was the red egg party time. We would hard-boil chicken eggs and dye them red color. Eggs symbolize new life because chicks come out of eggs. The egg also symbolizes strength, because an eggshell is very strong. And of course, red—the color of blood—symbolizes vitality. The red egg party reconnected the mother to the village and introduced the baby to the Clan Sisterhood. This time, the birth mother cooked up a huge pot of special herbal soup. This was her thank-you soup to her Sisterhood, giving them back some of the nourishment they had given her—maintaining the balance of giving and receiving is important—and to show she was back on her feet. This soup must have pigs' feet, chicken, and liquor cooked for hours in sweet and sour soup. Served so steaming hot you had to blow on it—*phoo, phoo, phoo—*before you could sip even one spoonful. Oh, and men could come to red egg parties to have some soup, say hello. And even the Little Sisters would eat a little soup, despite the liquor.*

The red egg party was also a special kind of speaking-round-and-round. Men usually left after the first serving of soup. This speaking started as each Sister cradled the baby. She would look into the baby's eyes, formally introduce herself by name, and state her family relationship. As if the baby understood every word. She then diagnosed out loud the baby's strength, skin color, size, and so on. Then she passed the baby to the next Sister. Oh, we were serious, like real doctors. The mother listened very carefully because this was how she learned from our collective experience, especially when the eldest Aunties spoke.

Sisters advised on what foods this baby should eat or which soups to drink for increasing health. If the baby had a cough that came from the chest, a Sister might say, "My first-born daughter had this kind of cough. Be sure to give her lots of the medicinal tea made from this and that plant. It cured her of the cough by the age of seven."

Sisters remarked on personality characteristics, like "This one is really smart." An elder Auntie might say: "See how his eyes watch and follow every movement. He should go to school, perhaps a university in Guangzhou."

Another Sister might notice, "This girl is kind of deliberate in her movements. She clutches my thumb very tight. My Sister is like that. She's really strong and will be a good farmer."

Or "This boy has a kind face. His smile is big and his eyes are soft. He will be a good son to his parents. Send money home all the time."

In this way, each Sister knew the baby's strengths and needs and could help care for the baby if for some reason the mother could not. Like Kow Woon, when the Japanese airplane killed her family. My mother already knew her like one of her own when we adopted her. You see, in this way, in our village, there's always someone to care for a child for an afternoon, a moon cycle, or for life.

Little Sisters learned a lot about each baby from the red egg party speaking-round-and-rounds, training us in motherhood even as little girls. Which is good because we babysat when the Aunties went away to market or worked the fields.

Then everyone gives a lay see or hung bow—a red envelope, very pretty with gold characters—with money inside for the baby. Money symbolizes the support of the village for every child. A slang term for money is "water." By giving money, the big trees were giving of their own precious "water" to the baby shoots until they were strong enough to get their own water. Red, the color of blood and life force, means vitality. Gold symbolizes the providence of family, friends, water, sun, good harvest, peaceful times, and material wealth. This is the same sentiment when grown-ups give red *envelopes to kids during Chinese New Year—the older trees giving of their own water to our young shoots.*

But you were born in the United States, in a hospital, not in China, even if it was a Chinatown hospital named Chinese Hospital.

Your paternal grandfather immediately gave you a power name, Poy Jom. Poy means someone who stands strong, is thoughtful, and can figure things out. Jom has the water symbol in it, signifying someone who is placid on the surface, but whose waters run deep, possessing a deep reservoir of wisdom and resources. Your family name, Lee, is comprised of two Chinese characters— tree is on top, and young or new life is on the bottom. This is like the tree of life. Toisanese are like that—we have many branches throughout the world, but we grow from one tree.

Your grandfather also gave you an English power name, William, after the English monarch, King William the Conqueror. He knew from his own harsh life as a Chinese American that you need a power name to succeed here. All your given names—Chinese and American—are power names. And because your American middle name is also Poy, your Chinese and American names are linked.

Your birth here was very different than it would have been in the village. I tried to keep the traditions, as I promised my mother. But it was much harder to do so since most of my Sisters were back in China. There was no midwife, but at least Dr. Chun Hong Gum-feng was a woman—Toisanese too! Very nice lady. And she assisted the birth of every baby in Chinatown for many, many decades! Yes, I stayed at home for thirty days. But there wasn't a Clan Sisterhood to help me during the thirty days' isolation. If we had stayed in China, I would have moved to your father's village and become a member of the Lee Sisterhood, and they would have made my soups for me. But there weren't enough Lee Aunties or Chun Aunties here for a Lee Clan or Chun Clan Sisterhood. The new-style Chinatown Sisterhood was thrown together with Sisters from different

villages—Wong, Fong, Lee, Chun, Lew, Lum, Tom, and so on.
Well, they were mainly the wives in the apartment building. We all
seemed to understand the same things anyway, and they knew what
to do. So I guess all the Toisan Sisterhoods are similar.

Another difference was that I had to cook all my own soups and
foods. Oh, the neighbors would help me out by buying whatever I
needed every day. They took turns shopping for me so I wouldn't go
out and risk chu feng.

At your red egg party, everyone remarked how big you were,
nine pounds at birth. We called you Ai *(Big)* Bee-bee *and* Lao
(Adult) Bee-bee. *"Ai" because of your size. "Lao" because your*
features were well formed, like an adult's. The Sisters considered
you wise and intelligent beyond your years. Everyone said you were
strong and so would grow up healthy. Maybe because the Sisters
were not really my Sisters in the village, they didn't speak as much
or in such detail as back home. This was America, and our motley
Clan Sisterhood did the best we could.

Two years later, we had Richard's red egg party. Richard was
sweet-tempered, obedient, and healthy, many said. Richard was
handsome, others said. And mainly, how lucky I was to have two
sons. Then, something terrible happened. No one was watching
you, William, and you knocked over the pot of hot soup. Thank-
fully, it only scalded the right side of your ribs and not your face.
That's how you got your scar. I know you don't remember anything.
I try not to think of it either.

Heahhh—this never would have happened in the village. I don't
know why, but a put-together Clan Sisterhood wasn't as alert,
didn't watch out for each other as well. Maybe we felt a little fuzzy
because of the bigness and strangeness of San Francisco. Maybe
we felt less powerful, not so important, because Chinatown was
much more complicated than home. We could only try our best, and
it was mostly good enough.

Thirteen years later, your youngest brother, John, was born,
and that was the last red egg party I gave. Everything was happy,

happy at that one. Who could have thought I would give birth at thirty-five—and to a third son? Nobody!

Still, the early years were wonderful years. Only a few sad things happened, like the hot soup and your scar. Every week, I wrote letters home, sometimes sending photos and sometimes money, just as I had promised my mother. The letters they sent back said they had sent the photos back to the village and how help-ful the money was. You see, they were now living in Hong Kong, all five of them squeezed into a small hovel in a very run-down part of town. Every dollar I sent made a difference. But it wasn't easy sending back money. Your father made me write down every cent I spent: seven cents for salt, fifty cents for a bundle of chopsticks, twenty-five cents for beef, and so on. He turned out to be a cheap-skate, making me account for every cent, forbidding me to send money home. But I did it anyway. I would lie, say I forgot to write everything down. This is the only thing we ever argued about—money.

To make my own money, I worked part-time as a waitress near Union Square and later on Washington Street near Grant Avenue. Chinese restaurants, of course. Later, I sewed clothes in a China-town sewing factory. You and Richard slept next to me or played on the floor, lost in piles of cut-up fabric. Your father picked up the two of you on his way home from work so I could attend American-ization classes in the evening. I loved learning the American lan-guage and all about America. I really enjoyed America.

Working, attending Americanization classes, raising babies—you just don't know how much work babies require of a mother—shopping, cleaning, cooking, washing clothes, writing letters home, missing my family, and arguing about money. That was how it was when you were babies. I was no lon choon—*a lazy bug sunning on a branch. But when Richard was about three years old, I couldn't do it anymore. I started crying for no reason. Some days, I couldn't do anything. I quit work. I dropped out of Americanization classes. For a few months, I dropped Richard off in the afternoons to a Clan*

Sister from the village. He cried every time. I felt bad because a Toisan mother should always take care of her children herself. It's best for the child. No one ever cares for a child the way a mother will. That's the Toisanese way.

But your father insisted on the babysitter even though she cost money. He wanted me to get well. He felt bad, I could tell. Like he had let me down or failed to protect me. But I got better and soon could take care of Richard too. I never went back to Americanization school. I only worked a little once in a while. Who had time anyway—with two boys? And then you entered kindergarten.

CHAPTER 10

MRS. RANSOM'S
FORTY-EIGHT STEAKS

That was the day I crossed over, the day of my formal introduction to the American language and the American way of life. My first attempts at complete American sentences were made on that first day—in reciting the Pledge of Allegiance.

"Okay, children, we will now pledge allegiance to the flag of the United States of America. Please stand up, everyone," said Mrs. Ransom, the gentle, soft-spoken kindergarten teacher for Washington Irving Grammar School. Thirty or so Chinese American kids remained firmly seated, silently staring at the teacher. Not one of us understood a word of American.

"Hmm, well, let me help you," she said as she moved from person to person, gently taking each one by the hand, helping us to our feet.

"Now, all of you stand up." She held her arms wide, palms up, and pumped them up higher toward the ceiling. We understood. This was the signal for us to rise.

"Now place your right hand over your heart," said Mrs. Ransom.

No one moved.

"Here, like this," she said as she placed her right hand over her heart. "Like this." She gently took a right hand here and a right hand there, placing them over the heart.

Most of us placed our right hands over our hearts, but I placed my left hand, going the other way. "Billy, let me help you." Mrs. Ransom had pinned a name tag onto my new school clothes. Prior to today, I had always been called by my Chinese name, Jom. Father had said "William" was what everyone would call me in school, so to be called "Billy" instead was news to me. Mrs. Ransom had assigned me this nickname as if it were the most natural thing in the world.

"Okay, everyone. Please repeat after me: I pledge allegiance."

Silence.

"Okay, everyone, look at me. Look at my lips," she said as she pointed a finger to her lips. Mrs. Ransom bent at the waist so we could see her lips better. Her lips were the brightest lipstick red.

Mrs. Ransom was the first Caucasian I had ever been able to examine up close and for countless hours. This is why, even to this day, her image remains so clear in my mind. She was quite tall, at least a foot taller than my mother. And she was slender. Her ash-blonde hair fell evenly to her shoulders, curling up at the ends. She wore a tan, short-sleeved V-neck sweater that disappeared into the waist of a tight brown plaid skirt, which in turn blossomed out to midankle, just above her black high heels.

She repeated the first line several times. Then she made a circular motion to include all of us, making eye contact with each and every one of us. She slowly opened her lips to start again.

Suddenly, all at once, we hollered out in unison, "I pleck al-leak-gance."

"To the flag," continued Mrs. Ransom. Again the inclusive circular finger.

"Toot dah flack."

"Of the United States of America." Mrs. Ransom kept going.

"Ahf dah Uni-ked Steaks of Amal-lee-ka." We bravely blurted it all out until we reached the last word of the pledge.

Mrs. Ransom then reviewed the design of the American flag, telling us that the red and white stripes represented the thirteen original "steaks" and something about each star representing one of the forty-eight "steaks" making up this huge country called the United "Steaks" of America, to which we had just pledged allegiance.

She went on to say that there is a father of the entire country, known as the "pres-za-dent."

"Can you say pre-za-dent?" she coaxed, pointing to her lips and then making the inclusive fingering circle.

"Pleh-see-dun-tah," several of us bravely attempted.

"The president's name is Ei-sen-how-er," she said. "Can you say Ei-sen-how-er?"

At this point, we sucked in our breaths, unable to say a sound. She seemed perplexed that we stopped after doing so well with the pledge on this, our first day.

The reason was that Chinese American family names are monosyllabic: Lee, Chan, Wong, Ng, Fong, Kwok, Kwan. The longest Chinese family names were limited to two syllables—Leong, Louie, Owyang—and those names were rare.

So here was Mrs. Ransom telling us there's a guy who is the father of our country whose family name alone is four syllables long. Then he sports a title that is three whole syllables long, and we don't even know his first and middle names yet, which we knew he had to have! And just how long were each of those names? Why, he had enough syllables for several families! We were boggled mute.

Finally, Mrs. Ransom said, "But everyone calls him Ike."

Thirty kids, on our first day of kindergarten, suddenly released our collective breaths—loudly. "Ike, Ike, Ike," we gladly chanted back, over and over, so relieved that we didn't have to use a four-syllable name with a three-syllable title to refer to just one person. Even if this very important man was the father of our big country of forty-eight steaks.

I first found out I was going to kindergarten in late January of 1956, forming a midyear class. Mother explained that every kid had to go to school when she or he became five years of age. I asked whether Richard was going too. We were so close, sharing all our toys, racing, and wrestling with each other all the time—I couldn't imagine going to school without him. She explained that Richard wasn't old enough yet, but Henry Lee from the Chinese American restaurant down the street and Donald Soo from next door would be attending school with me. Then we went shopping for new clothes and new shoes.

Although I was born in America, I had spoken Toisanese exclusively for the first five years of my life. Toisanese was our household tongue, the only one spoken by our neighbors as well as the merchants along Grant Avenue. I did not start speaking "American" until that first day at Washington Irving Grammar School. We called the language "American" because we knew what English sounded like: The British in Hong Kong spoke "English." Later, in the 1980s, when I spent a great deal of time in England, I discovered that the English agreed with us that Americans did not speak English, but rather a dialect they labeled as "American."

Mother registered me inside the school auditorium. I came to know this auditorium well. We played there when it rained, and it rained a lot in the winter months. Mrs. Lau, a Filipino-looking Chinese American teacher, translated for the mothers, most of whom didn't speak American. She spoke Big City Cantonese and didn't seem too friendly or very respectful of the Toisanese mothers. She directed us to the kindergarten room, across from the auditorium. Mother gave Mrs. Ransom my forms and said goodbye and that she would pick me up later. Some of the kids were crying as their mothers left. I was scared too, but I didn't cry.

After completing kindergarten with Mrs. Ransom, we moved up one floor to first grade. Our next teacher was the very warmhearted Mrs. Stephens, who introduced us to Dick, Jane, Rex, and Spot, reading, 'riting, and 'rithmetic. We finished second grade with Mr. Walsh, a dapper, slender gentleman who regaled us with his clever jokes and stories about his garden snakes and his warty gourd, which was on display at the science table. Richard started kindergarten about then, with Mrs. Ransom. Having heard what I had been through, he was a little bit more prepared, a little less shocked at kindergarten goings-on. Later, my classmates and I moved up to the third floor for fourth, fifth, and sixth grades. Education was like climbing a ladder—the higher the grade level, the more stairs to climb.

All too soon, American became my dominant language. I still spoke Toisanese with Mother, though. Mother listened as Father tutored Richard and me in the evenings. Even with her promise to teach us written Chinese, Mother knew we had to master American first. For my part, it seemed natural that we were switching from Toisanese to American. Everyone in class had spoken only Chinese when we entered kindergarten, but as the teachers smoothly guided us over the linguistic divide into straight-ahead American, it felt like that was how life worked, that this was the natural order of the universe.

Mother constantly contemplated the most opportune age to enroll me in Chinese language school. Wait too long and she risked my becoming "Americanized."

In the 1950s, Chinatown had about five Chinese language schools. Chinese school started at 4 p.m., an hour and a half after grammar school let out. Most Chinatown kids attended one. As I progressed in American school, Mother undoubtedly noticed that her two sons were speaking less and less Toisanese. Worse, from her point of view, we were incredibly enamored of all things American. As it turned out, Richard and I were equally resolved not to enroll in Chinese school. Our battle with Mother ranged over three summer vacations. Since I was older, Mother's efforts focused mostly on me.

That first summer, I informed Mother that I simply could not fathom the necessity of it. After all, I was conversant enough to talk to her, shop on Grant Avenue, and order takeout from Chinese restaurants. Besides, everyone else on the block spoke

American. I listed them on my fingers: Sam of Sam's Cleaners and his friend Molly, Charlie of Charlie's Bail Bonds, Wallace the Carpenter, Mr. and Mrs. Jackson of Jackson's Bookstore, and the beat cop Danny the Wop. Even kindhearted Benny of Benny's Smoke Shop—and Tagalog was his first language.

I pulled out all the stops: "Chinese school takes time away from American school homework, and I won't win my scholarship to college," I said. "This will be all your fault if you make me go to Chinese school."

Richard listened with supportive bemusement, hands in his pockets, standing with me. With Richard being two years younger, Chinese school was still remote for him. But he knew that my arguments were his. My desire for free playtime after school was his desire. He was as happy as I was when I prevailed that first summer.

And I prevailed the second summer using a new twist. I discovered that it was Cantonese, not Toisanese, that was taught for the first two years; from the third year forward, it was Mandarin. So I marshaled new arguments. Well, everyone in Chinatown spoke Toisanese, so what was the point of learning Cantonese? Only Hong Kong movies at the Sun Sing Theater were in Cantonese, and learning Cantonese to understand Hong Kong movies better couldn't be more important than doing well in American school.

And then by year three, I dramatically stressed, Chinese school taught exclusively in Mandarin. That was practically a foreign language as far as Chinatown was concerned. What was so important about Mandarin, a dialect no one used in Chinatown? I mean, we're in America, and we have no plans to go to China or anywhere near it anytime soon. Just what was the point of Chinese school when you thought about it all the way through?

But the tide turned by the third summer. Mother's happiness was important to Father, who still felt guilty about her emotional breakdown. And Father was not against us going to Chinese school. Even though he was firm that his sons would stay Americans, he thought that we should know our Chinese heritage and be fluent in Chinese. After all, in his youth, he had achieved some merit as a writer of classical Chinese poetry. This genre of classical poetry is extremely difficult to compose. It is organized as a poem puzzle, with each word representing a number of concepts, he had explained. Depending upon their placement in the poem's structure, the meanings change—a kind of Scrabble game of literary, cultural, and philosophical allusions with double-score and triple-score brain-tickling delights. He believed that speaking Chinese and knowing Chinese civilization would actually enhance my chances of winning that ever-important college scholarship.

Mothers being mothers, and with the Clan Sisterhood tradition and all, Mother must have called a speaking-round-and-round. All I know is that one afternoon in the late summer of 1959, Mrs. Soo next door, Mrs. Yock from around the corner, Mrs. Lee of the restaurant down the block, Mrs. Lum from down the street, and my mother all escorted each of their kids to the front of our apartment building. In a phalanx formation, they force-marched the whole lot of us, nine kids, to Nom Kue Chinese Language School, two blocks away—on Sacramento Street between Kearny Street and Grant Avenue. Only after we were enrolled and seated in our classroom and the teacher had called the class to order did this Amazonian honor guard demobilize.

I have a confession to make. As a child, I was often ashamed of the Toisanese dialect. Of course, I spoke Toisanese at home without reservation. But in the company of non-Chinese neighbors and against the perfectly enunciated American of television, Toisanese seemed unmusical, clunky, and too loud. In contrast, the American language flowed mellifluously, so easy on the ear. It was the language of modern times, speed, military victory, industrial capacity, and amazing technology, a language so unlike Toisanese, the language of farmers in some God-only-knows-where backward old village in China.

My shame always was deepest when our patient, beloved, otherwise kind public school teachers reprimanded us during our rare lapses into Toisanese. These rebukes inevitably happened at recess, the time when we gave ourselves over completely to the freedom and joy of play. Spontaneously, someone would slip into the briefest happy flurry of Toisanese. As the recess teacher, scowling now, spun around in the direction of the offending sounds, she'd shake her large, loud, brass recess bell furiously as she rushed into the offender's face. She'd shout over the clanging: "This is America. Speak only American. You will sit on the bench until recess is over."

Sometimes, a teacher caricatured Toisanese in the most awful way, twisting her neck and moving her head back and forth and sideways like a chicken, as if to say, "What self-respecting person would want to speak this gibberish?" The few times I was benched for speaking my first language, it didn't seem to matter that I excelled in reading and writing American. The teacher somehow forgot that I had spoken American every other minute of that day and every day since the beginning of the semester. These thunder-cracking harangues condemned Toisanese as a transgression equivalent to coming to school while burning up with chicken pox and coughing in everyone's face. A gentle reminder would have sufficed, but was never forthcoming. In this milieu, I began to doubt the worth of my first language, the place of my family's origins, and, finally, the place of my parents in American society.

It took me many years to feel right, once again, about speaking Toisanese and then many more years before I felt good about being a Toisan Chinese. My awakening began tentatively when I entered Chinese language school. My acceptance of my background surged ahead in the late 1960s during the civil rights movement, when many people of color reconnected with the roots of their suppressed heritage. In my childhood, however, not only was the America of the 1950s arrayed against the speaking of

Toisanese, so too was the rest of Guangdong Province, the home of Toisanese. Guangdong's official dialect was Cantonese, and Cantonese speakers considered Toisanese inferior.

Even more invalidating was the fact that Mandarin was China's official language, and all Cantonese were forced to learn it. Linguistically, Cantonese and Mandarin are two radically different languages, as different as French is from Latin despite their links as romance languages. As for the relationship of Toisanese to the Cantonese language, Toisanese is a dialect of Cantonese. Just as Parisian French speakers feel assaulted by spoken Quebecois French, so too do Cantonese speakers consider Toisanese an embarrassing variant. Official China, which had little use for Cantonese, knew nothing of Toisanese. As if salting a wound, China had historically considered the province of Guangdong a distant backwater in the lowest corner of the empire, a place to exile unpopular magistrates, rebels, and criminals. For Cantonese speakers, Toisan villages were their backwaters.

Because of Toisanese's reverse cachet as a hillbillyish, coarse, down-in-the-delta variation of Big City Cantonese, there are no Toisanese novels, poems, or operas. There is no legacy of Toisan royals with ornate Toisan summer palaces. The prolific Shaw Brothers Studio of Hong Kong did not make movies in Toisanese. Bruce Lee never slipped into Toisanese. There are no Toisanese television series, and no Toisanese pride movement is clamoring for one. Toisanese sounds signify sweaty, impoverished, backcountry peasant farmers working oxen in mud the whole day long, with syllables that are harsh to the normal ear and spoken at a decibel level equivalent to shouting. In truth, the normal volume of spoken Toisanese is a shout. When spoken angrily, the listener is sometimes finely sprayed with spittle. People coming from Toisan who wanted to pass for better in Guangzhou or Hong Kong dropped Toisanese and picked up Cantonese as if shedding soiled, ill-fitting, rough cotton work clothes for the blue silk garments of scholars and merchants.

And yet most of the first Chinese American pioneers were Toisanese. Arriving in numbers in the 1850s to join the California Gold Rush, we stayed to build the first transcontinental railway from the West Coast, as Irish immigrants built it from the East. Grimly, we stuck it out through the 1880s, a reign of terror of anti-Chinese legislation, antimiscegenation laws, race riots, lynchings, and torching of Chinatowns up and down the West Coast. The horror of life for California's Chinese residents was so unrelenting that it gave rise to the then-popular expression "He didn't have a Chinaman's chance." Beginning in the 1900s, we eventually settled into an uneasy, institutionalized Jim Crow segregation within the surviving Chinatowns.

These Chinatowns prospered and became havens for later waves of Chinese immigrants: in the 1950s, refugees like Mother fleeing from Communist China; in the 1960s, refugees like Grandmother Chun, who had been stranded in Hong Kong after the 1949 Communist assumption of power; in the 1970s, Mandarin-speaking Taiwanese and then ethnic Chinese Vietnamese boat people; and finally in the 1980s and 1990s, Mandarin-speaking mainland Chinese moving to America for freedom and opportunity.

Through all those periods, the sons and daughters of the original Chinese Americans, the Toisanese and Cantonese who built and maintained the Chinatowns, welcomed each wave of newcomers. These pioneers had not only built safe havens, but their children went on to become doctors, lawyers, decorated war veterans, US senators, a state governor, best-selling authors, movie stars, and Silicon Valley moguls. Their names are part of our culture: actors Anna May Wong, Bruce Lee, and Jason Scott-Lee; former governor Gary Locke of Washington State; and best-selling novelist Maxine Hong-Kingston.

Over the years, I sensed that the linguistic characteristics of Toisanese might reflect the inextricable, interdependent bond between the Toisan land and its people. Like the language of the

Basques of the Pyrenees, the U'wa Indians of Colombia, and the Hawaiians and their islands, our tongue became inseparable from our homeland. Because the Toisanese people and their dialect are unofficial and underrecognized, our character became unpretentious and practical. We became tough-skinned to life's difficulties. We focused with an incredible drive on family, land, home, education, and abundance.

Our dialect reflects life wrested from the mud, clay, and stone of wet delta land and the need to be heard over vast stretches of fields. Not surprising then that the sounds of Toisanese syllables come wrapped up like clods of dirt embedded with stones and held together by the long, sinewy grasses used for cooking. Sentences explode out of the mouth like a mortar barrage, with consonants, vowels, all the tones meshed into a tight, barbed clump of earthy linguistics. Toisanese can arc over rice paddies, penetrate a flock of noisy geese, cut through a stand of bamboo trees, and curve around a hill. As the sentence lands, the remaining barbs of sound hook your eardrum so you know that, indeed, you are being addressed and the reasons why.

The dialect was designed for survival—year after year, day after day, sometimes minute by minute. A self-reliant village of farmers needs to know immediately of any emergency, and the Toisanese shout served as our warning system, one that could carry over the curvaceous metes and bounds of our countryside. "A levee has just burst! A week's labor seeding a field will be lost unless all hands run to shore it up," or "Sell-lenn, your youngest daughter just fell and sprained her ankle! Hurry back, she's crying loudly!" These messages would boom and echo across the fields.

During World War II, Toisanese warnings were of destruction and death. "Danger! Danger! Japanese soldiers are raiding. Run to the hiding place in the hills. Make no noise. Don't come back tonight." In the land of Toisan, there were no excuses for failure. There could only be survival, and thus Toisanese evolved to guarantee survival. A nuance-free language whose meanings

72

were harshly, crudely, and loudly clear—where layered linguistics of hidden meanings has no place—served its speakers well.

In contrast, Big City Cantonese was melodic, like a stanza of music in its seven tones and spoken at a normal volume. The one-upmanship of city sophistication propelled its colloquialisms. It was the language of overly clever merchants and the prickly double entendres of the social elite. Big City Cantonese was spoken in urbane quarters, with the speakers wearing clean, fashionable clothes and using elegant manners. Its basis was politeness masking a withering wit, preferably while eloquently describing the subtle fragrances of this year's harvest of that rare tea handpicked by monkeys from misty high cliffs.

But even Big City Cantonese appreciated that the earsplitting, spitty Toisanese attained its oratorical finest reach when downright rude and disdainful to the bones of your family and especially your ancestors. It soared even higher when salty and sexually graphic. You knew you were told off when you were tongue-lashed in Toisanese.

Although Chinese school was the start of my eventual acceptance of my Toisanese heritage, it initially confirmed for me the shamefulness and distastefulness of the Toisanese dialect.

The Chinese school principal and the teachers trucked no Toisanese. My first-grade teacher, Mrs. Wong from Hong Kong, enforced this linguistic reign of terror with a drumstick. Rap went the drumstick, reddening your open palm, at the slightest offense. Speak Cantonese and leave Toisanese behind!

This created some problems with Mother, because she tutored me in a Toisanese-accented attempt at Big City Cantonese. I often cringed, imagining Miss Wong's sharp correction of my recitals the next day. In frustration, I continued my attacks asserting the futility of Chinese school with a righteous frustration.

In time, however, my Cantonese improved. I did well in both my recitation and written exams. Soon enough, as with American school, my resistance melted away.

Oddly, the written language of Chinese—a pictorial symbolic system—remained constant and unified, with Mandarin, Cantonese, and Toisanese all written as one language. I fell in love with Chinese classic brushstroke calligraphy; it not only captured my imagination and my artistic sense, but also validated my Chineseness. Unlike American words that can be sounded out from the printed page, each Chinese word is a unique picture character unto itself that has to be memorized as a separate creation. Different lines, boxes, dots, and commas constitute each word character, and each stroke has to be exactly where it belongs. To complicate matters, we drew characters with a classic bamboo brush dipped into black ink and held in an upright position that required twisting several fingers awkwardly along the bottom of the brush.

At first, my brushwork resembled nothing more than a series of mini-Rorschach tests. Eventually, I improved. With brush poised over rice paper, I learned to run my first stroke clean, from a tiny dot down into a flower burst and, with a flourish, to lift the brush off the page just so, without smudging or dripping ink. Suddenly, writing Chinese—and being Chinese—was fun.

But it was only when we studied Dr. Sun Yat-sen and his Three Principles of Democracy that China and America seemed psychologically connected. Dr. Sun Yat-sen, considered the George Washington of China, formulated his principles from the writings of America's founding fathers, especially those of Thomas Jefferson. The good doctor had walked the streets of our very own Chinatown, tirelessly proselytizing for the funding that overthrew the last emperor, Pu-yi, in the democratic revolution of October 10, 1911. Our own local newspaper, *Geem San See Bo* (*The Chinese Times Daily*), Mother and Father's favorite daily, had advocated democracy and modernization in China for more than half a century. Suddenly, Chinatown's humble streets—packed with three-story buildings, vegetable and fish shops, souvenir stores, and functionally dressed men and women—took on a magnificent prominence. We had financed a revolution that ended thousands of years of monarchy in a vast nation of millions, a revolution that, for better or for worse, had propelled China into the twentieth century. China suddenly felt familiar, like a second cousin, and no longer a stranger.

As my interest in Dr. Sun Yat-sen grew, my Chinese school selected me on one Ten-Ten Independence Day to recite the Three Principles of Democracy. I somehow managed it—in flawless Cantonese—before the entire Chinese school. In time, the school taught us China's long history, nearly five thousand years of outrageous emperors and empresses who ordered up the Great Walls and opulent palaces and waged ruthless wars that built and destroyed civilizations; about major Chinese inventions—astronomy, gunpowder, silk weaving; and of the large fleets of ships that navigated by the stars and the first compasses, crisscrossing the oceans centuries before Columbus accidentally landed in America. There were indications that Chinese captains may have even reached the Americas before Europeans.

Teachers read from the poetry of Li Po and Chuang-tzu. We learned of Buddhism and Taoism, Asian religions that had played great roles in Chinese civilization. These religions sounded and felt Chinese, with Chinese-looking people in their paintings and statues, so unlike the Chinatown churches with their Caucasian Jesus and ivory Mother Mary statues surrounded by European-faced angels.

We were taught about the sage Confucius and his philosophy of Confucianism, a hierarchical system of social cooperation and obedience between levels of society and within families. It was this system that had united and built the ancient civilizations of China. Two of those rules, "Obey your parents" and, of course and inevitably, "Obey your teachers," were drilled into our heads.

In time, I understood more Chinese than I could speak and eventually could easily switch over to Cantonese. If Mother's intention was to keep me Chinese by sending me to Nom Kue Chinese school, she succeeded. Yes, there was more homework, as I suspected, but for the three years I attended Chinese school, it did not take time away from my American studies. Yes, there was less playtime after American school as feared, for we rushed home, gulped down our snacks, and flew out the door in one move. With our ubiquitous Chinese school bags in hand, we flapped down the street all the way to Nom Kue, desperately trying to make the 4 p.m. bell and looking for all the world like a flock of one-winged ducks.

As for Mandarin attitudes toward provincial bumpkins, well, if we had to, we'd master Mandarin, including the highest form, Beijing style, with its distinguishing and linguistically questionable "ar, ar, ar" word endings. But our migrations outward were and are always overseas destinations. We take on Vietnamese, Malay, Filipino Tagalog, English, Spanish, and American—whatever the tongue of the dominant culture is, Toisan immigrants will learn it and their children will master it.

For centuries, we have bravely gone forth to foreign climes, sunk new roots, spoken new languages, acculturated, and then blossomed for generations in our new home. This too is the Toisan way.

CHAPTER 11

THE SOUP DU JOUR IS CH'I

Toisan mothers must cook the special seasons-change Ch'i-adjustment soups for their children. Especially so when they are young, but also when well into their teen years. Our responsibilities go beyond washing, dressing, and feeding our children's physical bodies—we have to nurture the invisible Ch'i bodies. These are not food soups, like the vegetable soup that Benny the Smoke Shop man treated you to from the Star Cafeteria or like Campbell's Chicken Noodle Soup, which you and Richard loved as children.

No, these soups are like medicine, similar to the soups for rejuvenating postpartum mothers, yet very different. Even though they're medicinal soups, they taste delicious like American soups. These Toisan soups adjust and strengthen Ch'i energy for the climatic changes of the seasons so our children won't catch colds and flu. If eaten regularly during childhood, these soups will keep you strong and healthy throughout your life.

During hot summer days, I cooked oong-gwah hong *(winter melon soup). Winter melon soup brings down the yang heat in the body for it is* leang *or yin. The herbs are the same ones used in the rejuvenation soups for new mothers—*bok kee *(Astragalus),* hong-ong *(Codonopsis),* gee-doo *(red lycium berries), and* hung dow *(red jujubes). Lycium berries are good for your eyes—they keep your vision strong. Besides winter melon, I added peas, sliced pork, and eggs to make it sweet. Not sweet like sugar, but sweetly delicious from all the juices of the herbs and the meat mixing together over a hot fire.*

Another summer soup was foo jook hong *(bean-curd soup),*

also very yin and good for very hot days. I cooked it with the same herbs, but only for an hour, no more. Sometimes I added a piece of pork to sweeten the soup. You didn't like bean-curd soup, but I made you eat it. Sometimes you waited until the end of the meal when it was cold before you would swallow it down whole. Good thing bean curds are slippery and slide down quickly. But if you wanted to play with Sonney or Donald, you had to eat your bean-curd soup.

Most important was to adjust the Ch'i as summer turned to winter. After you and Richard started school, you two caught everyone's germs, vomiting for days with really hot temperatures. I started to cook lots of soups around fall. These soups raised the fire in your Ch'i so your body could fight off colds and flu. Ngow-mee hong *(oxtail soup) cooked with these same herbs was especially good for this. We boiled the oxtail for an hour and a half until it was so soft the meat slid off the bones. By then, the soup was so sweet. You really liked oxtail soup. You'd dip entire pieces into soy sauce, slurp the meat off the bone, and then suck the marrow dry. You'd lift up the bowl and gulp down the soup, your throat bouncing up and down. And then ask for another bowl. Well, that's the way you should eat oxtail soup, suck up everything.*

I also cooked soups for your father and me. Adults need soups too because as we get older, our bodies change, lose vitality, and don't heal as quickly. Gee hong *(turtle soup) strengthens the body. Lots of nutrients, like a multiple vitamin. Same herbs as with oxtail soup. You see, Toisanese always used the same herbs. Maybe it started because we were poor farmers, but really, there's no need to get so fancy with herbs, like Big City people do. They use this and that herb from Mount Emei, so-and-so tree bark from Szechwan, and this and that tuber from Xinjian—paying five hundred dollars an ounce and so on. Simple herbs with local vegetables and meats cost less and are just as powerful. The trick is to use your eyes and look for the glow of quality; use your fingers and feel the living Ch'i stored in the ingredients. That's how to make good soups.*

Turtle soup is best eaten just before winter. The turtle should weigh four to five pounds. The turtle should be alive with a healthy shell, shiny eyes, and active feet. The really important thing beforehand is to remove the intestines and organs that have toxins. And you have to remove it without spilling any of the toxins onto the flesh of the turtle. Otherwise, the soup tastes bitter. This is not hard to do once you know how.

For cooking turtle soup, we used the special lacquer pot that is used only for cooking herbal soups. It looks like a little bushel, reddish in color and covered with wires on the outside. Simmer turtle soup with the same herbs we always use, but add a lot of Chinese liquor to give it a very strong fire Ch'i. Cook it for about four hours. Eat it just before bedtime, after dinner has been digested. That way, the balance of the medicinal ingredients is not upset. Dinner foods have a very different kind of balance—don't mix dinner foods with Ch'i soups.

The first time I made turtle soup, the turtle lived in the sink for a few days. You and Richard played with it every day, walking it in the hallway, placing it in the bathtub full of water. So you refused to drink the broth. You were sad that I had killed your new pet. But that was okay, because turtle soup is really for adults. Kids have strong Ch'i, and turtle soup could add too much fire. But because you had been so sick the year before, your father and I decided you should have at least one bowl. "Turtle is a food, not a pet," I had to explain. You complained about the green color and the smell and so on. But we watched you drink it down until it was gone.

Sometimes I made ngow-now hong *(cow-brain soup). Like turtle soup, cow-brain soup strengthens the body, but it is especially good for removing the chill in the head area you get from chu feng, or a "blowing wind" that is so strong it tears holes in your energy body. Also, if you have a lot of headaches, cow-brain soup cures that. Toisan people believe that* seck, *or dampness, can gather in your brain, and cow-brain soup is good for clearing that. If you don't remove the dampness, you may not suffer right away. But when you're older, ohhh, you'll have lots of headaches and get sick all the time.*

Before cooking cow brain, you have to remove the red veins. This is not hard—soak it in salt water for a few minutes, and they just come off in your fingers. Same basic herbs, pour in a little white Chinese liquor, add chung-koon *(wallachi tree bark) and* bok kee *(Angelica root). Boil everything for about two hours. By then, the brain is white, smooth, and soft like tofu. This is an adult soup, but because I wanted to strengthen you and Richard, I served you small portions, about a rice bowl's worth. It was funny. You were so skeptical. But the soup was oh so sweet, and after you dipped a piece in soy sauce, you couldn't stop eating until it was all gone!*

Jee-gek hong (pig-feet soup) is definitely an adult soup—so much strong, white liquor in the soup, a child could get drunk. You insisted on trying it because you really enjoyed my soups. But one spoonful, your face grimaced; you said, "Ugghhh," and coughed it back into the bowl.

There are lots more seasons-change and Ch'i-adjusting soups—like yin wall hong *(bird's nest soup),* you chee hong *(dried scallop soup),* schloot ngee hong *(white fungus soup), and* hlee mee hong *(four-tastes soup). The four ingredients of four-tastes soup are* wai san *(Chinese yams),* len doo *(lotus seed),* bok hop *(lily bulbs), and* hah geen *(almond). The main soups I made for my children were winter melon, oxtail, bean-curd, turtle, and cow-brain, and that turned out to be good enough. You were the weaker child—more colds and flu than Richard. And you had tuberculosis when you were eleven. But by your midteen years, you were very healthy. Strong body and a quick mind. Straight As in everything, even gym. You played basketball for your junior high school. Not bad for a child with tuberculosis. Even now, you're still very healthy, alert, very strong, and everyone says you look ten or fifteen years younger! Good Toisanese soups, that's why. Strong Ch'i for life!*

CHAPTER 12

RAGTAG BOY SCOUTS

During the 1950s, our family lived at 638 Kearny Street in the heart of old San Francisco, across the street from historic Portsmouth Square. Surprisingly, this urban village, in a section called the International District, replicated the characteristic values of a Toisan village: safety, respect, cooperation, and above all, protection of children. People from all over the world lived here in a surprisingly respectful harmony. Thus, our street was emotionally familiar to Mother—a clean, well-lit, and compassionate place to raise kids. Trustworthy shop owners and caring neighbors watched over her kids, just as her own village had watched out for her.

Portsmouth Square itself was a museum of the early history of San Francisco. Monuments commemorated its genesis as the plaza for the founding Spanish town of Yerba Buena, the site of the first American flag raising, home of California's first public schoolhouse, and a favorite haunt of Robert Louis Stevenson.

Beginning in the 1850s, thousands of Chinese made their way across the square to a Chinatown growing along Grant Avenue. They came to work the gold mines and build the first transcontinental railroad, but stayed to farm, fish, build businesses, and start Chinatowns up and down the West Coast. By the 1950s, when I played in the square, Chinatown surrounded it on three sides. Our apartment building was among the remnants of the lawless Barbary Coast, like the historic Bella Union Theater where the great opera singer Caruso sang and the row of burlesque joints along Pacific Avenue still in business in my youth.

Across from the square was the old Hall of Justice—the city's police headquarters, jail, and courts. A block away from the square was the International Hotel and other bachelor hotels, home to scalawags from every nation and a community of Filipino American veterans. Nearby was City Lights Bookstore, the epicenter of Beat poetry.

It was here, on the square, along the International District, and in Chinatown, that I enjoyed an idyllic, wondrous childhood in the heart of a big city. Our parents never admonished us to stay away from our neighbors based on their race, ethnicity, or language. They encouraged us to get to know them and to tell stories about them, and then would drop by to thank particularly kind ones.

Like Benny Beltram, a Filipino American who operated Benny's Smoke Shop, an eight-by-ten-foot hole-in-the-wall stuffed to the ceiling with pocket-size goodies for neighborhood bachelors, winos, the nearby constabulary, and kids alike. Against his back wall and up to the ceiling, Benny displayed exotically named cigars from all over the world—Diego Garcia cigars, Bering Havana Tampas, Dutch Masters, Corolla Sports Deluxe, Bayuk Philadelphia Handmade Perfectos, La Flor de Tampa Conches Extras, Webster Dreams Special Seleccion, Dry Climate Brand Perfectos—stored in cigar boxes in clean colors of straw, white, burgundy, emerald green, or gold, bordered with thin multicolored ribbons or crossed with a wide gold or red sash, and some aromatic wooden ones with a brass hook to keep the cover shut.

On the left side wall, Benny sold America's favorite cigarettes—Viceroy, Lucky Strike, Winston, Kool, and Kent; rolling tobacco in glistening white sacks with drawstrings; round tins of Copenhagen chewing tobacco; Gallo's Thunderbird Port; and the *Racing Form*.

Dominating the counter was a terraced explosion of candies, gums, and cough drops—Mars Bars, Almond Joy, LifeSavers, Wrigley's, Smith Brothers, Juicy Fruit, M&M's (plain and with peanuts), boxed licorice twists, and more—tightly displayed and easy to see even at the eye level of kids. In front of and to the left of the counter, a water-cooled Coca-Cola top-opening fridge offered refreshing 7UP, Squirt, Dr Pepper, and, of course, Coke. Across from the soda pops, a wall rack gripped the scruff of bags of Laura Scudder's and Granny Goose potato chips.

Just outside, two tall racks of comic books leaned against the store's wall—Archie, Superman, Richie Rich, and Classic Comics, which introduced us to *Treasure Island, Two Years Before the Mast, A Tale of Two Cities, The Man in the Iron Mask,* and *The Count of Monte Cristo* before public school did and kept us quietly entranced for many an afternoon. On the sidewalk, next to the street, a news rack prominently displayed breaking headlines of the morning papers—the *Examiner,* the Hearst-chain flagship paper, and the *San Francisco Chronicle*—and later in the afternoon, of the *News Call-Bulletin.*

All day long, packages of tobacco, candy, munchies, bottles of wine and soda, and newspapers and comics flew over the counter in rapid-fire exchanges from 7 a.m. to 6 p.m., six days a week.

Benny's Smoke Shop was also an informal community center. Like the families in our building, Benny exemplified the village sensibility of treating others' children as a communal trust. In the summertime, we neighborhood kids met there to read comics and share sodas and chips. We earned extra money by running errands for Benny before deciding on the group's mischief of the day. Hike up to Coit Tower to pick berries and catch bees? Triple feature and steaming hot dogs with mustard and fresh-chopped onions on Market Street? Walk through North Beach to Aquatic Park to catch baby crabs, wet our shoes, and get in trouble with our mothers? Benny knew our whereabouts, so our mothers often checked in with him to find out where we were or left messages for us with him. Filipino men stopped by for letters from home and then dropped into a lilting, almost popping, Tagalog conversation, sharing gossip and arguing Filipino politics. Benny shifted seamlessly back and forth from English to Tagalog as customers shouted out greetings or cigarette brands. Every morning, gamblers bought the *Racing Form* and shared tips about the horses before trekking off to catch the trains to Bay Meadows Racetrack, returning late in the afternoon to celebrate with a bottle of Thunderbird Port or to grouse.

Over time, Benny quietly settled on Richard as his chief errand runner and slowly trained him on how to order goods, pick them up, and restock the shelves. Hence, Richard had more money than I did, which felt strange at first because, as an older brother, I was supposed to do better. But since we shared everything, his generous treats soothed the stings to my ego. Besides, Benny made everyone feel wanted. He treated us to the daily soup from the Star Cafeteria a few doors down. Our favorites were vegetable and chicken noodle. We'd voraciously dip the crunchy sweet-dough bun slathered with butter into the steaming broth. And every few days, he offered us soft drinks and chips.

Nor was Benny alone in this instinct. Molly, a blonde, buxom, big-haired Irish American woman, spent her days with Sam at Sam's Cleaners & Alterations. Sam himself was a grizzle-faced, bespectacled Chinese American who spoke American perfectly. They sat across from each other over Sam's sewing machine, which was positioned perpendicular to the front counter and door so Sam could easily crane his neck to greet entering customers while sewing, catch the afternoon sun, and, of course, pay attention to Molly. If Sam were hunched over his sewing machine, busily hemming pants legs or pulling thread through a buttonhole with his teeth, Molly would quietly paint her fingernails even redder or touch up her face with very red lipstick, powder, or eyebrow pencils.

But mostly they sat like royalty, the king and queen of Kearny Street, facing the street, legs crossed, shouting greetings, and joking with passersby. They shared bottles of Pabst Blue Ribbon beer and took turns blowing smoke rings through the other one's smoke rings. Meanwhile, we petted Sam's collie, tied up in front by the fire hydrant, and pretended she was the television hero-dog Lassie. We played hide-and-seek under the racks of dry cleaning that filled up the back of the shop, pushing our bodies through them as if on a planet with a thick atmosphere. The hiss and steam created by Sam's workers pressing clothing on the adjacent ironing boards suggested an even more mysterious landscape, like that of red planet Mars, which we knew from the triple-feature cinemas along Market Street. If one of us fell crying onto the concrete while playing outside, Molly would sit us on her lap and comfort us. But in the evenings, Molly left Sam's Cleaners for Smokey's Bar, where we could see her laughing, drinking, and smoking through the swinging door. Then she acted like she didn't know us as she went back and forth with different men, arms around waists, to her room at the Hotel Justice, a few doors away.

In an era when interracial couplings were taboo, Sam and Molly's unusual, undefined, and very public pairing was silent courage. They were not a traditional couple, but neo-outcasts, and perhaps living on the social margins rendered them tough enough to live as they pleased.

Sometimes Sam treated us to a hamburger from the Lee family restaurant next door, especially if we had run back and forth several times bringing him and Molly cold beers. Mr. Lee seemed pleased at each and every order, as if we were calling upon his best abilities. We watched attentively from the counter as he personally patted each new burger by hand, dicing fresh onions and pressing them into the patty before placing the patty on the open grill. As the patty sizzled, Mr. Lee deftly sliced a fresh tomato, rinsed the bright, green lettuce leaves in the adjacent sink, and lightly toasted the whites of the buns on the grill before slathering both sides with mayonnaise. He put it all together, sliced it into two perfect halves, and presented it to us on a white oblong plate with a side of crisp potato chips. All for twenty cents. Heaven was biting into a Mr. Lee hamburger.

The Compass Bookstore was on Clay Street, around the corner from Sam's Cleaners. Mr. and Mrs. Jackson owned and operated it, so everyone called it Jackson's Bookstore. The bookstore was a two-story cathedral stocked from floor to ceiling. A balcony that stretched along the four walls, dangling precariously over the main floor, held a slender second story of floor-to-ceiling shelves packed with hardcover literature. Everything was dark wood, cozy and quiet.

Wood. There was so much wood in Jackson's Bookstore—a light, shiny, quiet, cathedral-like world holding books, tons of books, thousands of volumes. Books made from wood, turned into pulp, treated, rolled out into sheets, cut into pages, printed on, bound between hard covers made from wood, and placed on wooden shelves and wooden display cases leaning against wood walls joined to wood floors and wood ceilings, wood ladders to reach higher wood shelves, wood stairs to reach the wood balcony with its wood railings with more books. Books that were eventually sold over a wood counter and paid for with dollar bills manufactured from wood.

Mother once explained that wood is one of the five elemental forces in Chinese culture (the other four elemental forces are fire, water, wind, and earth) and that each of us has a personality that is mostly of one element, so our character is stamped that way throughout our life. That's why it's important to know your element type, so you can know your strengths and weaknesses.

Mother said I was a wood element personality because my face reads wood, very placid and almost poker-faced, the visage of a contemplative, quiet person who would not be satisfied with the basic understandings of life, but would always want to know more, to go deeper.

Is that why I felt so at home in Jackson's Bookstore, this temple constructed of wood, chock-full of ideas, history, and imagination, there to mull at my own leisure, with each inspiration individually bound in the form of a book made from wood?

Mr. and Mrs. Jackson played European classical music all day long as they stacked and stocked books, explained titles to customers, and rang up sales on the brass keys of their noisy old cash register. The Jacksons took time to point out certain books, especially history books, explaining their contents to us. We didn't always understand, but listened anyway, and got into the habit of perusing books. This early and easy experience made books seem like friends, confidants who would tell you everything you ever needed to know, like pals who could entertain you endlessly. Still, we habitually ended up among the pulp fiction with its horrific covers of ghouls rising from graves against a full moon, or vampires carrying women into the midnight, or of women who looked surprisingly like Molly, cigarettes dangling from their reddened lips and holding a smoking pistol over a dead man lying at their feet. "Had our Molly ever shot a man dead?" I asked myself one day. She certainly was tough enough and sometimes gave overly familiar customers at Sam's Cleaners a look so chilling it could kill.

In the evenings, the local beat patrolman, affectionately nicknamed Danny the Wop, paused during his brisk rounds of twisting and rattling the handles of closed shop doors to make sure we were okay as we played hopscotch and foursquare outside our apartment building. Sometimes, he joined us in an ever-so-short game of toss or gave us change for potato chips and ice cream.

There was a small contingent of older African American men who shared the bachelor hotels with Filipinos. They began their mornings with bottles of Thunderbird and cigarettes from Benny and then whiled away the day sunning on the benches in Portsmouth Square. Or they gathered in front of their friend's shoeshine stand across the street from Jackson's Bookstore.

Ralph was tall and gaunt, forever gracing everyone with a smile. Killer Diller was mean, always growling at us, and sometimes pretending to chase us with a butter knife, behavior befitting his nickname. Yet once, when a very mean white man, a stranger to our neighborhood, shouted racially derogatory names at us—an occurrence so odd that we froze in confusion rather than consternation—and charged menacingly at me, Killer Diller came to the rescue. He shouted, "Leave that boy alone," and placed himself squarely between us. I had been paralyzed with fear, and if Killer Diller had not intervened, I am sure I would have been injured. That was the only time he looked at me with open kindness, with unconcealed concern in his eyes. "You all right?" "Yes," I shouted and, "Thanks, Killer Diller!" as I ran off with my pals. I knew then that Killer Diller, for all his histrionics, could never hurt us. He was our Scary Man, and we were his kids to scare, but always in play.

On sunny Sundays, we woke up to the robust sounds of African American spirituals soaring up from Portsmouth Square. Perhaps young eyes see more sharply, and gazing out our windows, I could make out Killer Diller dressed in a fresh suit with a red carnation, along with Ralph and the other bachelors in their glistening Sunday best arrayed along the green-painted park benches. Large African American women adorned in outrageous hats and shiny red, blue, and black dresses beat out rhythms on their clanging tambourines as they led the assembled in shouts and calls, prayers, praise, and song. Ralph and Killer Diller would raise one hand to the sky while the other rested on their hearts, shouting hallelujahs and praising Jesus. Sometimes, they leapt up to dance around, both hands shaking in the air, faces uplifted to the sunny, blue heavens.

Nurtured in this milieu by resilient, canny survivors, our neighborhood gang acquired an unusual optimism and resourcefulness. Is it any wonder then that we started our own Boy Scout troop?

Several weeks earlier, Donald Soo and I had visited the Boy Scouts of St. Mary's Catholic Church and School. Donald lived with his five sisters in the house next door and was my best friend of the "outside-the-apartment-building club," just as Sonney

Chong was my best friend of the "inside-the-apartment-building club," a four-story home for eight families.

But one night, Donald and I went to watch Sonney go through his paces in his Boy Scout uniform at St. Mary's Catholic Church and School. As visitors, we sat on the top of foldout tables, as quiet as could be. Lined up perfectly, the troop recited the Scout's Oath, passed uniform inspection, and then drilled. Several merit badges were awarded, and later they worked on tying sailors' knots.

Donald and I yearned to sign up for Boy Scouts, but couldn't because our families couldn't spare the money.

But one school night, as we sat around the apartment's central stairwell chatting, studying, and playing games, Sonney flipped through his Boy Scout manual with me. He taught me the Scout's salute, three middle fingers of the right hand straight up next to each other and the thumb curled over the pinky. Then I practiced the Scout's Oath, reviewed the manual sections about hiking, marking the trail back with twigs or stones, and starting and extinguishing fires. We discussed what it meant that a Scout is always prepared. On another night, we practiced tying knots.

Soon enough, Richard learned the knots too. Then Sonney's sisters, Maxine and Marie, joined us. We all memorized the Scout's Oath. Soon Donald and his sister Ruby joined us every night. Then Henry and Harry from the restaurant dropped in.

One day, someone suggested, "Why don't we start our own Boy Scout troop?" A giant lightbulb lit up over all of us. Yes, why not indeed? What did we need? Well, we needed Boy Scout manuals, Boy Scout kerchiefs, pocketknives, flags for each troop, and Boy Scout uniforms with caps. The merit badge activities we could take straight out of the manual, and we could practice in the hallways of our apartment building.

For the flagstaffs, our mothers contributed old brooms and mops about to be thrown away. We sawed off the old bristles and mops with pocketknives. To make the flags, Mother gave us clean cotton diapers saved from our childhood. Cut diagonally, they made perfect triangles for the troop flags. A skilled illustrator, Sonney drew animals on the troop flags for Eagle, Bear, and Snake Troops. I headed up Eagle Troop and Richard headed up Bear Troop. Drop-ins and less-devoted members lined up as Snake Troop. With the side rails from a crib, we built a lean-to command post against a banister. A large 7UP box and a hand-crafted stool served as a desk for Sonney. He was Scout Master, no question ever about it. He had the training, the uniform, and the only Boy Scout manual.

But as the weeks passed, we dreamed of having our own manuals and uniforms. Richard and I approached Mr. Jackson of Jackson's Bookstore to buy some used Boy Scout manuals. "You see, Mr. Jackson," we attempted to explain, "we started a troop in our building. We did it because we couldn't afford to join a bona fide post, like at St. Mary's." Mr. Jackson rounded up several old manuals that were in fairly good shape. He took only fifteen cents. A few days later, he gave us a couple more for free and *presto!* we each had our own manual. Next acquisition—neckerchiefs. We saved our pennies, and eventually Sonney ordered Boy Scout neckerchiefs through St. Mary's for each of us.

Every night after homework, we assembled as Boy Scout Troop #638, Kearny Street Post, just outside my family's apartment door. We stood at attention in our assembly area, Richard and I in front of our respective troops as Sonney inspected and drilled us. We were so organized, serious, and sharp that the adults started to watch us nightly—big smiles on their faces. Like a panel of judges, they commented on our drills—crisp right turns, about-faces, at-attention, and salutes to Sonney. But it became clear that, except for Sonney, we all wore ragamuffin street clothes, the Boy Scout kerchiefs our only unifying feature.

Apparently astounded that our interest did not wane, the adults must have discussed getting uniforms for us. Mrs. Chong knew the cost, and that put a stop to the talk of uniforms. But my mother didn't stop thinking about it. After all, she lived by the Eighth Promise, to take care of her children regardless of the circumstances.

Unbeknownst to us, Mother had stored the Chinese Nationalist Army uniforms her mother had given her so many years ago on a high shelf in our bedroom. One day, she and Father brought them out, handing them to us. The boxes erupted into a disarray of snatched garments. We saw they were khaki-colored uniforms too, with a little more green than the official Boy Scouts, but to our delight, they were close enough in color. Our second thought was that we wouldn't fit into adult army uniforms, but to our surprise, the jackets, shirts, pants, and trench coats looked like children's sizes. "Wow," I thought, "the Nationalist soldiers must have been small people—like the munchkins in *The Wizard of Oz*."

And so we lined up in our uniforms, courtesy of Chiang Kai-shek's Chinese Nationalist Army, an army often composed of small underfed teenagers—and therefore, our size.

When refugees flee, they take only what they need: food and drink, money and gold, addresses and phone numbers for people in cities they might go to, and perhaps a warm jacket and a change of clothes. What had possessed Mother to carry these bulky uniforms over so many difficult miles, from Toisan to Guangzhou to Hong Kong to America, several apartments, and finally up three flights of stairs to this apartment?

Was it the dream that the Nationalists, with the help of their American friends, would one day retake the mainland that had kept her hanging onto these antiquated uniforms? Was this part of the fourth promise to her mother, to keep the dream of Sun Yat-sen alive? Or was it in honorable memory of her older brother, a beloved teacher and Nationalist official who had died for the Nationalist cause—either driven off or thrown off the roof of our village home during the Communist assumption of power?

Guided by the imperatives of her Eighth Promise, she must have weighed the old Nationalist dream against her self-reliant children's concrete needs of today and then cut the lingering sentimental ties to the closed reality of her former life, its dying dreams. Her life was now in America. Her children needed uniforms here, now, today, so they could be Boy Scouts of America. Not China, not Guangzhou, and not even Toisan, but the Boy Scouts of America, in America, their home.

And that's how the Kearny Street Boy Scout Troop came into being. We exulted in our status as bona fide Boy Scouts. We recited the oath, tied knots, and left trail markers throughout our building. We drilled endlessly and tightly in our narrow hallway and tight alcoves. We practiced being prepared, storing water bottles and packaged foods in case of an earthquake. With the uniforms, we were no longer poor kids.

Our neighborhood had given us the gift of resourcefulness. But it was Mother who had magically legitimized us. Now we were just as good as the official Boy Scout Troop at St. Mary's, each one decked out proper and grinning from ear to ear. Mother bestowed this gift not just on her own sons, but also upon all the children in our Clan village–like three-story apartment building.

CHAPTER 13

THE TOISAN RULES
FOR HUSBANDS

There weren't many unmarried Chinese women in America. Not in the 1950s. Many more Chinese men than women, I mean for Chinese who weren't born here, who didn't speak American well. You see, American-born Chinese women wouldn't marry immigrant men from China. They wanted to move out of Chinatown after college, not be stuck in a marriage with someone less Americanized. For them, Chinatown was for weekends—to visit their parents, buy Chinese food, enjoy Chinese movies, banquet with friends, and so on. They wanted American-born Chinese husbands, people like them. That was the way it was, and so there were lots of eligible Toisanese bachelors.

I had promised to help my family get to America, but I couldn't sponsor them until I was a citizen myself. Marriage to a Toisan bachelor who was an American citizen, however, could get my two sisters here right away. I set out to find a husband first for Yoong and then for Tien, my youngest sister. This was during the late 1950s, when the immigration laws were so tricky that sometimes an overseas wife would be denied a visa.

I put the word out—to the Clan Sisters in San Francisco, the merchants on Grant Avenue, and all the family associations.

We didn't marry for love, you know, or for good times. Go-betweens arranged marriages. I became the go-between for my sisters. What I looked for in a Toisan husband was:

1. **Kun-lick**—*A determined worker, not easily discouraged. A saver, not a spender.*

2. **Jett**—*Truthful, reliable. Not a troublemaker.*

3. **How sheen foo**—*A good, strong body of average
   height and build. Someone with character who could
   put up with all kinds of difficulties, day after day,
   without giving up.*

4. **Guai doi**—*A man who is not flamboyant and had no
   bad habits like gambling, drinking, or womanizing.*

5. **Leck doi**—*Intelligent enough to work and take care
   of the family, but no need for brilliance.*

*The Wong couple introduced Mr. Shleen-wah Wong to me.
You remember the elder Wongs—they lived across from us at our
Kearny Street apartment and later moved to North Ping Yuen the
same time we did? They knew Mr. Lai, who used to visit us. Mr.
Lai was a very nice man with a car who took us on Sunday outings.
But he was too short, all hunched over all the time. Also, he had a
hearing problem, and later there were rumors he had a wife in
China anyway. Not for my sisters.*

*Anyway, elderly Mrs. Wong knew I was prospecting, and
Shleen-wah was a Wong too, possibly a relative. So she arranged a
first meeting between us. A getting-to-know-him meeting without
talking about marriage. I cooked a special meal and, as it turned
out, Shleen-wah Wong was very nice. In World War II, he served in
the American army, fighting the Japanese. He was captured and
tortured. For months. Once he was buried up to his neck in dirt as
a punishment. For a long time, he said. But he survived and received
some compensation from America for his hardships. Maybe
because he was Chinese American and not a white person, the Japanese soldiers treated him worse. Still, Shleen-wah was strong and
healthy. And he had all the qualities of a good Toisan husband. He
was a chef. He was frugal and ambitious—saving money to start
his own business. He smoked a little, but that's all. In those days,
everybody smoked cigarettes, even your father.*

But there was one problem. Mr. Wong was older, much older

than Yoong. About twenty years older, as a matter of fact. So we met a couple of more times so I could be sure, always over dinner at our home. Finally, I decided to show him a picture of Yoong. He thought she was very pretty. And I think because he had gotten to know me, he assumed that Yoong would be just as nice and as capable a wife.

That was why I cooked dinner for him, dressed nice, and treated him nice. I knew that if he liked me, he could get to like Yoong. After all, Yoong was in Hong Kong, and he was here. In those days, most people still traveled by boat—President Lines mostly. Airplane travel was new and expensive—only for rich people. You couldn't just fly over and have a long weekend date. Besides, Mr. Wong was not romantic at all, just very businesslike. He still wanted children, and time was running out. Basically, he wanted a reliable wife more than fun.

I agreed to tell Yoong about him. I wrote her a long letter with a photo of Mr. Wong. Yoong wrote back that she didn't mind his age. So I turned it over to them to decide the rest. After several letters, they agreed to a meeting. Mr. Wong went to Hong Kong, and the next thing you know, they were married, and he returned to sponsor her immigration.

I was confident that the match would turn out fine because, well, Yoong is matter-of-fact about life. She doesn't need a lot of fun, and she doesn't like to spend money. Very frugal. Yoong wanted security, to be taken care of. Mr. Wong could provide security. Also, Yoong looks older than her age, older looking than me even though I am the first sister. The way she is, she seems more like an old person anyway. Perhaps too for Yoong, it was a plus that Mr. Wong felt his time was running out.

Mr. Wong even asked your father to partner with him. He had the money, but didn't speak American well. Your father spoke American well, but mainly he was very comfortable dealing with white men, since that's what he did all day in white-owned restaurants—chatting, debating politics, and joking back at white people every day. Well, Mr. Wong knew of a grocery store for sale near Hyde Street and California, you know, where the dang-dang cheh—*the cable cars—turn the corner before going down to the Financial District? They even visited the store several times, but your father decided to invest in another business. Mr. Wong bought an apartment building instead, near the same corner as the store.*

Mr. Wong died sometime in the 1970s. Yoong still lives there, in the sunny penthouse, alone now since her two sons left for college and then jobs. Yoong is financially secure, collecting the rents from four apartments. The building keeps going up in value—from the original fifty thousand dollars to several million dollars now.

She's become a cheapskate. Stays home most of the time, counting her money. Me, I'm not like that. If I have money, I take the train with your father to the Bay Meadows Racetrack and watch the horses. We gamble ten or fifteen dollars for fun. Win or lose, no problem. Or we ride the bus out to Serramonte Shopping Center in Daly City. If we have just enough money, we don't even hesitate—we eat the buffet at Sizzler.

Or I'll fly to China and visit my Clan Sisters. Lots of good times there. If I come back broke, I stay close to home, gossiping with my Chinatown Clan Sisters. Lots of places in Chinatown for low-price pastries fresh from the oven with coffee or a three-course lunch with beverage. Take a walk to Fisherman's Wharf or downtown to look at the Macy's windows and hunt for sales. Why not? Life is good!

But Yoong is not like that. She doesn't like to spend money, even though she has so much now. That's why Yoong and Mr. Wong were a good match—they were both frugal. Hung onto money. Didn't have too much fun.

My youngest sister, Tien, is very different from Yoong. She's prettier, very playful, fiery tempered—a very quick thinker. I knew she would be happier with a man who respected her opinions and treated her as an equal rather than one who wanted to be in charge and put women down. So, Mr. Richard Lee was a good match for her. Same name as your brother—Richard Lee. Lots of Richard Lees in America. He was pleasant and mild-mannered, in his early twenties, about the same age as Tien.

At first I didn't think of him as a husband prospect. He was just a struggling college student who lived next door to us. No job, no money. Mr. Lee was so poor, he had to share his small room with another student. He couldn't afford to eat in restaurants and he couldn't cook. So I invited him to join us at dinner. Mr. Lee's favorite food was fish pan-fried in black bean sauce and chopped onions. He salivated when he smelled the dish. He was always so hungry, he'd wolf it down with two quick bowls of rice.

I guess I felt sorry for him, like for a younger brother. He was naïve too, a scholar with a gentle personality. That's why I always made his favorite dish. That kind of fish was very cheap—twenty-five cents for four small fishes, like the shiners you used to catch at Fisherman's Wharf. And four was more than enough to share. I even washed and ironed his clothes. You remember we had a washing machine at the time, the only one in the building? I was just helping him, not really thinking about his marrying my sister.

Many go-betweens had approached him, and he had refused them all. And that's what started me thinking. Maybe he would make a good husband for Tien. There must be some reason why all the go-betweens propositioned him. When I suggested that perhaps he and Tien might make a good marriage, he didn't say no to me. I think that was because of my kindness to him. Maybe he felt he owed me a favor. Maybe he had grown to like me, and like Mr. Wong, he thought Tien would be like me, that she too would cook good food for him, especially black-bean-and-onion-sauce fish! His eyes lit up at her photo—Tien was very pretty. And later, after several letters, Tien agreed to meet him.

Richard didn't have much money or a steady job yet, so he didn't meet all the criteria for a good husband, especially kun-lick. But he studied hard and read books all the time, and so I thought he would work hard when the time came. He spoke American quite well, although not as well as your father. Besides, as a college man, maybe he would do something else besides restaurant and laundry work. And everything else seemed okay. He voyaged to Hong Kong, and there he married Tien.

Well, as the years went by, Richard did work hard as a busboy at the Commercial Club downtown. He ended up as a restaurant worker after all! But he saved his tips and his thirteenth-month Christmas bonus, year after year. They moved into the North Ping Yuen housing project, just like us. I had told them about it when we moved in and it was still brand-new, like a rich apartment building with a sunny view of the bay. Later, he and Tien bought a nice house in the Avenues, the Sunset District, with my brother. It's now worth lots of money, probably about a million and a half.

It turned out Mr. Lee and Tien are more like equals. Mr. Lee is actually a bit timid and indecisive, but Tien's fiery will and expressiveness balance him out. Sometimes they sound like two sides of the same person, thinking out loud with each other and finishing each other's sentences. They really love each other.

So this one too turned out to be a good match. And so I fulfilled the promise to my mother to find my sisters good husbands.

Your father helped me all along the way, even though we did fight about money. But that's little stuff. He didn't mind that I prepared expensive meals for Mr. Wong. Or the cost of Mr. Lee joining us for dinner night after night. Or my doing Mr. Lee's laundry in a washing machine that Father paid for. Father knew it was right for me to find husbands.

And it was your father who helped me to pass my citizenship test so I could bring my mother and brother to America. Father found and paid for the immigration lawyer who prepared me for the oral test. Every week or two, I walked to that Financial District office to be tested on the last week's set of practice questions and to receive a new list. The lawyer assigned a Mrs. Wong, who spoke Cantonese, but not Toisanese, to work with me. She wasn't very friendly at first.

There was one major problem: I didn't speak American, and the oral test was in American. I didn't read American, and the study materials were in American. Your father worked all day and couldn't teach me, so he assigned you to be my tutor. He explained that you earned good grades in every subject, good enough to tutor me, and had time because you were on summer vacation. I think you were around ten years old then.

You both ended up as my tutors actually, because your Chinese wasn't that good, and that left Father to explain the test questions to me in Toisanese. They were mostly about democracy, which I knew about from Sun Yat-sen. Oh, there were questions about the three branches of US government, the election system, the most important presidents, the rights of citizenship, and so on. If the test was in Chinese, I could have passed it easy and saved a lot of money.

So your job was to help me understand in American. Oh, we tried so hard. You read each question, and I tried to read it back. You read each answer, and I tried to read it back. Day after day— impossible to learn both the American language and memorize the citizenship test in one summer.

One morning, quite frustrated, I started writing Chinese char- acters over each syllable, Chinese phonetic equivalents of the American sounds. That's how the idea came to us. I don't know who thought of it first, but we realized that each question and answer had unique-sounding key words. So instead of trying to remember every sentence perfectly, we realized that I only had to memorize the sounds of the key words. I furiously wrote in the closest-sounding Chinese characters over those key words.

If I heard the sounds "first pres-za-dent," I answered, "Wah- sing-ton." If I heard the sounds "free the slaves," I answered, "A- blah-hem Ling-kon." The one I had most trouble with was "kur-rent pres-za-dent." I tried to say, "Dwite-Dee-I-zun-how-wer," but his name was too long. But you told me that your teacher said you could call him "Ike-kee," and that became my answer.

Mrs. Wong didn't like this at all. She felt that I should answer everything in perfect American. I explained to her that we only had so much money and so little time, and I had to get my mother over. She was getting old, stuck in Hong Kong, and this was my promise to her. Even though Mrs. Wong was Cantonese and not Toisanese, an American-born who looked down on immigrants like me, I think she felt what I was feeling, missing my mother and my brother. I think she remembered how hard being Chinese in America could be, that sometimes we have to help each other even if we are not in the same social circles. At first reluctantly and then kindly, she cooperated. Instead of sending me home to perfect my language, she passed me and gave me the next set of questions.

Finally, the big practice day with the lawyer came. He was white, and I had to be able to answer all the questions in any order. I was glad you could stay in the room with me, as you had for every visit with Mrs. Wong. Well, both the lawyer and Mrs. Wong were smiling when we finished. He said I would do fine. I surprised Mrs. Wong when I shook her hand and said, "T'ank you velly much, Wong Tai-tai." She smiled back. "You're welcome."

Two weeks later, we dressed up nice and walked to the Immigration building. You found the right office, and a man called out my name, "Mrs. Poy Jen Lee." He was a nice man. I looked him directly in his eyes and kept smiling. At first he was a little surprised at my short answers; then after he struggled with it, I guess he decided this was okay. After a long time, we finished. He was friendly as he showed me the door. I was sure I had passed, and a few weeks later, the lawyer sent a letter confirming this.

We went to swearing-in day together. I took my new patent leather purse with brass locks from Macy's in Union Square, a celebration gift to myself. We walked to the big courthouse, up the wide stairs with two-story columns, and into the dark wood and marble halls. You found the courtroom—hundreds of people there, all races and ages, new citizens with their families and friends.

The guard said to stand up for the judge, but then the judge asked us to sit down before we even got up all the way. He congratulated everyone on becoming a citizen, then asked us to stand up for real this time and repeat with him the oath of citizenship:

*I hereby declare, on oath, that I absolutely and entirely
renounce . . . all allegiance and fidelity to any foreign*

*prince, potentate, state, or sovereignty of whom or which I
have heretofore been a subject or citizen; that I will support
and defend the Constitution and laws of the United States
of America against all enemies foreign and domestic; that
I will bear true faith and allegiance to the same . . . and that
I take this obligation freely and without any mental reservation or purpose of evasion; so help me God.*

*Then we recited the Pledge of Allegiance with him—loudly,
with every kind of accent echoing back and forth in that big room:
"I pledge allegiance to the flag of the United States of America,
and to the republic for which it stands, one nation under God, indi-
visible, with liberty and justice for all."*

I could hear you saying the pledge along with me.

*To thank you, I took you to Manning's Restaurant, a fancy
place with white tablecloths and bow-tied waiters on Market Street,
near the cable-car turntable. "Order anything you want," I said.
You did—all your favorites—chicken noodle soup, hot dog with
French fries, cherry Coke, and apple pie with vanilla ice cream.*

*A few years later, I sponsored my mother and brother into
America. I was so happy to have my mother near me again—I had
missed her so much all these years. Finally, we were reunited.
Finally, I had someone I could really talk to about my children and
my marriage, especially about your father's meanness.*

CHAPTER 14

BOGIE'S MAN

During my 1983 visit to Toisan, I was stunned to encounter a near-identical twin to my father. Same small stature and sinewy body. Same thinning hair above the brow. He was a teacher at the local grammar school. Unlike Father, his face was devoid of pain, frustration, and struggle. He seemed totally at peace in the world. Beatific, in a word. Gazing deeply into my eyes, as if nothing else mattered, he searched for our Clan connection. Only after he found it did we exchange the briefest of greetings before he nonchalantly turned back to his pupils, all quietly hunched over, whirling brushes on rice paper. In spite of his startling resemblance to Father, the feel of the teacher's presence was, perplexingly, more reminiscent of Mother, as if Father had been emptied of his volatile personality, then refilled with Mother's steady kindness.

And yet he wasn't related to Father, or at least he hadn't responded with specific recognition like my Chun Clan relatives had that same morning in the makeshift village square when they openly recognized Mother in my face. It was more like the teacher felt for our vibe of kinship rather than any specific blood relationship. Kow Woon also did not mention a blood relation, and so the remarkable similarity may have sprung from the commonality of our Toisanese gene pool.

Later that afternoon in 1983, I visited Father's ancestral home, a mini-townhouse of wooden construction. The tenant, Father's teacher from childhood and my parents' marriage go-between, invited me in and then left. He didn't know I was coming either, and yet his ease at my presence and his complete hospitality were as natural as if we had known each other all our lives.

But unlike in Mother's spacious house, little sunlight penetrated the interior of Father's childhood home. I had to move ever so slowly to avoid bumping into the furniture. Shiny farm tools, baskets, pots, and pans hung neatly on every wall. Mother's larger and sunnier home, although comforting, had felt like an abandoned sacred temple, its spirit fires burning low, patiently awaiting the return of the survivors of the dispersed Order to revitalize the space. This smaller, darker townhouse, though shadowed, felt lit up and energized by the thriving lives of the residents.

Unexpectedly, as I descended the steep stairs from the second floor, a sepia-tone photo of Father as a teenager confronted me, eyeball to eyeball. As in a graduation photo, his young face gazed upward, slightly to his left, exuding optimism and promise, someone so brand-new that his visage glowed despite the stairwell's dimness. Father was once beatific, like his near-twin, the village teacher. He wasn't always an unpredictable emotional pendulum.

I wondered, as I crouched in that stairway, about the cost to Father of putting rice on our table every day, of the tearing away at his psyche by a hostile society. If Father had stayed in China, would he be serene like his near-twin? Would he have encouraged me to write or to paint, just as he had composed poetry, instead of pushing me into a moneymaking profession? Would his essence, then, have been completely safe and always nurturing, like Mother's?

Perhaps that's the rub with difficult but not completely abusive fathers. I always wondered whether it could have been better and why it wasn't. Whether Father could have been more of a mentor and later, as I aged and wizened, whether we could have been friends, even buddies. For despite his difficult personality and his unpredictable rage, we inevitably reached back to one another. Many a time he would just call and suggest spending a weekend together. Or I would suggest an outing to some beach or nearby state park. On his seventy-seventh birthday, I invited him over for the day, and on an old upright birdcage piano left by the previous homeowner, I plunked out and sang "Happy Birthday" to him. He seemed deeply touched and then whispered, "No one has ever sung 'Happy Birthday' to me before. No one has ever played the piano for me before."

That was a good day, for on many others his volatility predictably blew up the bridges between us, and many a time I increasingly preferred to let them lay in ruins for an interminable period. It was usually Mother who brought us back together by cajoling me to come home for dinner or, if I was particularly resistant, by springing him on me at some restaurant, despite her promise that she would come alone.

Mother always admonished me, "He's sorry. He knows he was wrong. You know how he is—*mo lo, mo lah*—no sense, just say stuff. It's nothing now. It was said, it's out and over with. I've lived with your dad for years. He's just like that. He doesn't mean it. Forget about it."

Father always confirmed her statement with his downcast eyes. He could never say he was sorry, but his apology was in his demeanor. Over those reunion dinners, Mother and I did most of the talking, and he said little, if anything.

And then it would be fine again—until the next outburst. When I was younger, it was usually during these rages that I momentarily felt that fantasy most of us have indulged in at one time or another—of having been switched at childbirth in the hospital nursery, that these weren't my real parents—because my real father would have been kinder, understood me completely, and done better by me, emotionally, materially, and intellectually.

But of course they were my real parents, and certainly Mother never lacked in my eyes. So over the years, I settled into loving him, accepting his wit, grace, and gifts when Good Father was present, but never, ever making excuses for Bad Father's behavior. And no, it never stopped being confusing.

Physicality—in my earliest childhood memories, it's Father's strength that stands out starkly. First to rise every morning, he'd drop to the floor for thirty push-ups followed by sixty sit-ups. Father labored in restaurants, a supply man and busboy who lifted vegetable boxes, sides of beef, two-gallon cans of tomato sauce, and trays stacked with dishes, eight hours a day or longer. Only slightly over five feet tall, of a slender, compact build, his biceps were large, hard, and round like a curled fist. His body was taut, with sinewy muscles and bulging, dark-blue veins.

Father was a fierce walker. In my earliest childhood, he walked to work—even though the Meteor Restaurant was two miles away—and then home again. Rain, fog, or sunshine. On weekends he propelled us, one on each side like mini-versions of him, to Market Street—San Francisco's boulevard of movie palaces—to catch a double or triple feature. Clutching our hands, he'd launch off as we half-ran to keep up. Eventually, we got the hang of it, tossing our arms far forward with his and stepping large, like soldiers on a triple-time drill. Still my thighs suffered windburn from whipping through so many long blocks, and I'd scratch them while waiting in line for our tickets.

In play, he swung Richard and me around effortlessly and endlessly as we laughed and yelled, "Faster, faster." He'd hoist us high above his head to the ceiling so we could fly like Superman. At the playground, he'd push our swings way past the other kids'. When we headed home late and sleepy from a Cantonese movie, he'd cradle both of us against his shoulders and then climb the three flights of stairs to place us in our beds without waking us.

But Father would explode without warning. Several times when we were kids, Father became so angry that he beat Mother with his fists. Richard and I were so shocked the first time it happened, in the middle of dinner, that we stared incomprehensibly. We had no reference point for violence. We didn't know what was happening. Before we knew it, Mother had fallen on her back, futilely blocking his punches, crying like a baby, and promising to do better. Another time, Richard and I forced our bodies between Father's fist and Mother, thinking he would stop rather than strike his own children. Oblivious, he rained hurtful, bruising blows on all of us. It was heartbreaking to see our gentle, caring, and hardworking mother being beaten.

Even our play could shift surrealistically into terror when he raised us over his head in anger and threw us down like sacks of potatoes onto the mattress. These slams pained us mostly in mind. It was always the bed he threw us against, never the floor or the wall, as if Good Dad would always thwart Bad Dad, even during a rage so intense that Father could not or would not control himself.

But because his abuse was sporadic, I remember Father more as an upbeat, caring man who not only provided us with "three hots and a cot," but tutored us nightly in reading, 'riting, and 'rithmetic. Because the apartment lighting was dim, he set up a naked bulb over the dining table that was exclusively for our use at homework hour. Mother and Father subdued their activities during that time, staying as quiet as vigilant mice until our bedtime.

Saturdays were Market Street matinees, and Sunday morning was American food brunch, when Father cooked up huge, pungent meatballs in a zesty tomato sauce over spaghetti, ham and cheese omelets, macaroni with cheese, or sliced hot dogs in ketchup and onion sauce over white bread.

In the second grade, for my first current affairs assignment, Father taught me analysis by carefully picking apart a news story's key points and then reassembling them into a beguiling narrative. He patiently coached me that first time until I memorized my report. The next day, standing with my feet slightly apart, delicately holding the news clipping in front of my chest with a talking points crib note behind it (just in case), I confidently described the inventor in the photo, a young man proudly holding his prototype of an atomic-based device that looked like a Flash Gordon proton cannon. The teacher raved, and, after a few more successes, I joined Father as an inveterate reader of the daily paper. Soon Richard too excelled in current affairs, and daily we sat with Father on the sofa as he passed sections to us, pointing out stories of interest.

Ever so gently, Father guided us to earn grades of "Excellent" in every subject.

Over time, he fixed a singular goal in our minds: college on a complete scholarship that we could and would earn through good grades. You see, he explained, as a poor family, he could never afford to pay for his sons' college education. He never said this as if it were a shameful thing or as a judgment upon himself, but matter-of-factly. Life was clear—Father worked, Mother took care of the house, and his sons studied to earn college scholarships.

This became such an article of faith for Richard and me that we never doubted that one day the grand prize would simply float into our embrace. Born here. Raised here. Succeed here. College, our American birthright, would deliver us from life as restaurant workers, even if Father had resigned himself to this.

Father's favorite movie star was Humphrey Bogart, and late at night, when he thought we were all asleep, I could hear him softly singing "As Time Goes By" to himself.

Why Bogart and not all the other tough guys crashing across the screen in all those Market Street movie palaces? Because Bogart was the only Hollywood star that a Toisan-featured man could possibly identify with. John Wayne, Gary Cooper, and all the others were too impossibly tall, too barrel-chested, too fair-skinned, and too blond, brown, or redheaded. But Bogart—well, he was shorter, of slender build, with a slightly receding hairline, swarthy-faced, and with strong cheekbones—exactly like Toisan men and remarkably like Father as a young adult. Amazingly, Bogart's hair was black, as black as Chinese hair! And his suits hung loose, the way Chinatown men wore them.

Even more than his appearance, though, it was Bogart's roles that resonated deeply for Father. In *The Maltese Falcon*, Bogart the loner hero walked the streets of San Francisco, often ambushed by rough men and waylaid by cops and district attorneys, but still seizing his living against a cast of unknowable, twisted customers. Father walked these same streets every day and often at night and, along with many Chinese men, risked unprovoked attacks after dark. He also daily confronted the sneak-attack, racial, attitudinal whippings and verbal haymakers from white bosses, customers, and passersby. In *Casablanca*, Bogart was himself an immigrant, betrayed by love and stranded in a hostile, foreign land, far from family and friends. Like Bogart, my stranded father somehow made lemonade out of lemons.

And finally, in character, they were both as reliable as an unstoppable train, always on schedule. Father often repeated that his boss at the Meteor Restaurant considered him indispensable. "Oh, Lee, if I only had a few more workers like you," his boss would say, or "You'll always have a job with me." Wryly, Father remarked that perhaps he should be made a partner, knowing that that could never happen.

Yet, he never missed a day of work and turned his earnings over to Mother every Friday night. Every Saturday night, they handed the landlord his cash for, as my parents taught us, it was important to pay bills on time. Father's industry brought home the apartment building's first television set—a full-screen black-and-white Emerson—and then the first washing machine, from Sears, a whirling tub with a hand-operated wringer to squeeze water from the laundry. Father strove to stay moral and hopeful, to do the right thing by his family and himself. Always by his bedside was a well-thumbed copy of Norman Vincent Peale's *The Power of Positive Thinking*.

Mother suffered a nervous breakdown shortly after Richard's birth. What was surprising was that she had made it that far intact. Nor was this caused solely by Father's periodic rages. The decade of terror during the Japanese ethnic cleansing, the trauma of her older brother's suicide after the Communist victory, her adaptation from life as a working farm girl to one in a completely modern society, her attempts to master a difficult language in months, the sharp severing of the support of her loving mother and Clan Sisterhood—all this had traumatized Mother.

Over the years, I have seen Father's tenderness toward Mother prevail more often than not. In his calmer moments, he would feel guilty about letting her down, about not protecting her. That's why he paid for a babysitter for Richard even as he ranted about every unaccounted-for nickel and dime. He loved his Poy Jen, always had and always would. When I was around seven, he made the biggest demonstration of love a man could possibly make in that day.

This feat began when he became business partners in an auto repair business with a man named Kai Yep. We called him Yep Sook—Mr. Yep in Toisanese—or Bob, his American name. Eventually, we called him Bob all the time. In smaller, delightful ways, Bob was more generous with Richard and me than Father ever was, treating us to potato chips, sodas, and comic books and giving us his spare change. The business tanked, but Bob stayed in our lives. He was Father's best friend—a jovial, verbose buddy who openly admired Father's grasp of politics and world affairs. In fact, Bob was the only friend Father ever had.

Soon, with his freewheeling schedule, Bob was helping Mother with shopping, picking up Richard and me after school, or driving us to the beach, the zoo, or Golden Gate Park. Mother and Bob spent so much time together that the Chong kids started to insinuate that something more than friendship was going on. Evidently, much more was going on, for I caught them *en deshabille* several times, although as a kid I did not fathom the implications of partial undress in the middle of the day.

Father undoubtedly suspected, but in spite of his easily triggered rages, he never expressed jealousy, accused Mother of unfaithful behavior, or in any way cut Bob off from the family. I think Father knew he couldn't meet all of Mother's needs, socially, emotionally, or financially. And so, like all good Toisanese, he accommodated, so long as minimal appearances were maintained. He genuinely wanted Mother to be happy, and if happiness was an unspoken triangle of sorts, well, so be it. Besides, Bob not only met so many of Father's needs too, but put up with his mood swings. Perhaps, as with so many other immigrant fathers, compromise was part of survival. He had no choice but to absorb the blows of the outside world to keep body and family together; now what could he do but accept this unkind cut to his uneven family life. One can only fight so many battles.

For his part, Bob did not seek to take Mother away from Father, nor did he try to commandeer our affections with his treats. All of our adults held it together for the entire family unit.

In many significant ways, Father exercised a good, strong influence, including this remarkable instance of Toisan flexibility and pragmatism. But he could not pass on to me the subtler, more potent Toisan ways. Summoned by his father at the age of thirteen to America, a society for which he had no preparation, he had to assimilate as quickly and as completely as possible. The price for the desperate bargain his father forced upon him was to jettison his Toisan ways.

In this way, it ended up that Mother, and not Father, was always our connection to the Toisan sensibility. Having reached adulthood before she left the village, she retained the inherent Toisan characteristics of compassion combined with industry and perseverance. Father was only half-formed and, perhaps because of this, he was Toisan interrupted—broken by his being thrust into America. He worked hard and persevered, but denied compassion by his father and struggling always to survive, his own compassion slowly dribbled away over the years.

So too had his beatific visage, as I realized as an adult, as I stood in midstride in his childhood home's stairway, gazing at his lovely teenage face.

Mother was our quiet yin influence, just as Father was clearly our yang influence. Mother embodied China, while Father personified America.

But when we were young boys, Father's yang was always more eye-catching, thrilling, and desirable. Going forth into the larger white world, hitting home runs, wisecracking, graduating from college with a good job, and moving into a nice house with a yard in the suburbs, just like Dick and Jane's, was graspable and doable. Brewing suspicious-smelling Ch'i soups, having the patience for new-baby speaking-round-and-rounds, endlessly sewing and shopping, and repressing all bad thoughts during Chinese New Year were not congruent with the messages we received at public school and through the television. So Richard and I took our lead from Father.

Father also sparkled in ways that other Chinese American fathers did not. He was a freethinker, a radical. He told me about a white classmate, a girl, who initially tutored him during his houseboy days and then sought his company outside school, often inviting him to bike with her to a matinee on his rare Saturdays off. This was a brave kind of crush, for in the 1930s, interracial liaisons, even puppy love, were illegal and against all social sanctions. These were acts that justified violence against any male of color, regardless of age, throughout America. It took bravery for a Chinese houseboy to be seen with a white girl so often at school and then in the town. If he could have done so, he would have married white, I am sure. Or for that matter, any color.

Atypically, Father had turned his back on Chinatown society. This was radical in the 1930s and 1940s. It wasn't as if he had other options, like signing on to the *Social Register*, hanging out at the local Irish tavern, joining the Union Square Optimists Club, or even playing cards at his own white-dominated union hall. He refused to tolerate not only his own exploitation and that of other

Chinese Americans, but also the petty politics, egotistical airs, and vicious gossip of so-called Chinatown leaders. Father preferred striking out on his own, even if it meant being without a community.

Father was also unusually well read—*Time, Newsweek*, and *Life;* books on history, politics, and self-improvement; and the daily paper. He often returned home and described a rousing political discussion at work. In time, his coworkers bestowed on him the respectful title of Professor for his grasp of history, politics, and current affairs—and his relentless argumentation. Often, after a Saturday matinee, we'd stop at Union Square and listen to the spontaneous, noisy, public debates that were so much the life and hallmark of that square then. A speaker would step up onto one of the numerous concrete rims of the raised lawn and launch into oratory. Someone else would jump up alongside him and argue the other way. Audience members would hoot, cheer, hiss, and clap, hollering out their own broadsides. Always rousing, sometimes caustic, and oftentimes comical—regardless, the debates invariably ended with a handshake and the applause of an appreciative audience. Later, Father would explain the issues to his perplexed but enlivened sons.

As a union man, he spent Saturday mornings manning picket lines in support of strikers at other restaurants. He also passed out campaign literature and went over sample ballots with Mother. Passionate political views and picketing were second nature to him and, by extension, comfortable to me. Later, in public school, the teachings about the First Amendment guarantees of freedom of speech, press, and assembly seemed obvious—my father lived them for me.

My father's teachings remain alive, healthy, and active in my life today. But I and his other two sons owe him a different debt than we owe to Mother. Father assumed we had just better get on with the business of being Americans, and the sooner the better. He taught us American values and the American way, but he also taught us we could be patriots without being parrots. Our Americanization came quickly and soon. Only over time have I come to prize equally what Mother gave me—wisdom that I couldn't see, didn't grasp, and denied as a child under the rush and crush of assimilation. Beneath my father's larger-than-life American example, my mother's immutable Toisan ways eventually seeped through, making me the person I've finally become.

CHAPTER 15

TWO BUSES DAILY

Why did I visit you every day at the tuberculosis ward for nine months? Because I'm your mother, that's why.

In Toisan, we say that only a mother can love her children the best they can be loved. We don't trust child care like they have in America. Leaving your children with a stranger makes me go, "Ugggh! What kind of a mother would do that?" In the village, if a mother is working in the field, she will come home several times, even if her own mother is watching the children.

A mother must be with her children every day and throughout the day.

Yes, I took the bus from Chinatown all the way to San Francisco General Hospital in Potrero Hill. Every day, rain or shine, chilly or warm. One hour each way and change buses too. Yes, our visits were only an hour long. Two hours on the bus every day just to see my son for one hour. Sometimes our visit was shorter when the bus was slow. One time, the bus broke down, and I could only see you for five minutes. Then it was back to the bus stop. But this is what a mother should do for her children. I never thought of it as a sacrifice. I was always happy to see you, to know you were fine, ate enough food, had a good teacher, and that the nurses were nice to you. That's what makes a Toisan mother happy—that her children are happy.

It wasn't such a bad bus ride—quite safe in 1962. Everyone was nice, and no one ever bothered me. I passed all the neighborhoods on the way to the city hospital—Mexicans, white people, black people. So interesting to watch all the people. So different and yet so much the same. After a few months, I met a Chinese janitor who worked at the hospital. He gave me rides home and in exchange I food-shopped for him, which he couldn't do because he worked during the day. Nothing special—roast duck, barbecue pig, some vegetables once in a while. Sometimes Bob came with me. By then, his car had broken down, or he would have driven me every day, I am sure.

There was no question that I would visit you every day—no matter how long they kept you. Originally, you were only to stay two months. But still, I didn't want to let you go. I said we could take care of you, but the doctors insisted you had a serious case that needed lots of attention. Also, they were concerned that we might catch it.

Finally, I agreed. And before you knew it, nine months had passed. But it didn't matter—I would have visited you every day if it was nine years. That's what it means to be a Toisan mother.

CHAPTER 16

VISITORS WEAR MASKS

In 1962, I unexpectedly found myself in a new village—the tuberculosis (TB) ward of San Francisco General Hospital. The residents were a cross-section of the children of San Francisco's working class—Mexican, Irish, Italian, Chinese, and African American children—all from families who could not afford to pay for private long-term care.

The nursing staff made up the elders of this village. The white registered nurses (RNs) were nominally in charge, but I soon found that the African American nurse's aides, who were assigned to menial chores like changing sheets and cleaning up after meals, had equally important roles in the village's life. The only men were the Irish American schoolteacher, Mr. Sullivan, and the African American maintenance man, George (their names also reflected the class and racial structures of the times).

The time I spent in Ward 75 turned out to be an early rite of passage. At the age of eleven, I was unexpectedly wrenched from a comfortable home and community and exiled into an unknown environment. This alteration, on a less drastic level, was not dissimilar from Father's move to America at age thirteen or Mother's as a rather young twenty-one-year-old. As if caught in a family pattern, I was cut off from my parents and brother and set adrift in the company of strangers. Initially fearful, I took comfort from the promise made to me by the public health doctor that I would be home in two months—shorter than a summer vacation, I thought—and Mother's promise to visit me daily.

In the tradition of my Toisan parents, I discovered that unanticipated, wrenching change drew out the best in me. Schooling was my main responsibility, as I knew well. In my letters to Donald Soo, my best friend and classmate, I grilled him on his subjects, tracking his responses against what Mr. Sullivan was teaching me, to make sure he taught me the same subjects at the same level of difficulty. I built model airplanes—gifts from Mother; devoured a donated childhood collection of Tom Mix comics; learned to sketch from Ron Nagy's *Learn to Draw* series on the local PBS television affiliate, Channel 9; drew my own comic strips; and faithfully watched the *College Bowl* question-and-answer contest every Saturday night to test and increase my knowledge of the world.

Mother visited every day, rain or shine—the only parent who did. For the first few months, when I was kept in isolation because of the severity of my condition, Mother wore a mask all the time. Despite her truncated appearance, her clockwork visits still anchored me safely to the outside world, assuring me that this was only a temporary limbo. We didn't always have a lot to say, but I was always eager to see her smiling face. Every day, she brought me a gift—comic books or airplane models. At Christmas, she delivered my gifts, and on Chinese New Year, she passed along my relatives' red money packets. Eventually, we fell into a quiet routine of playing checkers. Most of the time I won, or she let me, and after my promised two-months-max hospitalization was long past, I began winning with a vengeance, as if punishing her for failing to stick to her guns about home care. When I badgered her about my release date, she simply smiled through my whining. She seemed to understand—doctors had delayed her too when she was trying to come to America. She never threatened to visit less. She never complained about her two-hour bus trip through rain, fog, or winter's bite.

Everyone else visited every few weekends. Since kids were not allowed into the ward, Richard and the Soo kids gazed up from five floors below, and we shouted in happy conversation. Even from that height, I could see that Richard had changed. He strutted a bit, seeming more sure of himself and, yes, definitely more independent. My little brother was no longer so little. I felt sad that he might not look up to me as much. But when he spotted me, he laughed gleefully, whirling up and down and waving so mightily with both hands that he resembled a propeller hat trying to fly up to touch me.

With the exception of Mrs. Ross, the kind, day-shift head nurse, I came to trust the African American nurse's aides more than the white nurses. They felt familiar, loving, and indulgent, like Chinatown mothers. Daytime Dorothy, the big, loving nurse's aide, became my surrogate mother, as she did to all the children. She held and comforted those who broke down crying because of homesickness. She gently painted red, stinging Mercurochrome onto our scratched knees. She looked the other way when I spit out the beets I hated. She loudly reminded the RNs that we were still children when they were overly picky about rules. George, the maintenance man, reminded me of Father. He was always diligently picking up and cleaning up after other people's messes, just like Father in his busboy job, and read us the news from the outside world every day, as Father had every evening.

Life in a TB ward is about waiting. Waiting for visits from Mother. Waiting, waiting—for the results from yet another saliva test, or another x-ray, or another lung-mucus test, where a tube that felt like fire was slid down a nostril into a lung. Waiting for that magic release date. Waiting was hard. Two months passed, and still I was not to be released. Three, then four and five months passed, and I gave up on a date. Once I broke down crying in front of Mr. Sullivan, sobbing that I missed my friends, my family, and my school. Another family, too impatient, showed up in force, grabbed their son, and fled out the door, because they had gotten so tired of waiting.

There were distractions. The most important came the day I

heard that a boy about my age was being admitted and, moreover, that he was going to take over my bedroom—the sole single room in the ward. My first reaction was visceral dislike—this was the guy booting me out of my room—even as I saw Arthur "Woody" Hudson wheeled in, flat on his back on a hospital gurney, and wearing a face mask because his TB was that dangerous.

Soon enough, Woody transferred out of his room onto the main floor. He spoke a rougher version of American than I was used to. He said he was from Hunters Point, a community of African Americans who had immigrated for the jobs at the bustling bayside shipyards during World War II. But in 1962, Hunters Point was the decaying "Dock of the Bay," the object of lament in Otis Redding's song. Woody fell into a fighting stance at the slightest perception of a verbal slight. Woody said he was tough, the best fighter in his grammar school. At first I wasn't willing to be his sparring partner, but he persuaded me that I should at least learn to take care of myself. He taught me how to protect myself against a flurry of punches, to dance around, and to throw quick, hard punches to the head and especially the eyes. He steeled me to take the pain of a blow, to keep fighting and moving.

Mr. Sullivan asked me to tutor Woody. Bit by bit, I came to impress upon him my less dramatic, but nonetheless equally significant skills. Settling back from his larger-than-life street persona, Woody learned spelling and the rules of grammar, eventually writing not only proper sentences but whole paragraphs. He also got a handle on long division and learned to remember dates of discoveries, wars, and statehood.

It was a small jump from learning school subjects to using his hands more constructively. Together we embarked upon the making of model airplanes, battleships, and statues of Frankenstein, the Wolfman, and Dracula. Woody learned to attach a propeller through the head of a Hellfighter plane with one drop of glue dangled delicately off the point of a pin, allowing the propeller to still spin freely. He deftly painted perfect drools of blood dripping from Dracula's lower fangs. Soon Woody began drawing and scripting his own comic books.

Woody's mother was delighted. Had my mother known what Woody was teaching me, she wouldn't have been as pleased. Besides his fighting skills, Woody already had a girlfriend. She wasn't his first girlfriend either, only the latest. He talked about kissing and lying on top of girlfriends. He said that was how people made babies, explaining that girls didn't have penises, but a soft, moist opening between their legs. I had heard something about this from some kids who played at our project playground, two Italian Americans who lived in North Beach. But Woody was not only detailed and graphic, he had done it.

From time to time, a kid would freak out in a raging tantrum, throwing things and striking out at the nurses. It was usually a boy, and George and the nurses would grab him, subdue him, and strap him down to his bed. A few times, Woody lost it too. Since he could really fight, he was a much more deadly proposition to subdue. Inevitably, it was Mrs. Ross, the day-shift head nurse, who was the bravest during these outbreaks. She rushed in and entangled her arms around Woody's arms so he couldn't pull a punch until he calmed down. Yet she was also the nicest, spending time with him to elicit his underlying feelings after the tantrum. She would do her best to soothe him, letting him know that he wasn't a bad child for having had the tantrum and that she was still his friend.

Not every head nurse was a Mrs. Ross. Among the many rules in the ward was the strict separation of girls and boys in the evening. Separated by the centrally placed nurses' station, we were not allowed to enter each other's sections after dinner. One Saturday night, the draconian Mrs. Logan set us up by inviting the boys to watch TV with the girls. Mrs. Logan accompanied the boys to the girls' side, then left only to summon the building's supervising nurse, who scolded us, turned off the TV, and ordered us straight to bed.

In shock, we managed to blurt out the truth, but the supervising nurse stuck by Mrs. Logan. A clearly upset Woody led our spontaneous rebellion, and to my surprise, I jumped right in. All the boys and girls refused to budge, like at a sit-in, with our arms crossed. We switched the TV back on, hooted, and accused Mrs. Logan of lying. The rebellion went until 9 p.m., bedtime, when we faded away to our beds.

It was the first time I had actually been wronged, and yet it was also the first time I had stood up! That was exhilarating, and knowing that there was a good nurse, Mrs. Ross, to whom we could and did appeal, was comforting. Like *The Wizard of Oz*, with its good witch and wicked witch, we knew we had an ally. She could and did set it straight.

This turned out to be a rite of initiation of an early kind—learning that standing up for truth is more important than compliant survival or even material comfort. As kids stuck in a hospital ward in the 1960s, we could have been punished in so many ways. This incident increased Woody's respect for me: I wasn't a "chicken" anymore. I enjoyed his newfound regard, but I wasn't sure that without his righteous presence, I wouldn't have "chickened out."

Toward the end of my stay, Woody and I raced to see who would get well first, yet neither one relished being left behind without the other. My earlier admission was no assurance that I would return home first—test results alone decided that. But I was the first to get the good news. I would be going home at the end of nine months.

There were rituals to leaving. The most overt was the doffing of the pajama-like clothing of the ward. Everyone watched the mother dress her child in spanking-new clothes and shiny shoes. Woody couldn't even look at me as I changed, keeping his back to me the whole time, unable to come into the good-bye circle. He was the tough guy, yet he was pushing away tears with his fists. Eventually, I went over to him. I gave him all my models and all my comic books. I told him we were friends and that I would write him. Woody and I shook hands and said our final good-byes, and I left.

Woody was released two months later. We talked on the phone, but never visited. Hunters Point and Chinatown were connected by the #15 Third and Kearny bus line, but our worlds were just too different.

The fighting skills that Woody taught me served me well. I was a straight-A college-bound "goody-goody" who had been hospitalized for ill health and who ran for school offices—prime bully material. But the first few times someone fired on me, I fired back and beat him. Thanks to Woody, I was never bullied in junior high or later in high school. I hoped that Woody's scholastics had benefited as much from my influence.

It turned out that Woody had transferred to my junior high school to renew our friendship, but one semester too late. Years later, Ruby Soo from the old neighborhood described an African American student from Hunters Point who had inexplicably transferred into a Chinatown junior high. He was always singing to himself, moving in a dancing kind of way, and wore a hat with a feather on one side. He didn't make any friends and disappeared at the end of the semester.

After grilling Ruby about his description, I knew that Woody had come searching for me, his friend. He knew my junior high school from my earliest letters, but had not figured on me graduating. By then, I could not track him down.

Years later, when I was clerking at the Employment Law Service of San Francisco, it turned out that our receptionist was from Hunters Point. I mentioned that l had a friend from there, an Arthur Hudson, whom I called Woody. Did she know him? She looked at me with a look that shouted out, "You can't be for real!" Then she told me Woody was her older brother. I gave her the same look back, then my home number and a message for Woody. But she was always vague about Woody. Yes, she had given him my phone number, that first message, and all my messages. She didn't know why he didn't call. Didn't have his phone number or address either. Didn't know what he'd been up to.

One day she quietly informed me that Woody had been found dead, drowned in the bay. All she would say was that he had apparently been involved in "some foolishness." How our lives had diverged. If only he had arrived at Francisco Junior High one semester earlier. I'm sure his mother sent him there in desperation, hoping I could influence him again. Might Woody still be alive today if I had been there for him? He had come looking for me. I felt loss and guilt for not being there for my friend.

But by then my own life had taken such an unexpected, tragic turn that it was all I could do to keep it moving, stay alive, and reenact a stand against abusive authority. But this time on my own.

CHAPTER 17

RIGHT FEELING

Nom kee—*right feeling*—*we had that from the start. We liked each other—enjoyed each other's company. He took care of me. Would I have married him if I had met him first? Yes, of course, because we had nom kee. Yes, I loved him. But I loved your father too. Still do. They had different qualities. They were different kinds of men. You know, there were other men who wanted to spend time with me, asking me out to eat, buying me clothes. But I ignored them. You remember Mr. Lai, with the green car—he used to drive us on weekends when we lived on Kearny Street? Well, after a while, he used to ask me out all the time. Just him and me. During the week, when your father was working. Treat me to a meal, go shopping downtown, and so on. I never went with him or any of the others—no nom kee.*

He was introduced as Kai Yep, and Bob was his American name, and that's what we called him. Bob came at the right time. I was still shaky from my nervous breakdown—it was around 1956 or 1957. For a long time, I hadn't been all that well. He treated me to coffee and cake in Chinatown. He helped me with food shopping. Just little friendly things that made me feel good, alive, and fine.

Did your father know him? Of course he did. That's how I met him—through your father. Bob was his business partner in a garage. The garage failed, but they stayed friends. Bob, too, read the newspapers avidly, and so they spent hours yakking away. You know how your father likes to talk about World War II, how Stalin tricked Roosevelt, how Communism wasn't that bad for China, and all that? Bob didn't know as much and would listen to your father for hours. That made your father happy, to have someone like a student.

Sometimes they went to movies together or fishing at the piers with fishing poles made of bamboo, just like in the village. In time, Bob became part of the family, often sleeping over on our couch.

Bob was a rogue. He didn't like to work a regular job, but he made money. He had spirit, wasn't afraid to go anywhere and talk to anyone about anything. He had his own car then and took me everywhere, places where most Chinese didn't go in those days. Bob didn't dress in dull Chinatown-style, but was very "sport," wearing cowboy boots, bolo ties, and dark sunglasses. And he was big for a Chinese. Broad-chested with strong arms, strolling with his head and chest forward, like a bull, and afraid of no one. People respected him on the streets without knowing why. Even white people would make room for him. In those days, Chinese had to make way for white pedestrians coming their way, but not Bob. He stood up to rude people, including white people. He wasn't a troublemaker, and he didn't look for trouble. But he got a lot of respect.

Bob did do some work for the tongs, those so-called Chinatown businessmen associations. Some of them are hok seh woy—under-world, you know. But Bob did little tasks. Drive around the big shots. Watch a gambling-house door in case of robbers. Pick up an order from the restaurant for the bosses. That kind of thing. Oh, there was some stuff he wouldn't tell me about, because sometimes he had "some business," then disappeared for a few days. He told me he used to drive down to Los Angeles to pick up a car-trunk load of marijuana from Mexicans and drive back to Chinatown. But that was a long time ago, he claimed, in the early 1950s, before we met him.

No, he was not really a gangster, but a runner. He never hurt people. He hated violence, because Bob's own father was a very violent man. One time in China, his father smashed a chair over the head of Bob's younger brother. That brother was injured for life, spending many years in a mental institution. Bob was so afraid of his father that he learned how to please him, to calm him down so he would never have his own head broken in like his poor brother.

And he escaped from home as soon as possible through an arranged marriage while a young teenager.

His family had money. Oh, his grandfather was some kind of big shot with offices in Beijing, Hoisin, Guangzhou, and Hong Kong. But the Communists executed him. He had treated the common people badly, and the Communists did that—executed a lot of brutal rich people. Some of the family's money left China with Bob's father. His father had that liquor store on Stockton Street near Broadway, around the corner from the housing project. You know, where the #30 Stockton bus used to stop on the way down to Market Street. Bob helped out there once in a while too. He always had some money. Enough to enjoy life.

He was very different from your father. Bob didn't work eight hours every day and come home tired, like your father. Bob didn't mind spending money on treats, like your father, who would always make silly excuses never to eat out. "MSG isn't good for you. You cook better than the restaurants," your father would say. Bob lived like a free man. He spent money on me. Drove me to Golden Gate Park, to the ocean, or to visit friends.

And Reno, oh yes, Reno. For a few years, we went to Reno a lot to gamble the night away. Reno was magic. I could forget about everything—housework, your father's temper, worrying about my sons, trying to get my mother and brother to America. In the 1960s, it was cheap. The buses cost only six dollars and gave you back the fare in chips plus tickets for a buffet dinner and breakfast. We saw the shows—happy singing, fancy dancing, and pretty lights. Stayed up two or three days without sleeping, spent twenty or forty dollars at most. Win or lose—didn't matter. Sometimes even your father joined us. Then one year, I started to lose a lot of money. I was hurting the family. So one day I stopped. I just stopped and never went back.

You know your father had a mean side, from when you were little kids. Very mean. He got angry about little things, usually money. "Neah-neah-neah," as he muttered about this and that spending. "Jah-jah-jah" this and "jah-jah-jah" that as he shouted at me. He even beat me. That's another reason why Bob and I got closer. Bob wasn't like that. He treated me like a lady. Remember, Bob hated his own father's temper.

One day I just got fed up with your father's temper. I didn't want to be hit anymore. We were on Kearny Street then. Bob was in the room that night when your father started in. You know how he gets. Hunching forward. Index finger jabbing. His face reddening as he talks faster and louder. He threatened to hit me and rolled his fingers into a fist. He's so strong from his work that he could really hurt me.

So that night I took a risk. I told him to shut up, that I was tired of his complaints and his "neah-neah-neah" this and "jah-jah-jah" that. I called him all kinds of the worst Toisan names—"leen how" (demented), "fook" (brainless), and so on. He called me the most horrible Toisanese names you could call a female, mostly the kind you say about women's sex, so I won't repeat them. This was really the angriest argument between us. I picked up a chair and held it over my head, ready to hit him. I knew he would get angrier, for I had spent weeks thinking this through. Now every-thing was going along exactly as I had planned, and I was counting on Bob to step in and stop it before it got out of control.

That's exactly what Bob did. As your father lunged toward me, Bob stood between us. He placed a palm against your father's chest and the other in my direction, separating us. He urged us to calm down. Please stop arguing—the children are sleeping, they have school tomorrow, and the neighbors will hear. Do you want the police to come and take you to jail? He said many things like that in his calm, soothing, reasonable voice, the same voice he must have used to calm his own violent father. Well, eventually your father did calm down, and when I knew his rage had passed, I put down my chair. After that, your father never hit me again, never raised his fist to me again.

Well, he stopped hitting me, but he never stopped picking on every little thing. Still "neah-neah-neah" and "jah-jah-jah" all the time. When you and Richard were in junior high school, he started in on you and Richard every night. Sometimes he punished you two by locking you up in the clothes closet for ten or fifteen minutes. Really for nothing. But he didn't hit you. Eventually, you two went to friends' houses and the library just so you could study, returning only in time for bed.

It got so bad, you even told me to divorce him. Do you remember what I said? "Don't ever speak to me of divorce. We are Toisanese. We do not divorce." Divorce would have destroyed him.

You know your father worked very hard for the little money we had. His bosses didn't always treat him fairly either, you know. And the one time he injured his shoulder at work, the one time he needed the union's help, they took their time and didn't process his claim for many, many months. Never sick a day, worked on his days off, and never went away on vacation, preferring to work for overtime pay when he could. Your father's only entertainment was movies, newspapers, and cigarettes. He didn't complain about any of that.

That's why over the years, when he picked on me about this and that, I just ignored him. It's the sounds he makes, like frogs croaking. I pretend I'm listening, but I'm not. He "jah-jah-jahs," and I answer, "yeah, yeah, yeah!" and go about my business.

Did your father and I make a good match? We've been married for fifty years now. We know how to live together, and we will live together until the day we pass over. We were first and we had it the toughest, that's all.

If Bob hadn't been there, though, I think maybe I might have gone crazy. But he made life good for me.

You know, Bob really loved you and Richard. He watched out for you two on the streets in case anyone was picking on you. He bought you snacks and toys. When your youngest brother, John, was born in 1966, Bob was as much a father to John as your own father. John was sick a lot as a baby, and Bob watched over him all the time, like he would with his own child. He took him to doctors and ran out any time of the day or night to get his medicine. He stayed over on the sofa if John had a fever, getting up to check on him. He would babysit when

I went out with my Clan Sisters. When John grew older, he drove John and me everywhere. He treated John to everything kids like.

Do you remember how I took care of my brother's children when his wife left him? She left with a gambler, said she had made a mistake marrying too young and never had any real fun. My brother told her that if she left, she could never return, and she had to give up the children. She agreed, and so Ada, Victor, and David—all under ten years old and about John's age—stayed with us. Well, Bob took care of them too, just like he did John. Those were good days. The streets were still safe. We walked to Fisherman's Wharf to watch the guitar players and the jugglers. John really liked the Man in a Jukebox. You put a quarter on a hand that stuck out of this colorful box, the size of a phone booth. The man inside made some warm-up sounds, asked your name, and then joked and sang silly songs about your name. There were summer art and music fairs in Washington Square and carousels and Ferris wheels at Portsmouth Square during Chinese New Year. We drove to the zoo, the beach, and Golden Gate Park, and to drive-in movies. In summer, when it was warm and still light—say around 9 p.m.—Bob walked us down to Clown Alley on Jackson Street and Columbus Avenue for hamburgers and French fries. What a treat that was!

Yes, over the years, Bob was very much part of our family. Sometimes he lived with us. Other times, he had a hotel room. That's how it was for over thirty years. He was your father's friend. He was a second father to all my kids, and he was my boyfriend until he passed over in the early 1990s. There has never been another one.

PART III

INITIATIONS

(1964–1972)

CHAPTER 18

SPEAKING IN TONGUES

Our new twelve-story, half-a-city-block housing project became a vertical Chinese village. Just as new-car owners are time and again uplifted by their new car's smell, we were enraptured by our new "no-smell" apartment, for Chinatown was redolent with the century-old odors of too many people, restaurants, and food stores sharing tiny quarters in sunless buildings. North Ping Yuen (Peaceful Gardens) was subsidized housing with million-dollar views—how delightfully miraculous: a third of the apartments, including ours, looked out onto vistas of San Francisco Bay and the East Bay hills. But best of all, each family had its very own kitchen and private bathroom, rare for Chinatown. "First class," as Mother put it—and we woke up every morning smiling.

We washed our clothes in a rooftop coin laundry center and drip-dried them on adjacent rows of shiny metal cables. This was culturally sensitive laundering—although Chinatown mothers welcomed the convenience of washing machines, they treasured the fragrance of sun-dried laundry.

On the multilevel playground and courtyards, little kids gleefully shimmied up monkey bars, seniors danced tai chi in the sun, and housewives watered bok choy in their garden patches. We played hide-and-seek endlessly, running hunchbacked along the balcony ramparts of all twelve floors, our presence given away only by the slapping rhythm of our tennis shoes and tittering. Rival teams tirelessly thwocked baseballs, stopping only when our mothers, craning over sky-high balconies, shamelessly hollered our rarely used Chinese names to call us to dinner. Sometimes it took the threat of a spanking with the ubiquitous chicken-feather duster—visibly shaken from on high—to pull us away.

But underneath this calm existence, my parents' differences festered. Noticing that my father could still manage to stifle his tongue when we studied, I gratefully buried myself in books until bedtime. Endless study equaled endless quiet.

Then at other times I couldn't stand their triangle. I wanted my family to be like the Nelsons in *The Adventures of Ozzie and Harriet* and the Cleavers in *Leave It to Beaver*. I lashed out at Mother, "Make Bob leave. He doesn't belong here."

But Mother could not respond as she had in my Ward 75 days. Still recovering from her traumatic teen years and at that moment managing both a raging husband and a complex triangle, she needed every ounce of her spiritual reserves for herself, energy that used to flow to us. In my thirteenth year, Richard and I began searching elsewhere for this nutrient.

Others might have filled in when my parents could not. For younger kids, the women of North Peaceful Gardens became a nurturing amalgamated Clan Sisterhood that watched over our vertical concrete village.

But my journey was further complicated because I had started to disconnect from Chinatown, becoming a living conundrum, a Chinese American—one who wouldn't and couldn't be Chinese and was at best a qualified American. My first personal act of Americanization was wriggling free of Chinese school. My conceit was to consider myself as American as my white teachers and as all the white suited-up professionals who streamed past my home to San Francisco's Financial District every day, and to whose ranks I aspired—physiognomic features to the contrary be damned. I limited Toisanese dealings to my mother and Chinatown merchants and competed in public-speaking contests, honing my American enunciation to a fine point.

There was a brutality to this choice, because the mid-twentieth-century brand of assimilation was also about rupture: amputating our ancestral history, culture, and first language; feeling ashamed of our racial origins and our parents' ethnic ways; and, finally, feeling ashamed of our community because we were not "real" Americans. Yet, as a teen, I was not able to identify this unrelenting pressure on my spirit. The daily workaholic mastery of school subjects helped repress this painful paradox.

In the 1950s and early 1960s, you couldn't walk through Chinatown without tripping over a China missionary, specialists in saving the souls of heathen Chinese. Expelled en masse by the Communist government in the 1950s, many relocated to America's Chinatowns. By my eleventh summer, an indulgent Richard and I had been saved so many times by so many zealous ministers of so many denominations that we could have sold time-shares in heaven.

In our search, we followed our old Kearny Street friends into an Assemblies of God mission, one that had just opened next door to our old apartment building.

One night, the Reverend Mrs. Baird placed her hands on my head; I fell to my knees and lost myself in a new spiritual sustenance—glossolalia.

With our new "family," Richard and I made the rounds of Assemblies of God youth camps, country churches, skid-row soup kitchens, and nearby Bethany Bible College revivals. With my spirit now freshly stuffed, my nascent talents blossomed, and soon I was organizing the Friday-night youth services, preaching in our whitewashed basement chapel, reciting from memory long passages from the King James Bible, and finishing the night with my laying-on of hands, imbuing others with Holy Spirit energy. Before long, the Bairds turned me loose on the Assemblies of God Northern California circuit, as a pulpit-pounding teen-preacher sensation. Here, I honed my leadership skills even further, confidently sermonizing to white audiences in suburbs and farm communities and learning how to schmooze after the services, as we raised money for the mission.

But then Rev. Baird mixed into this spiritual elixir some disturbing ingredients, toxic tastes that could never sit well with someone raised with my mother's compassionate, nonjudgmental trust in providence and flexible yielding before life's twists and turns.

One Sunday, she gleefully preached that the book of Revelation prophesied that only 144,000 saved souls would ascend to join Christ at the end-time; the rest would suffer through the seven years of trials and tribulations. That left out every other Christian denomination and, by the numbers, almost three-quarters of the Assemblies' own baptized members. Although I was sure I was on God's A-list, and Rev. Baird assured us we were, this triumphant elitism gainsaid the communal Toisan village sensibility that was, despite my estrangement, as integral to my core being as all the goodness of Mother's childhood Ch'i soups that still resided in my cells. I was trying to feed that, not replace it, and these so-called revelations repulsed me. Upon reflection, they felt unnatural when compared to Jesus' all-embracing new gospel.

But it was their social doctrines that were the real revelations. One day, the visiting Rev. Fife preached that the Bible mandated the separation of the races. "The book of Ruth says so. Right here!" he snarled when I questioned him, his fingers jabbing at his authority. The absence of the grace of the Holy Spirit in this last teaching broke the spell of the mission.

Richard quietly left. I followed when Brother Fife commandeered my pulpit one Friday night when I questioned the church's infallibility in all things. He then completely demonized me in front of twenty-five members of the Friday-night youth congregation, my closest friends for the past few years, and shouted that Satan had possessed me. Well, every good fundamentalist knows what to do in Satan's presence: Stand up, throw up your hands, pray loudly, and get filled with the Holy Spirit. My voice and reasoning now drowned out by this Pavlovian call to fearful prayer, I somehow managed to extract myself and, one step at a time, slowly climbed up those familiar stairs for the last time into the night air as the strains of this prayer ritual released their final hold on me and I turned toward the lights of North Beach and home.

Yes, I had grown from the Ward 75 Saturday-night kids' rebellion. I could stand up for what was right, and on my own.

In my odyssey, other tongues, intelligible voices, had been speaking to me and I was listening. Those voices included the Committee Theater Improvisation Troupe, City Lights Books, the anti–Vietnam War movement, the counterculture, and most important, as it would turn out, the Southern civil rights movement.

No doubt, part of my nomadic search was part of any young man's "checking it out." But it was more desperate than that, for I was searching for an "answer," a new "tribe" or "village," the proverbial balm of Gilead.

I was fifteen when a few friends and I first wandered into the Committee Theater's black-painted lobby, mesmerized by enlarged reproductions of Jules Feiffer–like editorial-page cartoons hanging like banners from the high ceiling. There she was, Jules Feiffer's slender, leotard-clad dancer pirouetting in her ode to spring. And more shockingly, two towel-draped figures, Uncle Sam and Premier Nikita Khrushchev of the Soviet Union, taking turns ravishing the globe, personified by a very barely clad female lounging on a bed, Mercator map lines etched on her curvaceous behind.

One of the staff invited us in gratis. I couldn't stay away and became a fixture, sitting off to the side on the high stools where the cocktail waitresses rested during skits. Relying on suggestions from audience members, the troupe tackled the hot issues of the mid- and late 1960s—and their shows became my private seminar on race relations, sexual freedom, drugs, religious hypocrisy, and the Vietnam War. In time, I enrolled in their student troupe—the Wing—and unexpectedly became a member of a family of kindred spirits who guided me in my curiosity, commiserated with my occasional confusion, and laughed heartily at my pithy improvs.

Mother encouraged my theater participation. Perhaps she was pleased that Richard and I had finally left a church that wanted to control our every waking moment—a criticism she had voiced with increasing frequency—but more likely it was because she trusted our instincts to ultimately select the right people and experiences from our rich neighborhood smorgasbord. Soon I expanded this first theater experience—and my worldly vistas— by volunteer ushering at the American Conservatory Theater, a delightful immersion into the plays of Eugene O'Neill, Arthur Miller, Ibsen, Shakespeare, and other playwrights of the Western cultural pantheon. Mother cooked dinner a little earlier on ushering nights, and early dinner nights grew in frequency as I increased my ushering to pop concerts, forgetting myself in the harmonies and the thought-provoking lyrics of Peter, Paul and Mary, Simon and Garfunkel, Joan Baez, and Joni Mitchell and the lush cascades of sitarist Ravi Shankar, flautist Jean-Pierre Rampal, and classical guitarist Andres Segovia.

When I wasn't at the Committee, I was half a block away at City Lights Books, the book-stuffed narrow townhouse of a store, the historic home of the Beat poets, a center of contemporary writers, and a depository of obscure poetry journals and Old Left periodicals filled with diatribes. City Lights became my new library, offering writings, an intellectual atmosphere, and a cool, bohemian attitude that the Chinatown branch of the public library could not.

The clerks, often lost in their own reading, didn't mind that customers stayed for hours without buying a single book. I did buy books from City Lights, books not part of the high school curriculum suggested to me by an English teacher, Robert Winkley. The books included a collection of short stories by Ernest Hemingway and *Brighton Rock* by Graham Greene, two authors who had roamed and experienced the world. Had Mr. Winkley detected a certain restlessness for knowledge and, possibly, travel in my daily journal assignments? But what captured my imagination were the books on black America—and City Lights had them all. Alex Haley and Malcolm X's *The Autobiography of Malcolm X*, Ralph Ellison's *The Invisible Man*, Claude Brown's *Manchild in the Promised Land,* and Richard Wright's *Native Son* all fascinated and horrified me with the bleakness and terror of life in urban black America. This literature stunned me, and I felt a call to action—America wasn't supposed to be like this.

Martin Luther King Jr. and the courageous Southern civil rights struggle drew me, for I had cherished the idealism of Christ, a lover of all humanity, a nonviolent rebel—someone who did not quote the book of Ruth to justify racism. But in 1967, there were few African Americans in Chinatown–North Beach and no recruiting station for civil rights workers, certainly not for a sixteen-year-old kid.

Anti Vietnam War activities, on the other hand, abounded. I often awoke on Saturdays to the chants of marchers in the distance. I passed a church with draft resisters chained to the front gates and scores of supporters gathered in vigil, guitars "twangin'-and-sangin' " in the glow of lighted candles, the warmth of solidarity. At City Lights, star-spangled banner peace symbol pins were sold next to buttons urging "Tune in, turn on, drop out."

But antiwar protests did not immediately speak to me. My mother had fled Communist China: Commies were bad guys.

Besides, I couldn't imagine that our nation would ever send us into an unjust war—or one America could not win.

Father did not agree with my naïve views. Having volunteered for the last good war, World War II, he recognized that Vietnam was not a just war. Father discussed how America had broken its promise to the Vietnamese people to allow democratic national elections once it became clear that Ho Chi Minh, the popular freedom fighter and a Communist, would win hands down. He highlighted articles and editorials from *Newsweek* that disagreed with the official policy in Vietnam. But at sixteen, I didn't see the war as a real part of my life. I stayed focused on my studies, perfecting my Motown moves, getting to "first base" with girls, and running for school office.

I was more drawn to a third movement—the counterculture, marked by multicolored psychedelic announcements for human be-ins, free psychedelic concerts in Golden Gate Park, and weekend triple bills at the Avalon Ballroom, the Fillmore Auditorium, and Winterland. The bands were outrageously named—Grateful Dead, Jefferson Airplane, Sly and the Family Stone, Janis Joplin's Big Brother and the Holding Company, Quicksilver Messenger Service, Big Mama Willie Mae Thornton, Moby Grape, and It's a Beautiful Day. Everyone was welcome, and a "light show" was promised at every happening. I picked up every new psychedelic handbill from City Lights and slowly wallpapered my bedroom into a psychedelic mural.

One day the Gallyot Brothers, Richard and Raoul, my schoolmates and offspring of North Beach beatniks, invited me to my first psychedelic happening. Jimi Hendrix, John Mayall's Blues Band, and Albert King shared the Winterland bill. In the cavernous stadium interior of the old Winterland ice rink, the three hundred or so concertgoers danced freely throughout the arena, grooving on one another, often with their backs to the bands and the massive light show. The stage was simple, built with the same kind of rickety risers used for our school gym dances, and barely two feet high.

Nothing had prepared me for any of this—and especially not for Jimi Hendrix, three feet away, eyeball to eyeball. "Freak," I thought. "He's faking it; he can't play," I thought. He sang "Foxy Lady" and then "Purple Haze," pausing to croon that soon-to-be-world-famous signature line, "Excuse me while I kiss the sky"—and then he did. I was close enough to kiss his magic guitar—and almost did. Jimi challenged everything about me, and yet he seemed to be whispering to me alone, "Young brother, check it out. Check it all out."

I did check it out—at the Summer Solstice Festival of 1968. That sunny day, an inner voice whimsically whispered, "Go to Haight-Ashbury—*today!*" Upon hopping off the #7 Haight Street bus, I discovered that everyone was streaming down Haight Street and into Golden Gate Park for a human be-in gathering at the Polo Fields with free music and free food. Someone said they were celebrating the summer solstice, the day with the longest daylight of the year.

A documentary film crew picnicking on a lawn invited me to join them. Daniel was a quintessential hippie—a long-haired and bearded blond wearing tattered jeans and a tie-dyed T-shirt. His girlfriend, Christa, more smartly coifed with a Dutch-boy haircut framing her patrician face, wore a clean white blouse and tight tan pants that slid into a pair of perfectly shined riding boots. They nonchalantly lit up a marijuana cigarette. Then Daniel started to dance without warning or inhibition, as Christa sat nonplussed, pulling on the joint. I asked Christa, who obviously was from a well-off family, why she had become a hippie. I thought that becoming a hippie was a kind of religious conversion, like becoming a Christian or a Hare Krishna devotee. "There's no real love in my family," she replied without drama. She and Daniel were tired of materialism, tired of the phoniness and expectations they had found in their well-off Chicago families and their high-priced university education. So they had dropped out and decided to just "be."

The stadium-size Polo Fields were awash in a sea of humanity. I quickly lost my new friends but made others. Wandering around more observer than participant, I felt a heightened state of awareness suffused with feelings of happiness, peace, curiosity, and excitement. This was how we should all live, in mutual love and respect, sharing and looking each other in the eyes always. This was certainly the way my mother lived—generous and accepting of others. Despite my father's vocal miserliness, he too often surprised us with his giving acts, his spontaneous kindnesses, and his unrelenting commitment to housing, feeding, clothing, and educating his family.

In the late afternoon, the emcee announced that a group called the Diggers was serving free food outside the Polo Fields. Hungry, I wandered off in search of the Diggers. Some folks were grilling chicken over an open-fire pit. Potato salad, bread, cheese, and pies were spread out on a table, free for the taking. Nearby was a rack of shirts, coats, pants, and dresses, also free. Everything was free, as much as you wanted, no questions asked, and no one looked to see if you were taking too much. No one cared. A bearded guy sizzled chicken on the huge, ground-level grill. He asked for volunteers, and soon I was stoking the flames, grilling, and serving. There was only this one Digger and people like me helping. Like Jesus at his Sermon on the Mount, we were inspired to feed all the hungry and to clothe the lightly clad as the late-afternoon ocean breezes started to move in. As in Mother's Toisan village, we pitched in to take care of one another.

The crowds started to walk to the beach, to ritually watch the sunset together on this longest day of the year. Knowing how chillingly damp San Francisco can get at dusk, I reluctantly caught the bus home. But the day left me warm inside. Exalted, my world had been rocked to the core. In spirit, these hippies reminded me of the motley, peaceful multitudes who had spontaneously gathered around Jesus, listening to their era's gospel—for we too were tuning in to the good news of our time, a zeitgeist of personal and social liberation. This was the part of Christianity I still treasured—Jesus' actual uninterpreted life. This was the harmony that had dropped out of my own family's household, cast off, as we were, from Toisan and adrift in America. In some indescribable way, I knew that what I was missing could be found within this tribe—even though I wasn't quite sure just exactly who they were—and, as my spirit vibrated, my heart exuded gratitude, and a contented fatigue settled into my bones.

CHAPTER 19

BENEVOLENT
AND PROTECTIVE

I didn't have much to do with the Chinese Six Companies, the "city hall" of Chinatown. They didn't have speaking-round-and-rounds or women in the leadership. I didn't know much about their role when I first arrived, only what my elder Clan Sisters told me. They said that in the middle 1800s, there was no Six Companies, but six separate ones. Each company represented its own Clan, and each Clan came from one of six districts of origin in the Pearl River delta, where all the old-timer Chinese came from. That's why a company is sometimes called a "district association."

Newcomers registered with their own district association. The association fed them, found them housing and jobs, and kept letters from home for those working far away from Chinatown. We Toisanese belong to the Say Yup District Association, because the Toisanese dialect is also referred to as the Say Yup dialect. Cantonese belong to the Sam Yup District Association, because their dialect is also known as the Sam Yup dialect. Each district association built its own headquarters, those three-story buildings with red balcony pillars wrapped with dragons and large gold-leaf Chinese characters carved into dark marble walls. They bought large Chinese cemeteries, just south of San Francisco, a long time ago, when many Chinese could not make enough money to go home. Father has already reserved our burial plots, so you make sure we rest there. Later, when the white people turned on the Chinese, the six district associations banded into one group. That was the start of the Chinese Six Companies.

Besides the district association, every Chinese belongs to a family association—Lee Family Association, Wong Family Association, Chan Family Association, Fong Family Association, and so on. You were considered relatives no matter which district you came from. Family associations organized summer picnics, Easter and Christmas parties with toys and candy, and loaned us money when American banks wouldn't or charged more. That's how we bought our first television and washing machine—with loans from the Lee Family Credit Union, the largest credit union in the United States in the 1950s.

And they sponsored banquets every Chinese New Year. We always ate at the three biggest Chinese New Year banquets—I was a Chun by birth, but also Lee and Wong, since my sisters and I married into those families. The tickets were so cheap, almost free, for a fancy ten-course banquet on plates so large that everyone took home leftovers. My sisters and I took turns taking the Johnnie Walker Red bottle home. With so many banquets, our husbands always got a bottle and then spent a whole year finishing it. We saw all our relatives from the old village at those banquets, especially those who had moved out of Chinatown. Everyone came back to Chinatown then—to show off their babies, brag about their kids in college, tell who got married to whom, shake their gold watches and jade bracelets to show how well they're doing, and just catch up on everything. Some years, the banquets were so huge we took up three floors of the largest restaurants, even closing the downstairs to tourists.

That's about the only time I ever saw anyone from the Six Companies—in front of the banquet hall, making speeches and smiling for Chinese newspapers. They loved being in the newspapers.

Then there were the business guilds known as the tongs. Restaurant owners, food markets, souvenir shops, import-exporters, and professionals belong to the tongs. Everyone knew some of the tongs were hok seh woy, dark-side organizations—"shadow people" who operated gangster businesses like prostitution, gambling, and smuggling. Our village didn't have "shadow people"—they're Big City kind of people, and best to stay away from them. Bob worked for them when he was a young man. He told me a few things, but I'm not going to talk about it. I was glad when he quit.

You know I used to play poker, and I got to be a pretty good judge of character. If I could have played a few games with those Six Companies men, maybe the tong bosses, I could have figured out what kind of people they were.

Oh, yes, I learned poker at that hotel on Montgomery Street we lived in when you were first born. At first it was just a way to pass the time, but I got good and started to win a few bucks every game. By the time we moved to Ping Yuen, I was really good. There were several games in the neighborhood, mostly women gamblers. I was in demand to play, because of my fast shuffling and dealing of the cards. I was always called to play out-of-towners from Sacramento, in for a fun weekend in Chinatown. Those ladies always wanted to go up against Chinatown's best. I was happy to give them an exciting game, a few card tips, and win their money.

By the time you entered high school, I was winning thirty dollars to fifty dollars a night, several times a week, for a few hours of play. Now that might not sound like a lot of money nowadays, but in the 1960s, that was good money. Steak was only twenty-five cents a pound, rice was twenty dollars for a fifty-pound bag, a 100 percent virgin wool sweater cost fifteen dollars at Macy's, and a brand-new bicycle was only thirty dollars. I was earning more than a Chinatown restaurant waiter working twelve-hour days. I was making as much money as your father on many a day. Anyway, I didn't end up saving any of it; I spent it on treats, clothes, books, and toys for you and your brother, and I sent money to my family in Hong Kong.

I'm a conservative gambler. If I have a strong hand, I push it. If not, I lay it down right away. Too much bluffing is dangerous, and that's how I win, because a lot of people think they're smart enough to bluff their way through the night. But if you watch people carefully, you see through them. Be patient, watch for the clues. The littlest things will signal if they're relaxed, content, and confident. Other times, I can feel the stress of a bluff. Or if someone is betting aggressively, I'll follow, matching their bets twice, usually, until I get the signs. Then I either drop out if the signs are they've got the cards, or I bet aggressively until they drop their hand. I always ask to see their cards either way.

Also, you learn to spot strategies—people use them over and over. For example, some players come on too strong to be telling the truth. They'll announce like it's a complete surprise, "Oh, what a good hand!" I watch for the signs. Do they have one pair or two?

Another common strategy is to place piles of money in front of you at the start of the game and bet so high that the other players drop out. Watch for the signs. If I had the cards and, after a couple of bets, was sure they were bluffing, I'd call them. This kind of strategy—intimidation by a show of money—usually works only two out of eight hands. You can beat this kind of high roller on the other six hands, and soon enough their piles of money disappear, and they leave the game.

Poker helped me to read people in life. That's why, although I never learned to speak a lot of American, I have no trouble going anywhere. I can read people and find the ones who will be kind to you, who will help you. If I judge wrong, I know how to drop and move on. That's why I made good husband matches for my two sisters, and when I get husband requests from Toisan, I always find good ones.

Yes, maybe if I had been able to play poker with the Six Companies' elders and tong bosses, I could have figured out what their game was. And the Kuomintang (Nationalist Party) officials too. They came over in the 1950s, just like me. Landed in Chinatown with their money, rich relatives, and corporations. Always telling us to keep America on the Taiwan government's side and attacking the mainland Communists. They seemed one and the same with the Six Companies. Play a few hands, and I would have known how to talk to them, too, about my sons and their desires to make everything better for all Chinese Americans. But they didn't want Chinese Americans to ask too many questions or point out bad things about Chinatown. They wanted us to bee men—give them face—so America would never doubt it was on the right side, the side of the good Chinese.

America loved Madame Chiang Kai-shek, the wife of the president of Taiwan. President Chiang was too Chinese—he was educated in Japan and Russia and couldn't speak American. But Madame Chiang was an American university graduate who spoke perfect American and a Christian who attended their churches. She was small and pretty and wore cheong-sams, those long silk gowns with the slit up one thigh. When Americans saw her, they felt protective toward Taiwan, like the Communists were barbaric Mongols who had taken China away from her and the good Chinese. That's what the Chinatown papers called the Communists, you know, barbarians and Mongol invaders.

That's the way the Six Companies told us to be, like Madame Chiang. But I was no Madame Chiang. I never owned a cheong-sam and would probably tear one squeezing it over my head. In their eyes, I was just a poor, stocky village woman. A Toisanese who didn't even speak proper Cantonese and not a word of Mandarin. Madame Chiang wouldn't listen to people like me.

She was one of three famous Soong family sisters. All very beautiful, very intelligent. I wish I could remember more, but each sister married a man who represented a different idea of China's future. One married a rich banker and settled in Hong Kong. Another married Sun Yat-sen and later became part of Mao's revolutionary government. Maybe she would have listened to the Clan Sisters. Maybe she would have joined our speaking-round-and-rounds.

When I was still a little girl back in Toisan, our parents gossiped about how rich the Chiangs kept getting, even in the middle of the Japanese war. I didn't know one thing from another—I was a kid, and I still don't know for sure. But that's what the villagers said, that the Chiangs were corrupt, getting rich off American aid while the rest of China suffered. You know Chiang Kai-shek wouldn't fight the Japanese—he kept retreating and retreating until he ended up way in the lower backside of China, so far back he was almost in Burma.

Yes, my older brother the teacher was a Nationalist member, not because he believed in them, but to keep his job. He wasn't an official, just a member. Only rich people could buy an official position, so they could get even richer. No, we just went along. The smart ones, the intellectuals, they left Toisan to learn about the larger world before deciding which side was better—Nationalist or Communist or some other way. You couldn't know one way or the other in Toisan. Get along, take care of the family, and harvest the crops—that's what we knew.

The Six Companies used to announce parades and rallies in support of Taiwan. Nationalist Party dignitaries would ride down Grant Avenue and speak at Victory Hall, something like that. Yes, my Clan Sisters and I lined the streets, but it was out of hospitality for another Chinese person visiting America. Yeah, they had those baskets we were supposed to throw money into—to fight the Communists. Everyone lost interest after a while.

President Chiang was smart in this way; he knew how to keep the Six Companies loyal to him. He gave them seats in the Taiwanese legislature—overseas Chinese seats, he called them. He gave them exclusive deals to import Chinese food treats to sell in every Chinatown—like black mushrooms, bird nest and shark fin for soup, traditional herbs, ginseng—lots of stuff you can't find in America. Those Six Companies heads made millions. No wonder they ended up doing more for Chiang Kai-shek and Taiwan even though their main job was to help Chinese Americans. They wanted Chinese Americans to be good, not make noise or ask for too much, just mind our own business and take care of our own. That was okay with me—I was raising my sons to grow up well mannered, to stand on their own two feet.

But in the late sixties, everything started changing. You spoke out against the school principal, saying Chinese should have equality. That's when I wish we could have spoken to the Six Companies and the Nationalists.

They're powerful, so powerful to this day. And the entire Clan Sisterhood was just like me—weak within Chinatown. The Six Companies and Nationalists wouldn't have listened to the ideas from a speaking-round-and-round. If we were to try to shame these men into right action, like we used to do in the village, where would we stand day after day to scold them? Which was the right district, family, or tong association headquarters building? Who in the Nationalist Party headquarters on Stockton Street would care? That's one thing about those elders: They sure made it hard to figure out who really was in charge. Maybe it was an old-time survival strategy, but Chinatown became too complex. People didn't care as much about one another anymore.

CHAPTER 20

NEW YELLOW PERIL

I was fueled by a feeling of offense that, under my very nose, there existed societal agreements that dared to proscribe my personal choices because of my ethnicity and thereby desecrated the ideals of America's democratic scheme under our Constitution. This was the genesis of my political awakening—not idleness or boredom or looking for a new experience. A political awakening is not something manageable, like taking up a hobby. It's going to turn your life understanding. But I was that offended.

Perhaps that's what it takes to catalyze anyone to spend exorbitant energy and time on understanding one's own political environment, and knowing it in the same way we understand the layout of neighborhood streets—which areas are safe and which can be dangerous, and which times are optimum for driving around to shop, see the dentist, and pick up the kids, thereby avoiding traffic jams, the greater likelihood of accidents happening, and the vigilant traffic police who lay in wait during rush hours.

While there may be wealthy families who teach their children not to take their privileges for granted, but to understand and keep in place the political system that protects their privilege, as a working-class son of an immigrant family, I did not receive any such clear instruction from family or our otherwise able public and Chinese schools. So I never knew that an awareness of one's history and political fabric is as essential to doing well and right in life as the college education I was groomed for. For those of us similarly situated, and from the point of view of the hindsight of my years, I would only suggest that it is important that all Americans not only understand the theoretical fundamentals of our system of government, so aptly taught in our civics classes, but also the historical forces and the more current politics that may have shaped your community and affected the quality of your family's life. I believe that this is the "eternal vigilance" that is often cited as the price of enjoying cherished liberties.

And so I started to ask about the origins and the history of my community—how had Chinatown literally, economically, and psychically become "our place" in American society? Had we ever struggled to break free of it, as African Americans were doing in their civil rights movement at that very moment, the midsixties?

In 1967, I knew that San Francisco Chinatown was not the singing, dancing, syncopated idyll of the stage and movie musical *Flower Drum Song.* Yet the Chinatown of my youth was indeed safe, comforting, and nurturing. But a protective baby crib is still a crib, and once-protective sides can slowly become prison bars. In my midteens, I discovered that Chinatown was in fact an involuntary community, a protective refuge wrought into being by anti-Chinese pogroms during the 1880s that continued intermittently into the 1940s. Like a psychic crib, there were invisible bars that no Chinese American, not even American-born ones like me, could step beyond and freely aspire to all that is the birthright of every American.

Very simply, as I entered my later teens, I started to receive messages from Chinatown adults and my schoolteachers that I should lower my personal and professional ambitions. Don't think of Harvard, but maybe some local college—well, possibly the University of California, Berkeley, maybe. Perhaps you should major in medicine or accounting, they said, or start a small business—Chinese are quite mercantile in that way—but don't think of rising to the CEO post in a Fortune 500 company. Consider it an accomplishment to move into a safe suburb not too far from Chinatown, others said, and on weekends, stroll Grant Avenue with your kids, visit friends, and eat dinner with your parents. Politics, big business, the high arts, Hollywood, and pop music— forget about it.

Until this realization grew, my personal political environment was not of particular importance to me. Oh yes, Father discussed President Eisenhower and Vice President Richard Nixon endlessly. He had been openly enamored of John Kennedy's candidacy, glued himself to our Emerson television set during First Lady Jackie Kennedy's White House tour, and often repeated to me over and over, with a faraway look in his eyes, as if he were addressing the adulatory crowd himself, "Ask not what your country can do for you, but what you can do for your country." That made me consider joining the Peace Corps as a goal instead of city government, for national politics was a faraway story that did not explain Chinatown's place in San Francisco or assuage my recognition of the growing constraints on my life.

President Kennedy's vigor and idealism could not explain to me, for example, why, almost universally, all the teachers in the multitude of Chinatown schools, all the firemen, and almost all of the police were white Americans, even those serving the Chinatown community. And I might add, they invariably did so nicely, responsively, and with daily dedication. Yet, even with my straight-A grades, teachers' recommendations, and superb physical fitness, I couldn't have realistically expected to join the fire department or the police force, even if that had been my heartfelt answer to President Kennedy's rhetorical admonishment to ask what I could do for my country instead of for myself. If I were to become a teacher, another public service profession, I could never hope to become a principal, regardless of my level of skill and dedication or an advanced degree earned at nights and on weekends.

Yet, in my father's youth, even these limited career paths would have been welcomed. After her war-torn youth, Mother was ever grateful for Chinatown's pacific if small cocoon. But for me, born and raised American and indoctrinated to believe in the

Declaration of Independence and our Constitution as the major breakthroughs in political philosophy of the human experience in modern times, I was not so willing to be too readily deprived of my birthright. I wanted to know that America could work for me all the way, and if it couldn't, I wanted to do something about it.

Perhaps it's not so uncommon to wake up one day and wonder why reality is the way it is, why your choices are either boundless or circumscribed. How is it that you ended up living on the right side or wrong side of the tracks? Why can't you dream of becoming a national TV news anchor? Why must some hope at best for a union job as the night janitor cleaning up after that anchor? Why is it that the only industry in your town is a paper or a steel mill that is about to close, and what happened to the fishing industry and independent farms your two sets of grandparents recount aloud with such prideful nostalgia?

And so I wondered more and more—in my mind and then aloud. Who could tell me how Chinatown had come to this and why Chinese Americans were lesser people than white Americans?

Not surprisingly, it was Father, from the experiences of his own life and his continuing self-education, who began teaching me what I needed to know when he realized I was ready—no, when I desperately needed to know.

"When I was your age, I couldn't even shop in JC Penney's because I was Chinese. And now, you work there as a salesman." That was Father's response when I casually mentioned that I would be working at JC Penney's department store in 1968, during my seventeenth summer. Left unsaid was Father's deeper gratitude that I was not limited to a lowly backroom job like stock boy or janitor, but had a highly visible, public-contact position as a salesman on the store's main floor.

Father had been the first to relate to me the history of racism against Chinese Americans: burning out entire Chinatowns, mob lynchings, and mass murdering of Chinese pioneers up and down the West Coast, which began in the late 1800s; the chilling ethnic cleansing war chant of "The Chinese must go!"; and the anti-Chinese exclusion laws that remained in force through the mid-1940s. Chinese pioneers, once 15 percent of California's population, fled to a few Chinatowns, where the larger society waited for old age to finish what the mobs had not.

Even until Father's time as a young man in the late 1940s and early 1950s, Chinese Americans caught out after dark were fair game for a beating. Father carried a restaurant butter knife when he walked home from work late at night—"just in case." Like pre–World War II Jews in their European ghettos, we could only live, own property, work, and socialize safely within the confines of Chinatown.

Father said that the Six Companies faithfully protected and served the besieged community during those horrific decades from the 1880s through World War II. They built Chinese Hospital, Chinese language schools, and employment centers, where Father found his first job as a houseboy in Marin County and, later, other work before he joined the union. The Six Companies, the family associations, and the tongs (ostensibly merchant guilds) wisely bought up much of the property in Chinatown, then devised a clever, interlocking, labyrinthine ownership structure that boggled corrupt politicians and sly developers alike. This was part Toisanese cultural imperative (buy land for future generations) and part modern pragmatism (Chinatown sat on prime downtown holdings coveted by developers), Father explained.

But then, Father intoned somewhat ominously, the Six Companies struck a deal with the white San Francisco establishment. Chinese could not live outside of Chinatown and would stay out of city politics. Chinese would stop filing legal cases against discriminatory city acts and appealing all the way to the Supreme Court, as the Chinatown community had done in many such civil rights lawsuits throughout the decades, including the famous case of *Yick Wo v. Hopkins* (1886), a precedent-setting case still cited today. In return, the white power structure delegated Chinatown affairs to the Six Companies, as our own separate but equal city hall. Chinatown could have its own courts to settle internal disputes.

In 1968, that Jim Crow deal was as solid as the day it had been forged and as ruthlessly enforced by the Six Companies' elders as by white city fathers. The discriminatory nature of that arrangement was exemplified for Father by the Six Companies' refusal to pressure white-managed unions to defend Chinese American union members against ill treatment. "The union takes our monthly dues and penalizes us if we're even one day late, but it doesn't stand up for Chinese," said Father. But there was a quid pro quo, because Chinatown workers remained unorganized, which added to the wealth of the new Chinatown establishment.

One day it all came together for me: Chinatown or no Chinatown, we Chinese Americans have our own civil rights struggle to fight. With that realization, I felt connected, complete, and on the right track. Perhaps whatever was missing in Chinatown and in my life were one and the same.

The first act of my political awakening started at my high school, Galileo, which was located near Fisherman's Wharf and had a gorgeous postcard view of the Golden Gate Bridge. By the 1960s, Galileo was a Chinatown high school: We were 75 percent of the school's population of three thousand. Yet, Galileo High was also a richly inner-city school—diverse, cosmopolitan, and surprisingly harmonious. We streamed in from all over the city: African Americans; white military brats; Mission District Chicanos; wealthy, white private school outcasts; middle-class Italian, Irish, Jewish, and WASP kids; artistic beatnik offspring and neo-hippies; and of course, Chinatown youth arriving for class on foot, by bus, hanging off cable car railings, on motorcycles, in cars, and even in chauffeured Cadillacs.

The school felt as safe and nurturing as my housing-project home, for despite being packed into a four-story building that ringed a small Spanish-style courtyard, we got along remarkably well, puzzling over homework together, visiting each other's homes on weekends, and generally obscuring the social, racial, and class barriers of our parents' generation. The teachers behaved the same way as our mothers—teaching us, watching us, and reprimanding us. Just another urban village—it seemed that the American experience was a serial movement from one safe environment to another.

In the spring of 1968, I sought to win the student body presidency on an unusual platform—civil rights for Chinese Americans, support for the fledgling Black Student Union, and doubts about the rightness of the Vietnam War. I had stopped thinking of student body offices as another gold star for college and expected to be jeered off the stage. Instead, I was elected on the first ballot with 75 percent of the vote.

"What have I gotten myself into?" I wondered, for on that last day of spring semester, a vicious rumble broke out between the white athlete clique and a group of smaller Chinatown students whose martial arts training more than equalized the disparity in size.

All was not well at Galileo or, as it turned out, in Chinatown. I needed more guidance, more than Father could provide, and found it, ironically enough, in the heart of Chinatown. One afternoon, as I wandered along Waverly Place, a two-block-long alley parallel to Grant Avenue, the high-strung strains of a Chinese classical music society's afternoon rehearsals wafting from a balcony clashed with and then gave way to Western classical music. The source of the lyricism was an airy, well-lit European-style beer and cappuccino bar, newly opened, named Il Piccolo's. Co-owners Richard Barkley and his Chinese American wife, Alice, chose its alley location to shelter it from the tourist trade of Grant Avenue. Il Piccolo's was a perfect place for privately ruminating, sharply exchanging new ideas, and plotting change. I was thrilled to discover this secret intellectual oasis percolating within Chinatown.

Chinese American intellectuals gathered here over coffee, iced Il Torino liqueurs, and European brew to organize against both the larger white power structure and the conservative Chinatown community. Unlike our elders, who dressed in bland colors and oversized, pajama-style suits, these intellectuals stood out strikingly, refreshing prototypes of Chinese Americans of the future.

A half-century later, when the pages of entertainment magazines are stuffed with ethnically Chinese stars, celebrities, financiers, and power brokers, it's difficult for even me to imagine my generation's parched-throat thirst for acceptable Chinese American role models. Back in the day—surrounded by Charlie Chan, Fu Man Chu, a fey President Chiang Kai-shek, and the fashion-challenged, remote Chairman Mao Tse-tung—an early Bruce Lee incarnation was the sole exception, in a television series even he hated, playing the role of the Green Hornet's television sidekick (literally). My survival tactic was to not even think about it, but having a few slightly different guys around might have helped, role-model-wise.

When I was seventeen, Il Piccolo's gave them to me—abundantly—an embarrassment of wealth. Bespectacled, with salt-and-peppered bristle-cut hair and goatee, Rev. Larry Jack Wong was the steely leader and intellectual visionary of the bunch. Wicked-sharp Dr. George Mu, a PhD and an official with the State Department on home leave from the US Embassy in Singapore, unfailingly attired himself in starched shirts, pressed ties, and perfectly tailored herringbone suits. A graduate from the Oriental Studies Department at UC Berkeley, Mu was literate in classical and contemporary Chinese; fluent in Mandarin, Cantonese, and Toisanese; and a native-born American speaker.

Like me, Larry Jack Wong and George Mu were Chinatown born and raised.

Mason Wong, the Americanized son of a Hong Kong movie star, was a student leader at San Francisco State University (then a state college). A Vietnam vet who still wore his green fatigue jacket and lace-up combat boots, he reported that the war was so unpopular that units refused to fight, instead working out private truces with the Viet Cong. He told me about "fragging"—despised white officers being shot in the back by their own men.

George Woo, also Hong Kong born and a State University leader, was tall, broad-shouldered, and rotund, a Chinese scholar whose words and voice shifted seamlessly between dispassionate analysis, fiery rhetoric, and ironic humor. Bristling with a thick black beard, he resembled the fierce Chinese god of war, Kwang-kung, his intimidating visage unsoftened by thick scholarly glasses and a puffing pipe. He typically wore a silky blue, traditional Chinese cotton jacket—the *men nop*—all four jacket pockets stuffed with American and Chinese newspapers and books.

Alice Barkley, who graduated with a master's degree from UC Berkeley's School of Architecture, was thin and small—barely five feet tall, but still a strutting, laughing, joking dynamo. She clip-clopped around in her three inch heels, a cigarette in one hand, as she pumped cappuccinos, uncapped bottles of foreign beer, and poured Il Torino soda—all the while firing off a baker's dozen of incisive and comical bon mots into our free-flowing brainstorms for the new Chinatown. Her signature mane of black hair streamed down below her miniskirt and on some days was braided in a queue. Having heard of my civil rights speech, Alice brought me into this cabal as the precocious high school activist.

Despite my age, I won their acceptance with my sincerity and eagerness. Increasingly, they solicited my opinions and views to test my grasp of the issues and eventually promoted me to the "youth voice" of the group. I was the younger brother to the elder brothers of this Clan Brotherhood. But Alice was more than equal in this "brotherhood" and frequently their superior in intellect, eventually earning the very respectful moniker "Dragon Lady." The group delighted in filling in the gaps in my education, correcting my naïveté of the world. They also enjoyed corrupting me slightly, acquainting me with the superior qualities and higher alcoholic content of foreign brews over American beer. Their camaraderie gave me not only a historical and social context for my fledgling intellectual insights, but emotional support. I was not isolated. I did not have to act alone.

But they also warned that a desperate power struggle was about to erupt in Chinatown, for Mother's Toisanese values of compassion and group harmony weren't the only strand in the Cantonese cultural tradition. I learned that Cantonese and other Southerners were the rebels of China, that our Taiping Rebellion (arising in part to protest for decades of oppressive taxation) had swept through China in the mid-1800s. I knew, of course, that overseas Cantonese had largely financed the 1911 Chinese democratic revolution of Dr. Sun Yat-sen, himself a Cantonese. I had proudly recited his Three Principles of Democracy in Chinese, but it was my Il Piccolo's friends who explained them to me.

The first was the Principle of Nationalism—majority rule of Han Chinese with equal protection for national minorities, including even the Manchu people who had oppressed Chinese for three centuries. That sounded like civil rights to me!

The second was the Principle of Democracy—elective government with constitutional separation of powers, among them the executive, legislative, and judiciary. But there was a Chinese twist of two additional branches: a fourth branch to oversee national exams that would serve to staff ministries on the basis of merit; and a fifth branch of censorship to root out the corrupt and the incompetent. That sounded like government of, for, and by the people, I happily noted!

Finally, the third was the Principle of Livelihood—incorporating state ownership of land; regulation of economics to prevent extremes of wealth and poverty; and policies that ensured a thriving middle class of farmers, craftsmen, and merchants. "Sounds just like Benjamin Franklin's ideas," I thought. Dr. Sun clearly envisioned a responsive national party, like the democratic socialist nation of Sweden, not a two-party system dominated by corporate capitalism that widens the gap between rich and poor and squeezes out the middle class.

No surprise that the good doctor's political values were those of the village farmer: inclusivity, fairness, honesty, opportunity, and protection of the little people against the abuses of the wealthy. No wonder Mother treasured Dr. Sun Yat-sen as fervently as Americans cherished George Washington and Thomas Jefferson.

And so my cabal of political parents moved to the same democratic tune as I did. Rev. Larry Jack Wong and others who dropped into Il Piccolo's had been inspired by the Christian nonviolence of Dr. Martin Luther King Jr., and so I felt assured of their tactical scheme, a commitment to debate, nonviolent demonstrations, and change through transformation, not violence.

But, it seemed, the same kind of incompetent self-interest groups that had plagued the imperial system and taken control of Dr. Sun's Nationalist Party now reigned in the halls of the ornate Chinese Six Companies headquarters a mere half a block away on Stockton Street. Although Asian American veterans in Hawaii had aggressively ended Jim Crow by wresting political offices away from entrenched white politicians, Chinatown's own veterans buckled under to the ironclad Nationalist Party/Six Companies policy of not rocking the boat. Squeezed into the straitjacket of "the model minority," we added patriotic anti-Communism to our avid churchgoing Christianity and workaholic, quiescent, stay-in-our-place professions and businesses.

These were the unspoken constraints the Il Piccolo's regulars chafed against.

And who were the enforcers of this fealty? My friends explained: The local tongs were—including one major tong whose headquarters loomed ominously across the alleyway. From the 1850s to the early 1900s, the tongs openly ran Chinatown's slave-girl brothels, gambling parlors, and opium smoke-easies—and regularly paid off cops and politicians. Because of their roots in China's revolutionary underground network, nestling inside each tong was a secret society, now criminal in nature and known as hok seh woy, the dark-side organization or the "shadow society." In the 1950s, the tongs trashed pro–mainland Chinese newspapers and ran their supporters out of town. By 1968, most tong members operated legitimate retail businesses. Still, my Il Piccolo's friends portentously warned me not to discount them.

And so I signed on. I dropped out of the Wing, the Committee Theater's improv training troupe, and consciously moved those improv skills off the stage and into my own ground-level real life, the improv of political change. Those social insights gleaned from hours of reading at City Lights and the intellectual excitement of the possibility of change—well, I was about to deliver them home to Chinatown too. And in my heart, I nourished my spark of inspiration from Martin Luther King's civil rights movement, intending to help ignite the cleansing fires of nonviolent social change, a reform that doesn't require destroying anyone, not even the bad guys.

My parents welcomed my somewhat edited report that I had found some college-age friends at Il Piccolo's. "They are reformers," I admitted, but Mother only asked me to be careful. In truth, my parents had never forbidden me to explore and, unlike many Chinatown parents, had never insisted on my adherence to the stunting Hobson's choice that would make me work every free moment to bring money home. They also did not now forbid me to join this movement for equality. Besides, I was a good son and had even brought home our first color TV, paid for with my biweekly JC Penney's paychecks.

Mother became alarmed, however, when I told her that a group of young Chinese Americans known as the Wah Ching, or "Young Chinese," also convened at Il Piccolo's. Delinquent Cantonese-speaking immigrants from Hong Kong who preyed on their own community—shoplifting, small burglaries, and extortion—they forged an unlikely confederation with my Il Piccolo's friends, serving as a smoking gun and contradicting the Six Companies' assertion that all was well with the model minority.

In turn, the liberals could help the Wah Ching obtain government grants for job training and youth programs.

In actuality, these intellectuals had so very little in common with the Wah Ching. Except for George Woo and Alice Barkley, they didn't speak the same language and their connection was at times as tenuous as that of well-meaning white liberals helping inner-city street gangs. But in the intoxicating, rosy idealism of the period, and with George and Alice's persistent bridge building, the alliance held well enough, and both groups reached common political goals.

As I got to know some of the Wah Ching leaders, I couldn't help but admire the pragmatic caginess within their idealism. Like the Jets in the musical *West Side Story*, they cheekily grasped that casting themselves as a "social disease" had already produced not only public sympathy, but also real city dollars for picnics, dances, and music shows, as well as several well-paying youth worker jobs. With their politicized, intellectual allies, Wah Ching youth might well indeed receive language and vocational training that could lead to union jobs, hitherto unthinkable opportunities that could change their lives dramatically—and yes, move them away from crime. Sure, why not—with nothing to lose, they could always fall back into street life.

Yet another locus of activism was flowering several blocks away. A group of young adult American-born Chinese (ABC), all juvenile hall veterans, started a nonprofit organization, Legitimate Ways, Inc.—or as they called themselves, Leways (pronounced *lee ways*)—as an alternative for younger ABC at-risk street youth. I envied their *Easy Rider* motorcycles airbrushed with flowing dragons in reds, greens, and purples. I spotted them dancing to blues, soul, and psychedelic music at Winterland.

I felt at home with Leways members. Many were "Ping" kids, meaning Ping Yuen Project–raised, like me. Soon, I proudly displayed Leways' two identifying lapel buttons, a bright yellow button with bold black letters that blared out "New Yellow Peril" and a second one that declared "Leways—Unity," encircling a sage clutching the telltale Taoist staff of divine wisdom. At Leways, I learned to shoot pool and to jam a mean, noisy, and high-scoring game of pinball on a machine named Heat Wave.

As 1968 wore on, some older members of Leways organized into a militant leftist cadre—the Red Guards, named after Mao's youthful vanguard army but styled after the Black Panthers. They marched through Chinatown screaming that "political power comes out of the barrel of a rifle," quoting directly from Chairman Mao Tse-tung's Little Red Book, which they waved in the air as vigorously as street preachers waved Bibles. Setting up business in the Fountain of Youth soda shop, a Leways business, they displayed poster-size portraits of Chairman Mao, piles of the Little Red Book, the multivolume *Selected Writings of Chairman Mao*, and a constellation of red and gold Chairman Mao buttons.

In 1968, in the Chinese Nationalist stronghold of San Francisco Chinatown, where fluttering Chinese Nationalist flags defiantly dominate the roofscape to this day, this open display of Maoist paraphernalia was heresy and provocation. The Chinese Six Companies could tolerate Leways, but a base for Chairman Mao—never!

Mother had left China to escape Communism and, for her, the appearance of Mao's Red Book in America exhumed disturbing memories. While I was not drawn to the Red Guard as I had been to Leways, their fervent presence was a wake-up call to rethink my views about China, the United States, the world—a reevaluation encouraged by Father.

Although committed to Dr. King's nonviolent tactics, the Il Piccolo's leaders knew that in the collective DNA of our Chinese philosophy of governance, the Six Companies and the Nationalists had lost the mandate of heaven, that living balance of righteousness and harmony, of duty and reward, between ruler and ruled. Our history taught us that rebel forces inevitably arose to establish a new order under heaven, and the ruling group always responded violently. I felt it coming, the operation of this inexorable Chinese social law of reordering, but couldn't, or wouldn't, accept its inevitability. I only hoped that the sophisticated Il Piccolo's liberals could change conditions before the Wah Ching and Leways youth, injected with the virulence of Red Guard righteousness and Black Panther militancy, could trigger the counterattack.

Yes, I clung desperately, naïvely, to my hope that our differences could be worked out *en famille*. Why wouldn't the elders welcome our generation's campaign for the full equality they had always craved? the idealist in me argued. That was the Toisan way and, I thought then, the Chinese way—work it out for everyone. I could not have imagined at that time that these old men had grown so craven and would preserve the status quo—their vested, profitable way of life—by any means necessary, as events would later demonstrate.

It was against this polarizing backdrop that I finally threw in my lot with the Il Piccolo's activists to organize the first Chinese American civil rights march along Grant Avenue. Perhaps we could keep the lid on, change the community without violence. At that time, Grant Avenue was best known to America as a stage set for *Flower Drum Song*, a popular 1960s musical portraying Chinatown as a sunny, halcyon middle-class dream of a shiny, smiling, singing, and tap dancing "model minority." We expected the street to be filled with ABCs visiting from the suburbs and tourists that sunny Saturday, and we were not disappointed.

A lively group of around forty of us filed onto Grant Avenue. Other demonstrators waiting along the route quickly swelled our ranks to one hundred marchers, then close to two hundred. Our boldly lettered bilingual picket signs blared our aspirations for equality for Chinese Americans, long overdue representation at City Hall, declaring that, after all, we had been here for over a century. Others made specific demands: "Fair, Decent Minimum

Wage for Chinatown Workers" and "Adequate Education Programs." Several directly attacked the Chinese Six Companies: "Chinatown Is a Picturesque Slum" and "Rice Tubs: We Too Are Human Beings."

Then I saw the old-timers. They had turned out to watch us, these old men of another generation who had lived under the Six Companies regime. Gathered in clumps of two, three, or five, they idled curiously on street corners and in entryways or hunched over the ornate balconies of association headquarters. They tried to appear nonchalant. As we marched block after block, they seemed to number in the hundreds, watching us in silent amazement, with the neutral body postures they had learned to wear, like the drab suits they put on in the morning, to slip safely through another day. These were not the well-fed leadership, but the bent, wiry, wage earners—the survivors. I had expected them to boycott the march, but at that moment, I felt our connection—they had built this Chinatown for us, their next generation. They knew we were picking up their long-dormant fight for full acceptance in America. Walking tall already, I stretched my spine higher for them and chanted louder for them, as if reimbursing them for their quiet, shuffling dance, their tongues bitten still during a harsher time, so that we could fight another day.

On that warm summer afternoon, Chinese Americans actually outnumbered tourists on Grant Avenue. It was the only moment of that tumultuous time that I felt we were one community, one village, united by our common craving for full acceptance, facing each other in the silent exchange of a non-speaking-round-and-round. I really hoped this day's march would swing them openly to our point of view, transforming the Six Companies from the grassroots up. Maybe we could work things out: The Wah Ching and Leways youth could be trained for real jobs. The old leadership might accept the new vision of the Larry Jack Wongs, Alice Barkleys, and George Woos, maybe even ask my friends to join the leadership councils of the Six Companies.

We continued our march, past the Empress of China Building, Grant Avenue's tallest, with its bay views, oriental pavilion rooftop restaurant, and photos of the owner with stage and screen stars, governors, presidents, and foreign dignitaries feted there; past the souvenir shops where I had worked during my summers since the age of ten—China Bazaar, the Empress (where my old boss, Auntie Francis Wong, smiled and waved at me); past the Sun Sing Theater where, as a child, I had lost myself in Cantonese movies; and finally, we turned at the corner of Jackson Street, dominated by Lun Hing Supermarket, the only Chinese-owned-and-operated supermarket, and the Italian market, where Mother bought her live turtles, live chickens, and live fish. Chanting as we marched, we exercised the power of our voices, urging our community to reclaim its own voice and its rightful place in America.

Tourists reacted openly, some smiling as if amused, pointing curiously at our signs, and snapping photos with their boxy Instamatic cameras. A few drew back in repulsion, as if to say, first African Americans and now the Chinese! What's America coming to? This definitely was not the Grant Avenue of *Flower Drum Song*.

At the Portsmouth Square rally, my friends vehemently attacked the Six Companies—in both American and Cantonese—for exploiting their own restaurant and garment workers at "slave wages." With a term derived from the turncoat appellation "Uncle Tom" that militant black leaders hurled at moderates, they scornfully branded the Six Companies "Uncle Tongs." No one was reaching out to the Six Companies; instead my friends attacked them mercilessly.

I picked up the microphone and, perhaps aware of the risk to myself, stated that outspoken Galileo students were often transferred out to the school district's Siberia, a trade school with a very high dropout rate. Short of that, we were given the mushroom treatment—kept in the dark and covered with manure. I, instead, advocated change in the schools—Chinese American administrators, discharging openly racist teachers, instituting Chinese American history classes. I did level a weak sideswipe at the Six Companies, arguing that Galileo needed a principal who ate with the common people in their homes, not just in the banquet halls, and that the principal should be a Chinese American.

Triumphant, we reconvened at the community center basement and then adjourned to Il Piccolo's. "First round of beer on the house!" shouted Alice Barkley, as we roared, more alive than we'd felt in a long time.

The ante was quickly and mightily raised when the Big Money rolled into Chinatown that summer in the form of the War on Poverty's multimillion-dollar program grants. It was during these meetings that I finally understood that the chasm was unbridgeable. The two factions entered meetings screaming at each other, barely restrained by a few calm attendees from bashing each other's heads in with the metal folding chairs set out for every meeting. Distressed, I stopped attending them.

The Six Companies hated us young upstarts—"outside agitators" challenging their franchise over the lucrative War on Poverty dollars that would have automatically passed to them under the old Jim Crow system. My colleagues railed back at them, calling them "poverty pimps" and *fan hung*, or "walking rice containers," for their social habit of gorging themselves insensate at self-congratulatory ten-course banquets every night.

The standing Il Piccolo's joke was that you could always tell a seasoned Six Companies' fan hung's stomach from that of a nouveau fan hung. A seasoned one's stomach delicately arched out from just below his sternum and then curved like a huge teardrop into a perfectly round belly, the product of years of slow, careful banqueting. In contrast, a mere overeater's stomach gracelessly flopped over his waist belt, the proverbial male spare tire. The consensus was that George Woo had a ways to go, despite his already formidable girth.

Late that summer, we discovered that a contract had been placed with hit men from New York's Chinatown targeting four of our leaders: Mason Wong, George Woo, Alice Barkley, and Larry Jack Wong. By chance, an alert security guard at San Francisco International Airport detained the triggermen after puzzling over their sharply tailored, pin-striped, double-breasted suits, so unlike those of the drably dressed local Chinese Americans. The guard uncovered guns in their luggage and then alerted the police department to their final destination—San Francisco Chinatown. My reformist friends had survived.

At least for the time being.

CHAPTER 21

THE TROUBLES

I was very proud of you when you were elected president of the student body of Galileo. Why wouldn't I be—you were the one chosen out of three thousand students. All kinds of other races there—white, black, and Mexican from all over the city. And you were from Chinatown, from a working-class family too. Everyone congratulated my relatives: What a good son your sister has, to be selected. Why did the students pick you? Because you were very smart, that's why.

Of course I was very worried over the trouble with the principal. Very worried. You were a good student, and when he suspended you from school, I was shocked, confused at the news, because only bad people get suspended. My son is not a bad boy. You looked so hurt and lost. My first thought was that we should apologize right away, try to get along with him again, and just stay out of trouble. We're poor; and in America, just like China, we could not protect you. If we had had money, he would have phoned us, and everything would have stayed okay-okay. No trouble at all.

But you were an intellectual at heart, with a strong sense of right and wrong, not a real troublemaker. If something was wrong, you would say so, do something about it. That's your character, and I could stand with you. But it was about power. He had the power. We did not. In Toisan, principals have power, and it was the same in America. I didn't want him to hurt you in any way, especially your chances of going to college. I wanted you to learn the American way in college, then build influence to come back and fight another day when you could win. You were just a student, a child. You couldn't beat a principal.

*Everyone in Chinatown knew about the Galileo troubles any-
way. Many agreed with you, said that we should talk about Chinese
not being treated fairly, that it was time for a change. Said you
knew the history, were very reasonable in your criticisms. Even
some Chinese newspapers defended you*—The Chinese Pacific
Weekly, East-West Chinese-American Weekly. *Now my eyes can't
read so well, but in those days, I read Chinese newspapers all the
time. I knew what the community was thinking all the time.*

*But the Six Companies would never help. They're good only at
settling trouble in Chinatown—and only between Chinese. A white
person, a school principal—forget about them standing up to a
white official. Go hire a lawyer, they throw in your face. With
what—burnt rice crust? Like poor people had money for lawyers.*

*I was very worried when we went to the meeting with the prin-
cipal. My thought was to let him lecture us first. Then I would calm
him down, talk softly to him, like in a speaking-round-and-round,
and let him know you're a good son, a smart boy who's going to college, someone he would even be proud to have as a son. I wanted
him to know that we were a good family, hardworking, honest people, that we could all be friends. Then, if I had to, I would have
dropped to my knees and begged him to please let you back into
school. Yes, I would shame him, just like we used to do to bad men
in the village to make them take back their wives. He would think
it was his decision, but that was okay with me. But would a white
principal even listen to me? How could we work this out if he didn't?
I would go to the meeting even if I didn't understand American. I
would have your father translate word for word, even if he wouldn't
hear my words. I would do my best.*

*A lawyer came with us, and the principal got angry. Then he
met with just the family first, and I started to speak, to calm him
down first, and let him know William is a good boy. But the principal got up from his desk, charged at Father, and started to scold
him like a child, his fingers pointing in his face. Oh, he was big, this
principal, but that was the wrong thing to do. Father, who was*

agitated but calm when we got there, jumped up from his chair, and with his own fingers jabbing back like in a swordfight, scolded him back. The principal retreated behind his desk. Father chased him, speaking faster and faster, circling the desk, his face getting angrier. The principal sat down. He stopped talking.

CHAPTER 22

ALL-AMERICAN HIGH SCHOOL

Mr. Kearney was easily a full foot taller than Father, twice as broad in the shoulder, and at least fifty pounds heavier. But Father sprang from his chair, stretched his back and neck upward, squared off eye-to-eye, and then started in. "The old days are gone. Chinese are no longer second-class citizens. My son stands up for Chinese rights. He speaks for me, and I am proud of him." Then Father let loose an impassioned recitation of all the wrongs committed against Chinese Californians, a venting of the ills of his own life in the guise of history. Like the longest string of Red Devil firecrackers, he cracked and boomed out all the unspoken pain from the underpaid, underemployed, wretched labor that had kept his family together.

In that moment, I understood my father's rage and that he had never been angry with us—he just took it out on us—and in that flash of understanding, I forgave him all his transgressions.

To Mr. Kearney's credit, he listened calmly to Father's soliloquy. After a pause, Mother gently stressed that I was a good student, not a troublemaker, and college-bound. Mr. Kearney did not refute that, but said that my activities could be detrimental to my success in life. Well, at least all the adults were united in their concern for my future. Then our attorney, Sidney Wolinsky, head of the local Neighborhood Legal Services Foundation, convinced Mr. Kearney that rescinding the suspension was in everyone's interest. Mr. Kearney walked me over to the Boys Dean's office, handed me an eraser, and I rubbed out the suspension from my record.

Jubilantly.

That was how it was, those last six months of my final high school semester, like being strapped into the latest, extreme theme park thrill ride. Each tumultuous personal confrontation ran into another, and my emotions spiked and soared hour by hour. Only this ride had no terminus. Literary commentators say that exact dates, locales, and facts that have been cross-confirmed by official documents, letters, photos, and multiple interviews produce a good biography. In contrast, a memoir is at its best when it is a narrative of emotional memories. The cold facts are not to be too keenly exalted, and the better practice may be to regard confidently recited facts skeptically.

But I remember the factual flow of the events of 1968 all too well, including how Mr. Kearney and I became archetypal nemeses, contrary to our better natures. He came to personify old, institutionalized racism, and I, the prototype of a new generation of outspoken, reformist Chinese Americans. We were both caught in a larger drama, the birth pains of an emerging zeitgeist. As for trustworthy emotional memories, well, 1968 was undeniably an emotional maelstrom. In that storm, I often couldn't tell who was a friend, how to do the right thing, even what motivated me at times or what my feelings were. So it is the emotional memories of the time that I recall with some suspicion, and the cold hard facts of events that are trustworthy are quite clearly branded in my memory. And, yes, there are many emotional memories—they still burn freshly in my psyche, are confusing still.

Had I known how to look back then, I might have remembered the training-wheel emotional outrage of my Ward 75 rebellion against an unjust nurse, when we suffered punishment anyway—a penalty that was never openly revoked and for which amends were never made. I might have recalled the emotional bloodbath of the night my entire Assemblies of God community expelled me and then shunned me because I questioned their dogma, dared to have my own opinion. But, no, although thoughtful, I was as yet reflective and so wasn't better prepared for the emotional battering. As a book person, I considered change to be purely a mental process, that what was right was obvious and everyone would logically agree without much resistance. I had no foreboding of the contorted emotions to come, that it could feel like torture.

I began my final semester in the fall of 1968 with a feeling of dread as the days moved toward January 16, 1969, the day I would turn eighteen. The Vietnam War was escalating, the draft boards were calling up the William Lees of the world, and antiwar protests dominated the 1968 presidential elections.

I remember being so angry that I dressed down San Francisco's new superintendent of schools at a televised town hall meeting after he gave short shrift to my questions about long-delayed maintenance at Galileo. Then to my surprise, the next day he sent a chief assistant to survey my complaints, and two weeks later, I was even more surprised when workmen built out private counseling offices. I remember a feeling of awe as I observed the shock and pleasure of the principal, teachers, and students alike as these long-forgotten improvements were suddenly, well, there. At last, we could talk to our counselor without everyone hearing our business.

I remember happily internalizing a new lesson: that speaking out made the system work. I remember that day's triumph and then later ruing how fleeting triumph can be.

I remember feeling hypocrisy as I led Galileo's biggest annual ritual, the "Song and Yell" contest, which was an orgasm of school spirit. All three thousand students gathered in devotion on the football field for the single purpose of screaming their heads off. The football team was introduced—we screamed some more. Then the newly elected homecoming queen was announced—we screamed ourselves hoarse.

Hypocrisy, because the predominantly white football team disdained Chinatown kids and so considered Galileo a racially inferior school. Outrage, because one English teacher opened the first day of each semester with the stark statement that Galileo's reputation plunged when Chinese students became the majority, and was never admonished. I remember loathing rigged elections, the ballot box stuffing that always elected a white homecoming queen. I remember pride, renewed ethnic pride at how hard we had worked to keep the balloting clean. We managed to elect a Chinatown girl that year, Millie Gee, a Leways girl. I remember the disbelieving tears of joy streaming down her face as I crowned her and the happy feeling of honest victory that echoed in the cheers of the crowd.

I remember fear again when, after the rally, the retiring principal, Dr. Moreno, mentioned my speech criticizing him, and then relief when he said there had been truth in what I said, and also gratitude, for he had always set a fair tone.

I remember many, many moments of fear during that brief six months, of feeling misunderstood, of more standing up than I could have ever imagined, and yes, of more standing alone than I could handle.

I remember mixed feelings at hearing of the multiple slashings of the car tires of the English teacher who berated Chinatown students with impunity—new tires slashed time and again, as if avenging each instance of his despicable put-down rants. Horror at an arson attempt that left burn shadows on an already dilapidated rear hallway wall, an item on the superintendent's to-do list from that triumphant encounter so long ago. Despair when one lunchtime, students rioted in the courtyard, setting fire to garbage cans and smashing a number of office windows. I remember confusion and hurt when a history teacher branded me a rabble-rousing "Adolf Hitler unleashing his storm troopers."

I remember feeling clever when I placed on our student council agenda an item to discuss a one-day student strike as a way to channel the growing violence into peaceful protest. Then disbelief when Mr. Kearney summoned me into his office and suspended me, all within a half-hour. I remember devastation that I, a college-track A student who lived for academics and college, had jeopardized my scholarship chances. And humiliation, as I slunk slowly home, the culprit who had single-handedly sabotaged our family's aspirations, and shame, for I had flushed away my father's years of hard work for this chance of education that he never had.

I remember sharp betrayal, then stoicism at the unkindest cuts—from friends and classmates since kindergarten—a whispering campaign that I was a power-hungry tool of outside agitators. Then surprise visited again, as I felt no anger toward them or any need to explain myself. I felt tranquility in the knowledge that I had simply moved ahead in my social vision, that my class was the transition class, the last hurrah, the final remnants of the model-minority mindset.

I remember feeling protective toward my brother Richard, who entered Galileo during my turbulent last semester. I was aware that with two and a half years to go before his graduation, he could easily end up as the whipping boy for my activities. And I felt how heavy guilt's weight could be if that were to come true.

I remember feeling a growing hope when Mr. Kearney unexpectedly offered me a ride home one evening when I worked later than usual in the student body affairs office. Here was the man who had unfairly suspended me, the localized bad guy of the white-run school system, generously giving me a ride despite our clashes. I remember feeling puzzled because he drove only an "okay" car—a nondescript sedan that my own father might have afforded had he known how to drive—and because, in contrast, our class sponsor, on a teacher's salary, was known for zipping around in his green Ford Mustang convertible.

I remember my wariness relaxing as Mr. Kearney talked of how he, too, was from a hardworking family, of the importance of education to him, and of how he was about to complete his PhD after many years of night and weekend schooling. With that degree, he would continue his advance professionally. Very indirectly, he cautioned me against jeopardizing my educational chances because of my idealism . . . and, perhaps by implication, to stop jeopardizing his career. My body tensed at this oblique turn in his soliloquy, but Mr. Kearney ended by saying that he was learning a lot this semester, ostensibly from me, although he could not openly admit it. When he dropped me off, he gripped me in one of those painful executive handshakes. I tensed again but still recognized that he had reached out to me in his own gruff way.[1]

Finally, I also remember satisfaction that in less than six months, we had eradicated the stereotype of Chinese Americans as indirect, inscrutable, and conflict averse; and that, along with others, I had recovered those precious Toisanese qualities of direct, plain, and loud speaking.

Back in Chinatown itself, I remember growing skepticism toward all politics, but especially the presidential candidates swinging by Chinatown, then the nation's grandest media symbol of Cold War anti-Communism. Puzzlement as the Republican nominee for president, Richard Nixon, zoomed through Chinatown one more time with his trademark grin and arms pushed in the air like a rabbit-ear TV antenna. Disappointment and anger when Vice President Hubert Humphrey's entourage charged through the schoolyard of the American language program (that day's campaign backdrop for TV news), where I tutored when I wasn't working at JC Penney's, and knocked some of my immigrant kids off their feet. Guarded hope as Bobby Kennedy's insurgent motorcade streamed down Grant Avenue, and this time Catholic schoolkids did duty as the nightly news backdrop. I touched Kennedy's peeling hand—and felt numbness at first, and then destiny, as a bolt powered its way through my body. Thirty

---

[1] Years later, James Kearney, PhD, was promoted to principal of Lowell, the district's prized academic high school and one increasingly comprised of Chinese American students. Many Chinatown students of that era spoke with me of his growing sensitivity, understanding, and active support of their concerns.

hours later, I remember an unnerving, miserable paralysis at the news of the déjà vu-like tragedy—and then despair—because Sirhan Sirhan had assassinated our last hope, Bobby.

I remember all these events so clearly, and the emotional memories, they were all present too. It's just that, because there were so many all the time, I'm not sure I remember them in their right order. I was seventeen and I was zapped out.

CHAPTER 23

GRANDMOTHER SMILES

Did my mother arrive by boat or plane? Hmmm, well, it was the midsixties, so it must have been by plane. What I remember is my nervous anticipation, trying to hold back my happy tears, standing there impatiently. She was around seventy then, and I was in my late thirties, but I was acting like a little girl who had so missed her mother. She cleared Immigration, then Customs. We stood and looked at each other, our eyes locked. We held each other tight, both of us crying. She whispered my name, "Jen. Jen. Jen. It's been so long." I whispered, "Ah Mah. Ah Mah. Ah Mah."

Grandmother, my brother, Wah, and his wife squeezed in with us in our Ping Yuen apartment for the first few months. When word got out through the Chinatown grapevine that Grandmother Chun was in America, all the old Toisan Clan Sisters dropped by. Those first few weeks were so busy; they brought her fruits, candy, food, and red packets with money—just like Chinese New Year. Spent hours talking about so-and-so of the village, where they lived, how the kids were doing. Every morning someone took her to dim sum, and every evening someone else honored her with a banquet. Later, your father helped Wah find an apartment in East Ping Yuen, the project across from us. Grandmother moved in with him.

Maybe because I was so happy because of my mother. Maybe because all the Clan Sisters encouraged me. They said that with two grown boys, enough time had passed that, for sure, the next child is guaranteed to be a baby girl. I really wanted a girl; soon I was pregnant again.

I still remember when I got pregnant. You kept remarking,

"Mom, you're getting fat!" I didn't say a word, just "yeah, yeah." Then when I was seven months' pregnant, my stomach sticking out like a ripe winter melon, you said quite emphatically, "You're really too fat. Time to lose weight." Your body froze and your mouth dropped when I told you, "I'm not getting fat. I'm having a baby." Well, John wasn't a girl, but I was still so happy when he was born. You really loved John too, offering to babysit him when I played poker. I always gave you money from my winnings.

Grandmother babysat John when he got a little older, along with Wah's three kids, Ada, David, and Victor, all around John's age. That's the way it was in Toisan, elders watched the kids while parents worked. They fed the pigs, chickens, and ducks while we worked the fields. Elders tended the vegetable garden too. And all three generations lived in one household. We had to, because in China, the government didn't take care of old people. And there wasn't food everywhere like here in America. If left alone, elders would starve to death. We had to share the simple foods we had with each other. Still, living together was good. Someone was always home to watch the kids after school, clean their scrapes when they fell down—and kids always fall down—cook rice soup when they were hungry, or take a nap together in the afternoon.

Grandmother tutored John, Ada, Victor, and David in Chinese, spending hours going over every word until their pronunciation was perfect. She helped them perfect their calligraphy and memorize Chinese characters. That's why, even today, John's Chinese is better than my first two sons'. And all the children loved her, always laughing, hugging, and climbing over her in her favorite sofa chair. She looked like one of those Buddha statues with one kid on a shoulder, another hanging off an arm, and still another curled up in her lap.

My sisters and I cooked elder soups for her. Lots of lamb soup because lamb is very nutritious, but more importantly, lamb helps bow hoot—it warms up the blood. And bird's nest soup. Also pig liver soup.

We added the herbs gee-doo, bok kee fong, and ginger to a third to a half pound of lamb. Ginger is a great source of heat. In the special Ch'i-soup pot, slow-boil everything down to about three-quarters of a rice bowl. Eat after dinner. We cooked this soup every other week.

For the weeks in between the lamb soup, we served her bird's nest soup. Very expensive, around $1,000 to $1,200 a pound, but we use only an ounce each time so the bird's nest lasted seven or eight months. Add some white-meat chicken to sweeten the broth, and then cook it with the same slow-boiling technique as the lamb soup until you have one and one-half rice bowls' worth of soup. Serve three-quarters of a bowl with dinner and the rest first thing in the morning. A rare bird chews up and then spits back out the stuff to make the nests. That's why it's so expensive!

And pig liver soup. Very easy to make—boil it for half an hour in about a rice bowl's worth of water. Then let it cool down for five minutes. She'd drink it like a tea.

Because the Ch'i energy of elders is not as strong, be careful not to serve so much vegetable soup. Vegetables are yin, lowers their blood strength. That's why we made Grandmother lamb soup so often. We cooked her lots of fish dishes, because that's also good for elders. And steamed pork hash with shredded ginger topped with salt-preserved fish from China. But mainly fish dishes with her meals.

Grandmother had become sick in Toisan. The Japanese invasion and then the civil war put too much pressure on her. She was a little healthier in Hong Kong, but got well in America—there's so much food here and it's cheap. Only fifty cents for a pig liver. In China, do you think we could afford lamb and pig livers? No, animals were few and far between, and the rich always got to the good stuff first. And Grandmother had bad blood pressure—160 over 95, but a doctor gave her some pills. Between our soups and the medicine, her blood pressure went down to around 120 over 80. You know, that's a very good blood pressure.

Grandmother liked Bob, said he was a good man, saw right away that he made me very happy. She knew he was kind of like my boyfriend, of course. Many Toisan elders are like that; they see things clearly right away. They look in your eyes and face, and they know what kind of person you are, how intelligent and hardworking, whether you are kind or mean, honest or tricky. You know she just accepted everything about me, that I was a grown woman now, had raised two kids and about to raise a third. She didn't act like she was a mother and I was still her little girl; she never told me how to raise my kids or that I could have done better, like making the older boys stay in Chinese school. She showed me respect—or, as we put it—bee men, gave me face.

Not all grandmothers are like that, you know. Like your father's mother. When she first came over, she tried to boss everyone, tell us what to do and how to behave, and said we better believe in Jesus or we'd end up in hell. Tried bossing everyone until her dying day, saying she would leave her savings to whoever was nicest to her, always playing one relative off another. It wasn't that much money, but she used every little hook. It got to the point where even your father avoided her, even though she lived upstairs.

No, Grandmother Chun wasn't like that. The only advice she ever gave me was to try to understand why my husband was so grumpy after work. He goes out to earn the money; he puts up with demanding people all day; maybe he has mean bosses even, she said. It's not personal; he's not angry with you. So leave his dinner for him to reheat and ignore his noise—his home is the only place he can let it out. That's the way it is in Toisan households. People get mad, say mean things, and clear it out of their system. Then it's over. Forget about it. Don't bring it up again. That's true for everyone—parents, grandparents, and kids—the home is the place to drop your frustrations. We don't divorce, so we say mean words if we can't hold it any longer, but we let mean words pass too. But today I say that if a husband beats his wife, she should divorce him, even if this was unthinkable in Toisan.

Grandmother Chun wasn't curious about traveling to Los Angeles or New York. Not even to Oakland and Sacramento, the second city that Chinese historically settled in. She was happy staying around Chinatown with her daughters, her grandchildren, and the Clan Sisters. This is kind of a Toisan way once you're settled. Even today, my brother, sisters, their children, and their grandchildren live in the Bay Area. I like it that everyone's close by, even though we may not see each other for weeks or months.

Yes, we showed Grandmother the sights. She especially loved the Golden Gate Bridge, commenting what geniuses Americans must be to have constructed such a beautiful bridge. She smiled at the brilliant orange, an auspicious color that reminded her of gems. She thought white people were friendly since they seemed to always be smiling at her. Maybe they smiled because she looked like such a traditional Chinese grandmother. She was short and a little chubby. She usually wore a black cap with green oval jadeite in front, a traditional black outfit, and Chinese cloth shoes. When she saw her first black American, she commented that America must be a real big country and a kind one to let people from all over the world come and live here, including her own family. My mother never had prejudices about anyone. She taught us only to discriminate on the basis of a person's character—never on race, money, or religion. Even in America, despite so many difficult years, Grandmother never scolded, gossiped, or said anything bad about anyone.

Her time in America was good, very joyful. She was much happier in Chinatown than in Hong Kong. Of course, I was deeply sad when she crossed over. But at least we had reunited and spent her last decade together. I was the one who sponsored her immigration over to America, my silent promise to her during our mother-daughter Lucky Day, even as she said not to worry about her, that she was too old to start a new life in a new land.

CHAPTER 24

TREMORS

Grandmother Chun left behind a frayed China only to land in a community in the process of fragmentation. But age, unawareness, her daughters' love, and the Clan Sisters' attentions shielded her.

Despite our family's joy at the birth of John and our reunion with Grandmother, my eyes were on the streets. In early 1969, the discerning observer might have viewed Chinatown more as a breeding ground for insurrection than as a hopeful promise of a nonviolent civil rights movement in the making. Groups of youth favored one of several militia-style uniforms: College students stuffed leaflets in the four pockets of their George Woo–style blue or brown Chinese cotton jackets; New Leftists paced around in their Vietnam vet army fatigues; Leways' younger members rendered themselves indistinguishable in dark Derby-brand zip-up jackets with Ben Davis jeans, resembling squads of Viet Cong; and the Red Guards marched in surplus green army fatigues topped with dashing red berets. The Wah Ching high-styled it, strutting about in colorful Superfly-style knit sweaters over their black peg-leg pants and black pointed-toe dancing shoes. And everybody but everybody wore very dark sunglasses.

That Chinese New Year, the year of the Ram, the seething youth rebellion spilled out into the streets in an attempt to gut the community's biggest model-minority public relations event, our annual two-week-long celebration. Leways and Wah Ching youth alike taunted and harassed tourists along Grant Avenue. Random fistfights increased as the days ticked down to the grand finale, the Saturday night Chinese New Year parade, America's largest night-lit parade—in prime time on Grant Avenue. I witnessed scores of fights up and down the parade route, climaxing in a shooting battle as retreating youth, taking positions on the balcony ramparts of an older Ping Yuen project, pinned down policemen with rifle fire, mere yards away from festive Grant Avenue. The leveler heads of the Il Piccolo's activists had not won out; the intolerant ones now set the tone.

Meetings with city and public school administrators rapidly deteriorated into chaos, with officials sometimes forced to flee for their safety. Tom Wolfe, the pioneering new journalist, arrived in Chinatown in his trademark three-piece white suit and shoes to hang out at Il Piccolo's and Leways. In his book *Radical Chic and Mau-Mauing the Flak Catchers*, Wolfe described our local devolution from peaceful civil rights march into confrontation, including a nighttime school board meeting in Chinatown where the impaneled school superintendent and his staff fled after a cherry bomb blew up in front of them.

Soon the Barkleys announced that Il Piccolo's would be closing—they could no longer subsidize the café as a community place. It was a common belief that the Six Companies had quietly quashed program funding for a Wah Ching clubhouse and then a proposal to convert Il Piccolo's into a restaurant-training facility. That last night, there was a sad but spirited party, as intellectuals, activists, and youths alike paid our respects and full price for every bottle of European beer. One inebriated irregular rambled up to the Six Companies headquarters and, in a fitting but futile symbolic act, tossed beer bottles through its ornate windows. When Il Piccolo's closed, Wah Ching as a movement for social change was dead, and everyone—activists and youth—dispersed into the streets.

We knew the tongs had already been quietly wooing Wah Ching members, perhaps predicting that the demise of Il Piccolo's would show the youth who had the power.

Some Wah Ching youths had already hedged their bets. In

those final days, from the sidewalk tables of Il Piccolo's, we watched several Wah Ching move their personal belongings into nearby tong buildings. They refused to look at us, partly out of shame and partly in defiance—"Who are you to judge me? We tried it your way and got nowhere." One faction led by Sun Ngeen Look, or "Crazy Six," joined a tong based in Oakland. Other factions affiliated themselves with San Francisco tongs.

One spring night, while shooting pool at Leways, I was detained during an unprovoked police sweep. Although outspoken and confident of my rights, this solitary confrontation with an armed, uniformed policeman in all his authority terrified me, and I never returned. These sweeps shut down Leways in a matter of months.

As with so many other movements of the sixties, the places for thoughtful conversation and nonviolent social justice activities were closed down. The tongs' puzzling but aggressive recruitment foreshadowed a potentially violent fight for control of the community.

The price of change was rising across the board, as I discovered when Mason Wong, as part of an outreach to community members, invited me out to San Francisco State to observe a student strike and noon rally for an Ethnic Studies College. At high noon, we marched out into the student commons, the Quadrangle, with upraised fists, defiantly yelling, "Power to the people!" I had expected to observe, not march into the middle of the crucible with the college administration's most wanted. Sucked into the action, I ducked my head, hanging as far back behind the central committee as I could without splitting off, raising my right arm in an unconvincing "power to the people" salute.

And that was when the games began, as the San Francisco Police Tactical Squad systematically isolated, then beat to a bloody pulp, the heads of as many leaders of the Black Student Union as they could corner. I watched them swing their long, standard-issue, black, hardwood clubs reinforced in the center with steel pellets, up and down, from right to left, without restraint, as they chased down leader after leader. I had just sat in Ecumenical House for an hour with many of those now so seriously injured. There were few things to my youthful eyes so violently graphic as the sight of blood pouring down like a thick, red waterfall against the blackness of crushed Afros, agonized black faces, and the torn black leather jackets of the unarmed. That infamous day was later remembered as Bloody Tuesday.

Yet, that strike and a similarly violent one at UC Berkeley were settled in 1969 with the establishment of ethnic studies programs at both campuses.

That same spring, I received notification of my acceptance into UC Berkeley for the upcoming fall quarter—with a complete scholarship package. I had at least fulfilled this, my family's life-long goal. UC Berkeley was then one of the top ten universities in the United States, the only California school rivaling Harvard, Yale, and Princeton.

As I waited for the fall term, several Il Piccolo's activists invited me to cofound a new organization, Chinese for Affirmative Action, to be modeled on the NAACP. But at eighteen, I felt too whipped by the year just past.

The closing of Il Piccolo's and Leways completely demoralized me. With peace in Chinatown still a long time coming, I felt a personal sense of failure. Even a well-motivated, good heart couldn't substitute for my deficient political and professional skills. I was ready to ride out of Dodge. There would be no commuting for me; I'd live in a campus dorm full-time to meet, understand, and engage people and perspectives from all over America. Maybe one day I would return with the knowledge and connections that could change conditions. Or not.

Like my parents, I knew when it was time to leave the village. It was my turn to sally out into the larger, unknown world of America, and university was just the first step, as far as I was concerned.

CHAPTER 25

FIRST SON GOES
TO UNIVERSITY

I withdrew. Pulled down all the shades in the house. Sat in my arm-chair, not speaking except when necessary. Your father didn't know what to do with me. Bob did most of the shopping and the chores. Everyone thought it was because you left home for university, that I was sad because of that.

Not because of that—you were supposed to go to college. That's what your father and I wanted for you, especially your father, because that's the only way you could escape his restaurant jobs. You know, in my village, we had lots of middle schools and high schools and Hoisin had lots of colleges. There were even famous universities in Guangzhou and Hong Kong. Children's education was important for Toisanese. We believed that children shouldn't have to worry about making money until after college.

I was sad not because you left home, but because I had failed you in my duty as a parent. When a Toisan boy goes to college, a Toisan family is supposed to give him money. For books, housing, and food. For new clothes for the first day of school. For a car to drive. But no, not a red cent did we give you, we were so poor. We couldn't even drive you to Berkeley, because we had no car. Instead, one of your own friends took you there.

I failed you as your mother.

The few times you came home for dinner, you pulled up the shades. Said you didn't like the dark. Tried to cheer me up. But no use, no use. I pulled them down as soon as you left.

You sent us a letter, trying to cheer me up. I remember that letter, thanking us for teaching you well. You said there was a larger world out there, one we knew very little about. You asked us not to be sad at your leaving. You said that we could trust you to find your way, even if it meant making mistakes, that we could not always protect you. You said you always would honor and love us, and you would be home for Christmas and Chinese New Year. You mentioned nothing about not receiving money for college. I guess you didn't know this was our parental duty.

But when Chinese New Year's 1970 came around, I pulled myself out of the sadness. Chinese New Year's—always a time to let go of the bad stuff from last year. Always a time to think ahead into the New Year for all good things. That's the way it's been for more than five thousand years, ritual and celebration. Pay your debts. Make peace with your enemies. Put away sadness. Clean the house. Cut your hair. Wear new clothes. Adorn the house with plum branches bursting with blossoms by New Year's Day and pyramids of shiny tangerines topped with living green leaves. Then, bless children with shiny red envelopes of money, coconut candy, sweet ginger candy, and all kinds of delicious dried fruits. Every one of the ten days has a special significance. There's a best day to have a start-the-year dinner—the lunar calendar will tell each family that. There's an "everybody's birthday" celebration, when everybody becomes one year older, celebrating that once again, together as a village, we made it through another year successfully. That's why we rarely celebrated your personal American birthday—the community's collective birthday is the time for our traditional celebration.

But the most essential practice is no bad thoughts, no bad words, and no negative feelings of anger, sadness, or envy—for the whole ten days. Forgive everyone who offended you or harmed you in the past year. Pay off your debts—don't let them linger into the New Year. Always maintain a positive attitude, because how you think, feel, talk, and treat people during the first ten days determines how things will be during the next year. This positive attitude affirms the good of the past year and continues the flow into a joy-

ful and provident year ahead. This is how difficult situations change for the better, enemies become friends, and misfortune turns into abundance.

You were so happy when you returned home for Chinese New Year's Eve dinner. The shades were up, the house was bright and clean, the plum blossoms were flowering, and your red envelopes sat on bowls of shiny tangerines. I was my old self, soaking vegetables, cutting up white boiled chicken, and snapping orders at you for last-minute purchases.

You gave little John his red envelope money, then tickled him silly and finally swung him around and around like you used to do.

I guess you knew your mother's spirit was back—you practically leaped in the air for joy when I barked at you to go get the crackling skin pork. "Make sure the skin is crackling—lok, lok, lok," I reminded you, like when you were a boy. You never seemed so pleased to be ordered out to jostle with the last-minute lines of New Year's Eve shoppers. Like us, they must have the tastiest two pounds of the last roasted pig of the day for this, the closing meal of the old year. Steaming fresh out of the oven, chopped while still too hot to handle with bare hands.

Yes, you were happy and so was I again. Gung hay fot choy. Sun neen fai lok. *All good fortune in the New Year.*

CHAPTER 26

CLOUDS

My strongest memory of my first year of college is of clouds. Clouds of tear gas blanketing protesters throughout the year, as it did on my first day in Berkeley, when I joined People's Park demonstrators herded along by armed National Guardsmen, bayonets at the ready, half-tracks revved up for mayhem. Clouds of tear gas blowing through ragtag groups of antiwar students battling mano a mano with fully armed, helmeted police during antiwar protests, clouds that invisibly drifted into classrooms, libraries, and the student union, wispy remnants that clawed at our eyes and throats for hours after the arrested had been jailed and the campus police had punched out on the time clock.

Cumulous clouds gliding over the spacious campus, more clouds than I had ever seen in my urban upbringing. Clouds burnished Maxfield Parrish–beautiful by the neoclassical columns, wide peaked roofs, and marble steps of Berkeley's buildings . . . the golden light of the setting sun.

Clouds of marijuana smoke in the rooms in Davidson Hall, our coed dormitory, as America's middle-class children gathered in our generation's version of cocktail hour, listening to the Beatles' *Abbey Road* album, exchanging stories of our upbringing, flirting, clucking our dismay at the war (always the damned war), exchanging rumors about professors, and asking who wanted to carpool to Altamont, where the Rolling Stones were giving a free rock concert.

Clouds of mental confusion as Marxists, Maoists, conservatives, liberals, the Spartacist League, the World Law Federation, the Esperanto Society, Hare Krishnas, Jews for Jesus, Students for a Democratic Society, the Christian World Liberation Front, L. Ron Hubbard, street characters like the Soap Bubble Lady and General WasteMoreLand, and our outnumbered professors competed for our attention, our allegiance, our lives, and our souls.

The UC Berkeley campus, circa 1969, was obviously not my family's lifelong notion of bucolic academia.

So I didn't tell them.

Beginning with my Il Piccolo's friends, I had started to edit my reports of my doings to Mother and Father. But with Berkeley, I went beyond editing; I hid truths from them: the dangerous demonstrations, lifestyle experimentation, and the many fleeting liaisons. By my third quarter, I was barely visiting my parents' home, afraid to reveal how much I had grown—and grown away from them.

My evasions started the day my mother's soft words and mediating style had failed to soften my high school principal, and I thought, Bless her heart, but she just doesn't get this America. My father had already pushed me away from him when I was fifteen. In one of his bad moods and angry about something or other, he raged, "I will pay the rent, put food on the table, and buy clothes for you until you turn eighteen. After that, you're on your own. No more help from me." Mother wasn't there, or she would have set him straight about his Toisan duties. But from his perspective, it was a good offer. I would have five more years of family support than he had had. He was on his own at thirteen.

He didn't present it as a traditional passage into independence, but rather as a punitive edict. Still, Father's words didn't hurt me so much as shake me awake. Who likes discovering that his father considers him a financial burden, one that chains him to dead-end jobs? I simply took it as the truth—his truth from his own childhood and now, and my truth from him—and continued my turning away from Mother's nurturing Toisan perspective toward Father's harsh view of life. Okay, I will be on my own at age eighteen and—I silently upped the ante—free of you too. You won't hear from me, and you'd better not be telling me how to live.

As we counted down to the liftoff date, I felt a decreasing responsibility to let my parents know of my whereabouts and about my thoughts and friends. I prepared myself to honor my father's eviction notice.

Finally, I was on my own, paying my own way with a hard-earned scholarship and a part-time campus job planting and then cleaning up hundreds of tomato plants at the genetics department greenhouse. I opened myself to a larger America, aware that the intimacy of Davidson Hall would help me decipher the unspoken social mores, cultural codes, and implicit rules of mainstream America.

Despite the diversity of my San Francisco, it was not Middle America, and mainstream Americans remained a mystery. Davidson Hall introduced me to a new category, Jewish Americans, who looked white to me but not to WASPs, who considered them off-white. Nothing personified this split more than the relationship of my floor-mate James—later the editor of our nationally regarded *Daily Cal* student newspaper—and his dorm girlfriend, Rachel, from Los Angeles's West Side, an upper-class Jewish American enclave. Free to fall in love with James within the socially liberated zone of coed Davidson Hall, Rachel nonetheless soon succumbed to lifelong cultural mores and family pressure to date within the Jewish community. They spent the rest of that year as "friends," but James's heartbreak was constant, visible in his downcast eyes.

I surmised that, similar to Chinese Americans, Jews had faced prejudice, found strength in five thousand years of their own recorded history, and fostered strong communities to overcome the obstacles. Ironically, a philosophical dispute arose as to whether Asian Americans, the model minority, were really people of color, as true-blue an oppressed minority as others in the ethnic studies purview. Those skeptics viewed us as "off-white," or not "of color," a position of ethnic ambiguity akin to that of Jewish Americans.

Another big surprise was that not every member of a well-known blue-blooded dynastic American family was considered of equal peerage. Paul, who was from one such family, explained to me that children of men born into his family enjoyed higher status than those of men who had married into the family. Paul's father had married in, as it were, and so Paul and the others in his category had to dress in blue formalwear at the annual family reunion as a way of setting them apart from the "authentic" members, who dressed in formal black. Paul chuckled that the "blues had all the fun." My fondest memory of Paul, a son of privilege despite his misgivings, came about one afternoon as I rushed off late for work at the genetics department greenhouse on the other side of the campus. He agreed to retrieve my clothes from the impossibly slow dryer. Not only did he do that, but he also folded ever so neatly every pair of underpants, socks, jeans, and my T-shirts into piles and then arranged them in a neat row on my bed. An American blue-blooded prince fetching and folding my laundry! Father, once a houseboy, would never have believed it. Warm feelings welled up inside me, renewing my faith that most people were intrinsically kind at heart.

Unfortunately, the hardest lesson of Davidson Hall was that too many of my white dorm-mates lacked this second-nature tai-chi balance of give-and-take within relationships, a balance so intrinsic to my upbringing by Mother. Perhaps it was the difference between the communal-village sensibility of my Toisan heritage and the individualistic focus on acquisition, ownership, and privilege that constituted the upbringing of most of my white dorm-mates. Over the year, I increasingly felt ripped off, then increasingly disrespected. I waited in vain for the natural rebalancing, but to my surprise, the more I shared, the more I was perceived as a soft touch, a pushover, a weakling. I had to pull back, to not be so generous with my records, books, notes, limited funds, and stash. This withholding was not an easy transition for me, but I learned to harden as a first response, and then to soften only when sure of the person's character.

In the spring of 1970, I switched jobs to work at the new Asian ethnic studies program as the interdepartmental liaison—a role well suited to my multicultural urban upbringing—and as the sole male clerk-typist there (thanks to my typing classes at Galileo). In its return-to-the-community service orientation, Asian ethnic studies at least offered a course called Conversational Cantonese, whereas the classical Oriental languages department offered Mandarin exclusively. But it stood as a puzzling choice to me, like a bad compromise, since Toisanese remained the predominant dialect of the Chinatowns of America.

Then several professors proposed moving all the offices and classes into the community. Despite its Red Guards' "correct line" imperative, I discerned that the real and unconscious motivation behind the proposal was personal: These fully assimilated kids needed to be immersed in Chinatown to feed the starvation of their cultural isolation, to feel bone-deep good about being Asian American. I quickly piped up that since I had just come from the "hood," I'd gladly hold down the scaled-down campus fort—you know, answer the phones, pick up the mail—to the chuckles of my sympathetic fellow clerk-typists.

Later in the spring of 1970, President Nixon sent in B-52s to carpet bomb the neutral country of Cambodia, escalating a war he had promised to end. That same day, following the morning news reports announcing the bombardment, students managed to shut down the entire UC Berkeley campus by noon. Then clouds of tear gas once again roiled through the campus and over the streets as our growing ranks spilled into the community. Over the next three days, other campuses followed—536 of them, to be precise. On May 4, National Guardsmen shot and killed four students at Kent State University in Ohio, and days later other

Guardsmen shot and killed two students at Jackson State in Mississippi, a historic African American college. Many more students were wounded at each campus.

In response, students were more resolved than ever to keep the campuses shut down. But to what purpose, since it was our own education at risk? Again the clouds of confusion—practicality colliding with ideals, because no one wanted to lose a year's worth of academic credit. Several Berkeley faculty members led us beyond striking and proposed "reconstitution," a complete reorientation of the university's teaching purpose toward a full-time education of the truth of the war and community action to end it.

If ever a speaking-round-and-round took hold at Berkeley, it was during reconstitution. Department by department, then college after college, reconstitution was adopted. Everyone was equal—professors, students, men, women, people of color, whites, even campus workers who cared to join our discussions. We spoke, shouted, quieted each other down, and planned the next day's antiwar activities. Those final two months were the most comfortable of my freshman year, with their bonds of community and the exhilaration of acting together for the common good.

I was recruited to join an antiwar tour addressing Asian Americans at nearby campuses because I offered a different perspective: that of Chinatown's working class.

After a contentious but rousing forum at California State University, Sacramento, in an agricultural area an hour from Berkeley, Jerry Chong, from the old Kearny Street apartments, introduced himself. I was puzzled when he asked if I remembered him. He was unforgettable—the older brother I never had, whom I had admired for his brains, athleticism, style, and leadership. In the grab of our handshake, I felt as if I had beached back onto the safe shores of that stable epoch of my first home, our apartment building cum village.

Jerry filled me in on his time as a marine in Vietnam as the respected leader of a squad that often ambushed Viet Cong units in the night—a nervy game of hide-and-seek and search and destroy—one of the toughest tours of duty in "the 'Nam." That was when Jerry wasn't running patrols and operations during the day. He served with Mike Company, Third Battalion, Seventh Marines Regiment from 1967 to 1968 in the Dai Loc District thirty-five miles southwest of Danang City. Those hotly contested combat zones came to be known as Dodge City, Charlie's Ridge, Arizona Valley, and Hill 52, later immortalized in two novels, *Fields of Fire* by James Webb and *A Rumor of War* by Philip Caputo.

On too many mornings, he said, white American GIs stood in his way, staring him down and demanding to know, "Who's that gook, that slant eye? What's he doing, wearing commando stripes, carrying an M16 like he's worthy?" And later, when he and another valued IBM employee, the only other Vietnam veteran, wore black armbands on a national day of silent protest, the rave job performance reviews stopped, the personnel counseling sessions increased, and soon he was out of a job. Jerry explained that he was in his second year at the law school on campus.

My speech had struck home with Jerry. It was white Americans who had questioned his American birthright, Jerry ruefully recalled. His words penetrated more deeply than any well-written antiwar editorial. The justifications against the war were overwhelming, yet in quiet moments, I wondered whether I was cowardly, unpatriotic, or ungrateful for opposing the war. But no one could challenge Jerry's medals, and we were the same kind. Except for a few years' difference, I would have blindly fought alongside him. My nagging doubts disappeared.

When President Nixon announced America's withdrawal from Vietnam in January 1973, Cal students danced wildly on Telegraph Avenue and Sproul Plaza, chanting, "Ho, Ho, Ho Chi Minh, NLF has won again!" And upon news of Nixon's resignation during the Watergate hearings, we spontaneously danced and chanted yet another night. The campus quickly shifted into a more or less normal rhythm of study, play, final exams, and quarter breaks. I hitchhiked home on holidays, and family was only a phone call away. But I continued drifting away from the closeness of my family, relying on my familiar if temporary "families" in Davidson Hall, Asian Ethnic Studies, and campus activist circles. I was living out the pattern of centuries of Toisanese pioneers, casting out onto the seas of the larger world. My father, as if in instinctual accord, checked on me less. Mother, though, steadily insisted on my presence at family gatherings, solicitations that I patiently declined.

In the same way, Richard was already making his own life. In early 1972, I knew enough of the surface facts to conclude that Richard was walking a similar path, but not in my footsteps. He co-organized a student walkout from Galileo to the Board of Education, protesting the same issue of a Chinese American glass ceiling. But they succeeded—Stanley Tong, my high school geometry teacher and a popular sports coach, was eventually appointed principal. Richard also organized youth dances and street fairs. Yet he never visited me at Berkeley and wasn't interested in applying there.

Then he won a scholarship to San Francisco State University and planned to continue his summer job with Wells Fargo Bank on a part-time basis during the school year.

We had grown up as close as two brothers could be—running the streets of North Beach, Telegraph Hill, and the waterfront; walking to and from the same schools every day; avoiding or fighting off the same bullies; chipping in to buy the *Down Memory Lane* record collection from Reader's Digest; jointly collecting *Spiderman, Fantastic Four,* and *X-Men* comic books, and—in our last collaboration—*Playboy* magazines. As the older brother, I often overshadowed him—in strength, reputation, and, of course, priority in our parents' traditional eyes.

Richard didn't seem to mind my first-born ranking, since I wasn't a mean older brother. In critical ways, we were equals.

Once, when I was around ten, after our Boy Scout troop had wound down, one older neighborhood boy, a newcomer and a teenager whose father owned the local rice store, drew us momentarily into his *Rebel Without a Cause*–style juvenile gang. We started with a short spell of shoplifting toys from downtown department stores. Then he began to talk of "rumbles," the 1950s slang for fistfights with kids from other blocks—or what we now call gangs. His pitch sounded fun in a dangerous kind of way. But one Monday, our teenage would-be leader of the pack gleefully reported about his recent weekend in a place called Juvie, the local juvenile hall incarceration facility. At that point, Richard and I looked at each other, went home, and talked it over. If shoplifting and rumbling led to Juvie, this would cause a lot of trouble and distress for our parents, not to mention the punishments we'd endure for weeks. One of us suggested, "I'll quit if you quit." We did, convinced some of our old pals to stay away, and then wisely spent our evenings, once again, in our apartment building, studying and playing with the Chong kids, and our weekends with Father at the matinees and family Sunday brunches.

Like most brothers, we had our tussles, but they were rare and fought fairly, never to inflict damage, and at any sign of surrender, we stopped and went on to the next thing, grudge free. We harmoniously shared the same small project bedroom for eight years, happily tolerating the beat of Top 40 radio, the mysterious sounds of French or Spanish lessons on our tinny record player, the smells and noise of raising guppies, hamsters, and lizards. We ended many a night by falling asleep while sharing stories, life's lessons, and tomorrow's plans.

Our later conversion into the Assemblies of God church was in tandem. True, our old Kearny Street pals had joined en masse, but we lived now in the urban oasis of Ping Yuen. If either of us had hesitated, that would have been the end of it. But we went for it, and although Richard left first, without consulting me, his departure quickened the process of my own exit.

Richard's solo departure from the Assemblies of God mission was his first major step into his own life. From that moment, we slowly grew apart, at first imperceptibly and then by strides during my two remaining years in high school, as my interests in theater, music, the counterculture, and finally politics filled my time.

It was during this drifting apart that we fought our final fist-fight. Richard said something that seemed to be disrespectful to my older-brother status; or possibly in my resistance to his developing independence, I just took it as lip. We threw fists hard and fast, mightier than usual, as if we knew the fight was truly about Richard's autonomy. Soon we were on the ground wrestling. Then with a final fury—my last breath actually—I managed to sit on top of him, pin his arms to the ground, and shout, "See, I can still beat you. You're still my little brother, and don't you forget it." But we both knew that it could have gone either way that day. We never fought again. He was free now of my first-son authority, but I too was free now of having to watch over him.

Then, surprisingly, I repeated this same ritual of emancipation with Father, only our encounter quickly turned dangerous. Although Father wanted me to be on my own by eighteen, he didn't adjust easily to my burgeoning independence. One night he threatened me with discipline—unfairly. His justification, mirroring my last fight with Richard, was that I gave him lip. He screamed that he was still my father and as long as I lived in his house, I must obey him. Seventeen going on eighteen and full of myself, I refused his command to extend my palms for a chopstick whacking, a sharp but relatively harmless childhood punishment. I didn't deserve it, and I certainly wasn't putting up with any deliberately infantilizing punishment. As with my final fight with Richard, this was the last stand of Father's evaporating authority. My now-enraged father and I ended up shouting. Suddenly, he scurried into the kitchen, turned back, and rushed me, alarmingly armed with a small serrated steak knife. I just as quickly dashed safely into my room and bolted the door.

This fight wasn't like the one with Richard, where there was never a possibility of serious injury. One of us had to stop, and I knew it would be me. Father had rarely been able to extricate himself from his seizures of rage. I kept my door locked and then pressed my body against it to hold it in place. I hollered that I was holding the stout half of a cue stick. I whacked it loudly against the door to emphasize its destructive power. I screamed that I wasn't afraid of him anymore, that he could no longer treat me unfairly just because he was in a bad mood, and that I could really hurt him if I wanted to. *Thwock. Thwock.* He left, and within a half-hour, we had both calmed down enough that I could leave for some night air. Father was slumped in the living room armchair. He didn't look at me, didn't say a word. He never physically disciplined me again.

By the time I enrolled at Berkeley, I was living very much apart from these male members of my family.

In my junior year, I cofounded a very successful campus club, the Asian American Students Association. Middle-class Asians didn't invite me to their parties: I was a Chinatown kid—an undesirable, carless student from the projects who didn't go away during spring and winter breaks. I couldn't even afford a bicycle to scramble across campus to make all my classes on time. As it turned out, I found the few parties that I crashed to be downright boring—cocktail parties barely buzzing to a kind of soft soul Muzak. I wanted to amp up the happening vibe and create fun, stimulating events where everyone was welcome and, yes, that even the coeds who had rejected me couldn't resist. Our student group started with multimedia dances (akin to the early Winterland happenings), then poetry readings, jazz performances, and art events that expressed our Asian American heritage. Our swiftly growing membership swung the annual campus election of that year's Berkeley associated student union slate of candidates to a Chinese American as a copresident and a Japanese American as co–vice president.

As I was about to complete my bachelor's degree in architecture, I contemplated entering the school's master's program in city planning and urban design. The conventional academic wisdom was that most public housing projects inevitably devolved into devastated battle zones of drugs and violence, where community spirit and personal self-esteem degenerated along with the buildings. It could be otherwise, I knew, like the nurturing, self-contained community of my own North Peaceful Gardens Projects. Perhaps a new generation of urban architects who had actually been raised in public housing could design a new kind of safe, decent, and sustainable public housing.

That summer, I was about to fly overseas to visit the three faces of China: republican Taiwan, free-market colonial Hong Kong, and then the Communist heartland. Armed with a departmental grant to photograph the public housing spaces there, I would start my career by synthesizing the past with my future, a journey combining field research with a search for personal roots.

Now the only clouds over Berkeley were of the cumulous variety. Spring was finally peaceful and the lengthening days sunny.

PART IV

CHAOS UNDER HEAVEN

(1972–1978)

CHAPTER 27

SPEAKING IN CIRCLES

What mother wouldn't want her children to have the best possible future, not to be limited like your father's generation? Despite all the troubles with the principal, everything turned out okay-okay.

And so, Richard followed in your steps, speaking out about Chinese rights. He started by working an after-school job sweeping up and watering the plants on Old Chinatown Lane for the senior citizens of the Self-Help for the Elderly agency. Later he worked with the Youth Council and Wells Fargo Bank. He was going to college.

Those last two years before college, Richard was spending more and more time with his new friends. He went out of town on trips to Los Angeles and New York. "With the summer youth program," he said. One summer, he called to say that he would be a few days late returning home. It turned out that he was in a car accident and didn't want me to know. One summer, he went camping a lot and then stayed out later and later all the time.

But you did the same, so I thought this was normal. Everything looked okay-okay for Richard, as far as I could tell. But now looking back, of course it wasn't. The elders were getting angrier and angrier, calling the young people "bandits" and "lawless elements." Everyone was afraid of the Wah Ching. More kids on drugs. Where did all these drugs come from? So many so suddenly, like from out of nowhere? And guns were everywhere. How did so many guns show up in Chinatown at the same time? There were never shootings in Chinatown before. More and more burglaries, young men robbing old people. Your father was robbed several times on the stairs of our own Ping Yuen housing project, returning from work late at night. Aiyahhh—jow gow sli-lah, chaos under heaven! Chi-natown was no longer safe.

I should have followed the situation more closely. Things were changing from your time. What was wrong with me, thinking events would let him move right along just like you?

You know, in our village, if we saw problems coming, we could talk about it and change the situation. I told you about the speaking-round-and-round of the Clan Sisterhood, a way to fix all kinds of problems, even between two angry people who hated each other. Of course, back then in the village, we didn't include men because they didn't listen to women. Especially if a man was part of the problem. But once we decided on a course of resolution, we stood in front of his house and harassed him day after day, talking loud, shaming him, and pleading until he gave in. If it had been like the village, I would have known what to do. There would have been no trouble, no rebels, no war, and maybe Richard would not have . . . would not have . . . been . . . jailed. . . .

One day during the summer of 1971, a warning in Chinese was issued in Chinatown, calling for an end to lawlessness in the com-munity. A tong gave the warning and threatened that those young people who failed to comply would be stopped by any means neces-sary. By any means necessary. The warning was published in a full-page advertisement in Chinese newspapers and was posted everywhere—Grant Avenue, Stockton Street, all the side streets and dead-end alleyways of Chinatown. Everyone in Chinatown was ji-ji-jah-jah-ing about it for days and days.

Night after night I stayed up until Richard returned home. Sometimes he came back by 11 p.m., other nights, at 2 or 3 a.m., and sometimes he called to say he was sleeping at a friend's house. But at least every night, I knew he was somewhere safe. I wasn't the only one worrying. All my Clan Sisters worried every night. China-town was dangerous now, with the killings, and something terrible could happen just because your son was in the wrong restaurant on the wrong night.

I didn't think the bulletin had anything to do with Richard. He was like you, a reformer and a rebel, not a Wah Ching. He was not a lon doi—*a broken child, juvenile delinquent. Yeah, yeah, he was a good kid, saved money all the time, starting as a child. He collected rare coins—Lady Liberty head dimes, Indian Head nickels, and silver dollars. Worked at a bank, no surprise—he liked money, touching it and having it around. Going to college. It was that girl, that May Tom, who testified against Richard, who kept changing her story about what the gunman looked like. She even said the gunman shot with his right hand. Everybody knows Richard is left-handed. Has been all his life. Does everything with his left hand.*

Maybe I was too busy raising baby John, trying to have some fun when I could. Poker with the Clan Sisters. Going to Reno for a few nights. Maybe I wasn't thinking straight. Maybe I didn't watch over Richard enough. Maybe if I had, he wouldn't have gone to jail That's the one thing I feel bad about—I let Richard down. I let Richard down. It's my fault he ended up in jail. I just thought he was like William. Richard is leaving Chinatown, going to college, and so everything's fine. I didn't watch over him carefully enough.

In this way, I failed him as a mother.

CHAPTER 28

WAILING WALL

On the morning of June 16, 1972, when I read in the *San Francisco Chronicle* that a young man named Richard Lee had been positively identified as the main suspect in the slaying of another young man, Poole Leong, I did not imagine for a moment that my brother was that suspect. I paused at the coincidence, but with scores of Richard Lees listed in the phone book, I was unconcerned and didn't even call my parents to double-check. End of story, and what else is in the *S.F. Chronicle* today? I flipped to the *Doonesbury* comic strip.

Enjoying the trajectory of my rich student life and urban design aspirations, I had somehow compartmentalized Chinatown as the past. I muffled the alarm bells that must have been clanging inside as the media reported an alarming number of sensational murders in and around Chinatown. Police sources blamed a Chinese youth-gang war. Yet no one asked exactly what they were fighting about. Was there a Chinese American Hatfield-McCoy personal feud running amok? Were my old Wah Ching and Leways friends retaliating for unpaid gambling debts and bad dope deals?

I was living large in Berkeley—my time, my life. I didn't want anything to put the brakes on it, to force me to slip back. I wasn't consciously aware of this filter, but in effect, I was long gone from Chinatown.

Instead, I wryly editorialized in my mind that the Il Piccolo's sages had predicted this bitter fruit—your just desserts, Six Companies—and I sighed with the smugness of the righteous.

On the morning of June 28, 1972, my sanctimony collided

with a hard-core dose of reality. The *Chronicle*'s front-page head-line story reported that Barry Fong-Torres, the highly regarded and dedicated executive director of a Chinatown youth service agency, had been shot to death the night before when he answered the door of his own apartment. Barry Fong-Torres's murder put a human face on the murderous horror ravaging Chinatown. Unlike anonymous immigrants, Barry was someone I and the larger public could have roomed with in college, befriended at a cocktail mixer, or debated politics with over a beer. His brother, Ben Fong-Torres, was the famous *Rolling Stone* magazine journalist, who was once a role model for me.

The assassins left a scrawled note "Pig infomer (*sic*) die yong (*sic*) . . . "

This curious note caught my attention because it was an anomaly in the modus operandi—no notes in any language had been left at any of the preceding ten-plus Chinatown-related slay-ings. As if youth gangs wouldn't have automatically been blamed anyway, the misspellings blatantly signaled the public, the news media, and homicide investigators that there could be no other explanation than the Chinese youth-gang war.

The article also reported that four hours later, mere blocks away from the crime scene, a Joe Fong had been routinely stopped for a speeding violation. Routine, that is, except for one thing: My brother Richard Lee, a wanted man, was his passenger, and now the police were eyeing Joe Fong and Richard Lee for the Barry Fong-Torres murder!

What the hell was going on?!!?

Stunned, I clutched my one sure connection, Richard, and hoped that, like Ariadne's cord, he could navigate me safely through the labyrinthine puzzle of a now unimaginable commu-nity to uncover the facts and ultimately to prove his innocence, if innocent he were.

That meant reacquainting myself with Richard in, of all places, the city jail. The bail amount was surprisingly high, although

Richard wasn't a flight risk, since he had shown up at his bank job every day until his unexpected arrest. The young adult facing me through the thick Plexiglas window was not the confident, low-key, suited-and-tied, smiling bank teller I had dined with months ago at Johnny Kan's, where jackets and ties were de rigueur. The man in front of me was distracted, lost, and disheveled in his prison-issued jumpsuit. Then, as he focused on me, he seemed to grow hard, and his two dark eyes glowered at me, as if stripping away all notions of civility. I picked up the phone handset, but Richard carefully batted away my questions—"What was going on in Chinatown? Is it true what the papers are saying about you? Why and who killed Barry Fong-Torres?" But his lawyer had cautioned him against talking about the case over the electronically bugged visitor phone system. Still, he reassured me of his innocence, urging me to talk to his lawyer, James Martin McGuiness, instead. Some friends had retained McGuiness on Richard's behalf.

This was comforting news, for McGuiness was one of the city's finest lawyers, a dyed-in-the-wool defendant's lawyer who once willingly spent several nights in jail when he refused a judge's order to divulge confidential client information. If anyone could, surely James Martin McGuiness would rectify this nightmarish mistake.

McGuiness's young associate and a recent law school gradu- ate, Patrick Coyle, was of the view that Richard should never have been charged for Poole Leong's murder. Richard apparently had a solid alibi for that evening, one that accounted for his time and whereabouts—dinner with friends and then attendance at a grad- uation ceremony at Lowell High School, both events that had taken place on the other side of town at the same time as Poole Leong's slaying. The sole evidence connecting Richard with the slaying was the uncertain eyewitness testimony of a sixteen-year- old Galileo student, May Tom. Also, Coyle continued, descrip- tions of the assailant varied, and none of them matched Richard's. Moreover, everyone identified the shooter as holding the gun in his right hand, while Richard was 100 percent left-handed.

I suggested that Richard might be scapegoated, though, convicted through guilt-by-association gang innuendo. Coyle was confident he could make a successful motion to prevent this kind of prosecutorial tactic or refute it because Richard didn't fit the profile, and he counted out the reasons: no prior arrests or convictions. Responsible work history. Guilty men don't show up at work every day, particularly not in a bustling city hall branch serving cops, judges, and reporters! And Richard was enrolling at the local state university that very fall. It was obviously a case of mistaken identity, one that would be cleared up soon.

Momentum—personal momentum. So hard to cancel my life in the making, my trip to the three faces of China. Fear of regressing to an old reality. In the *Superman* comic books of my youth, a villain would trick Superman into a mean, crude, and ugly parallel universe known as Bizarro World. To return to normal reality, Superman had to trick the villain into repeating his own very strange name. What charm, what magic name, which strange incantation would deliver Richard and me back home where we belonged?

My heart was set on leaving for the Far East in a week, but how could I leave with my brother in jail? I considered canceling the trip until Coyle advised me that the trial date was early November and that nothing much would happen between now and then, except perhaps that the real killer might be arrested and Richard released.

Richard felt the same way, that there wasn't much that I could do whether I was in the Bay Area or not. Perhaps in our new independence and autonomous relationship, he felt that his problems were his, mine were mine, and that he had no right to upset my plans. Momentum, faith in your chosen destiny—all too readily I took him at his word and convinced myself that it was all right to go.

I flew to Taiwan and then Hong Kong with the hope of entering China. I never got into China because it was still in the midst of its cultural revolution. China Travel Services dawdled on the visa, until finally in frustration I gave up. However, the trip turned out to be fabulous. I had sharpened my Mandarin and spent hours at the National Palace Museum in Taipei, Taiwan, ogling Chinese art. In Hong Kong, I lived with relatives in a massive housing project named So Uk Choon, but, through Berkeley friends, I was introduced to every level of Hong Kong society. How had I ever thought a few days in Hong Kong would be enough? I shot hundreds of color slides and black-and-white photos and received a standing ovation from my school of architecture colleagues following my presentation. Still, this journey was nothing compared to the journey I was to undertake after Richard's trial.

At summer's end, Richard was still in jail. He lost his bank job and his scholarship. As the November trial date approached, Coyle informed me that, given the weak case, the firm had decided that Coyle could proceed to trial. The firm confidently expected that the trial judge would dismiss the case on the basis of insufficient evidence.

My parents and I attended the five-day trial until the verdict was rendered on November 1, 1972. Except for watching the *Perry Mason* series on television, we had no experience of the court system. We simply assumed that, just like Perry Mason, Coyle would catch a dishonest witness on the stand or the police would arrest the real killer at the last minute, and that *tah-dahhh!* with a magician's flourish, Richard would be absolved and justice served. That's how naïve we were. We pushed open the high double wooden doors that led into a cavernous windowless chamber, feeling like little toy figurines abandoned in a huge spare toy chest. The lack of windows and the overhead fluorescent lights made me feel uncomfortable, as if we were sealed off in a strange universe with its own rules and unpredictable denizens.

As I watched this trial, however, a dense, sinking feeling pressed me farther back into the rigid, hard wooden bench of the spectators' section: I recognized the vampires of anti-Chinese racism past rising from their coffins, gathering around for a blood feast—impatient to gorge themselves on the energy of someone at the prime of his vitality—as if the national civil rights movement were only a TV drama and as if we had never marched on Grant Avenue three years earlier and jump-started our own stalled march for full citizenship.

First, the trial judge disallowed the defense attorney to probe the mostly white jury pool on their overall and specific racial attitudes toward Chinese Americans. Then the assistant district attorney, apparently a highly experienced prosecutor, dismissed both Chinese Americans and African Americans from the jury. He then called, as an eyewitness, a teenage girl who had glanced out of a well-lit apartment into a dark courtyard. She couldn't or wouldn't answer a straight yes or no to a direct question unless the prosecutor prodded her several times. Then a white Chinatown police intelligence officer testifying as an expert on Chinatown crime never mentioned the decades-old gambling syndicates and, more important, the historic payoff scheme to police and, during some decades, to politicians. He also left out the tongs' recent recruitment of Wah Ching youth as thugs into their crime syndicates. Instead, he focused on detailing a youth-gang war between two groups, Wah Ching youth and something called the Joe Fong Gang. He stated that Richard Lee was Joe Fong's right-hand-man and killed unhesitatingly on Joe Fong's orders. He suggested that this slaying was part of a series that must be stopped to protect the terrorized residents of Chinatown and outraged San Franciscans alike.

If the reader is wondering why I appear more observer than participant in narrating the events of the trial, it's because I often was. I couldn't fathom why the prosecution persisted so aggressively despite the weak, circumstantial evidence. I didn't know Richard in the close way of our earlier years. I had been away from Chinatown events. I felt psychologically alienated. My old friends, now fearing for their lives, would not talk to me or bring me up to speed on the impact of the closing of Il Piccolo's and

Leways and the tong recruitment of competing Wah Ching factions. So the trial had aspects of a refresher course for me, as well the real-time determination of Richard's guilt or innocence.

The trial concluded with the testimony of an inmate facing charges for kidnapping and armed robbery in California and who was about to be returned to a federal penitentiary in Indiana to serve out an unfinished sentence. This young adult African American inmate testified that yes, yes, an otherwise tight-mouthed Richard had inexplicably confessed the crime to him in gratitude for being saved from an attack by other cellmates. Moreover, Richard had given him—in writing—a name of an outside contact who could help him buy a gun upon his release. That outside contact, a social worker with a respected youth service organization, was identified as the older brother of Joe Fong.

This linchpin of the prosecution's case was divulged at the last possible moment—as are all proverbial last-minute surprise witnesses. Coyle strenuously objected—and was overruled. Coyle then moved to exclude this testimony—this motion was overruled.

The surprise convict witness further testified that Richard had boasted that May Tom would not identify him for fear of retaliation from his gang, effectively dispelling the smell of the possibility of pressure by authorities as a way to explain her hesitant, almost inaudible answers. Yes, he admitted, he was a repeat offender in custody for kidnapping a Bay Area taxi driver at gunpoint, then forcing the driver to transport him and his girlfriend to Southern California, a drive of many hours. He insisted that neither the police nor anyone in the district attorney's office approached him, but that he had contacted them of his own volition. (Apparently in a fit of civic duty and good citizenship, I fumed.) He also claimed he had not been promised leniency for his testimony this day, nor were any promises made to his codefendant girlfriend, a Caucasian prostitute pregnant with his child.

Yet, this man who apparently had not been able to raise bail earlier and had not been promised any leniency strolled easily down the aisle when he finished his testimony, past my parents and me, glancing warily toward us, then sauntered out of the courtroom, apparently a free man.

That was the prosecution's case—the unsure, wavering testimony of a reluctant eyewitness, the selective expertise of a Chinatown-based police sergeant, and a surprise jailhouse snitch. The prosecutor then wrapped the gang war theory around this tenuous evidence, appealing to public outrage at the unsolved Chinatown murders. He used the young eyewitness's reluctant testimony to play up the community's fear of the retributive power of the Joe Fong Gang. He signaled the need for society, represented by the jurors, to put someone away and send a message to the gangs that their day of terror was over.

As it turned out, Richard's lawyer, schooled in the fairness of the Constitution and the system, so fresh to the practice of law, was not able to prevent, preclude, or defend against this inflammatory innuendo. Richard's case was Coyle's first murder trial. His innocence too was crumbling away from beneath him.

As for Richard's unlikely murderer's profile, the prosecutor characterized him as a Jekyll-Hyde personality, a polite, patient bank teller by day who transformed into an evil alter ego by night, robotically killing upon the orders of his Svengali-like leader, Joe Fong.

They had pulled out all the stops, and yet, as horrified as I was, I was truly amazed at the extremely circumstantial nature of the state's case. This was a case that should never have gone to trial. I thought that even this all-white, crusty, old-line San Francisco jury could see that. There would be a *Perry Mason* ending after all, but one provided by the jurors. The jury system was the idealistic linchpin of our justice system, those commonsensical peers who would sweep away every prosecutorial smokescreen and glean the truth through every legal sleight of hand.

But the prosecutor gave an amazingly spellbinding closing statement. He had the jury in the palm of his hands, even had me going his way once or twice. Despite the contortions of his case, his style was crisp, sincere, and rational. None of the jurors seemed to have any inclination to suspect that his reasoning could be faulty. "No wonder he removed all the Chinese American and African American jurors," I thought to myself. These are his kind of jurors, I realized.

I thought the final nail was being pounded into Richard's coffin, but I was wrong. The worst was yet to come.

In a distressing "coincidence" on the eve of jury deliberations, California attorney general Evelle Young called a major press conference to denounce Chinese youth gangs as the leading organized crime threat in the state, a story that played on major local TV and radio news broadcasts that evening and the next morning. On the morning jury deliberations began, the *Chronicle* reported:

> The Chinese youth gangs named in the California Department of Justice report on organized crime are believed to be responsible for at least 13, and probably 15, murders in the Bay Area since 1969. . . . Because of their widespread involvement in gangland killings . . . Chinese gangs are fast becoming threats in the state and other parts of the country in cities and towns having Chinese communities.

The attorney general's report replicated in all respects the contours of the police intelligence expert's Chinese youth-gang war theory. Was there some kind of secret script making the law enforcement rounds, I wondered? This report neglected to mention the Teamsters' Mafia-linked illegal pension dealings in California, then under active federal investigation. The report said nothing about tongs, gambling parlors, or the police payoff system. Chinese youth gangs, it appeared, were the primary bane of California's law enforcement.

Richard wasn't the only one imagining a well-orchestrated conspiracy. We were knee-deep in Bizarro World, and the insidious atmosphere of that courtroom now blanketed the Bay Area and all of California like a torrid, noxious smog that couldn't be blown away. Yet I kept hoping to trigger the magic phrase that would drop us back into the good old days. My parents believed in the justice of the system, my mom in the humanity of the jurors. We'll never know for sure how the previous evening's broadcasts and the morning paper may have influenced the unsequestered jurors. I do know that after only a few hours of deliberation, the jury found my brother, Richard Wayne Lee, guilty of the charge of the first-degree murder of Poole Leong.

I was stunned. So was my father. Mother was silent at first. What I remember most was my mother's reaction the moment she realized what had happened. She hadn't understood enough English to comprehend the announcement of the verdict, and we were too stunned to tell her in the courtroom. It wasn't until the bailiffs unceremoniously shooed us outside that I told her in Chinese, "Richard lost."

Mother then let loose a wail that rose, dipped, and rose again. She placed her hands against the marble walls outside the Department 22 courtroom, and, as if beseeching a God that had broken a promise to her that day, she started to wail loudly, then louder and again louder in an ever-rising aria of anguish. Between her wails, she retched out Richard's childhood name, "Dickie, Dickie, Dickieeeeeee!!!!" Between shrieking Richard's childhood name, she banged her forehead against the marble, her private wailing wall.

Mother had no soup to make that could balance the conflicting passions of justice and law, retribution and punishment, that were at play. There was no speaking-round-and-round to convene a healing discussion between contentious parties. She had had no role in the fate of her most precious treasure, her child. She could not speak to the dead victim and ask him to tell her the name of the real murderer. All she could do was wail.

I think that all courtrooms should have a wailing wall, a psychological pissoir, an emotional vomitorium, located just outside the courtrooms of justice, a place to get it out of your system when you've had more than your fill of the system. Legal justice seems so cut-and-dried. Yet it is not. Never for the defendant. Never for the victims. Or for their "others"—families, friends, and community. Not even for judges, prosecutors, defense lawyers, or the police.

But there is no such wailing wall. In the halls of justice, no one has permission to wail unchecked. We tried to comfort Mother, but to no avail. She could not stop, and we could not stop her. The male bailiffs in the courtroom, who had moved us out, stood there uncomprehending at first. They were men. Tough guys. Then they looked ready to forcibly move her out to the street. After all, other courts were in session, and the process of justice could not be disturbed.

Finally, three women bailiffs gently touched and then comforted Mother. One was white and the other two were black. "You got to have strength. You can't help your son if you don't have strength." They spoke to her in English, which she could not understand, of course. But Mother heard them, heard them when she couldn't hear Father or me. She heard them because they whispered the secret melodies of those who know hurt in their hearts. They were women and they were mothers. It was another kind of Clan Sisterhood, and it wasn't necessary to speak the same language.

They said they would take her up to see Richard. One of the male bailiffs objected that this was against procedure, but in a tone suggesting he wouldn't be a stickler about it. The women bailiffs called up to the county jail's turnkey and arranged for a visit. Because Mom didn't speak American, I could accompany her.

We rode the elevator up to county jail, escorted by the women bailiffs. We were shown into the cell, where Mom immediately grabbed Richard, hugged him, and started weeping. After a few minutes, she calmed down. She said we would visit him as often as we could. Bring him Chinese food. She urged him to be good, do his sentence, and when he came out, we would be there for him.

I said to Richard that what had happened wasn't right, and I was going to do something about it, find the real killer, seek to overturn the conviction on appeal, do something. Richard said he wasn't asking me to do anything, that I was under no brotherly obligation—"You don't owe me a thing." He stressed that I had my own life to live. This was his fate, and he would live with it as best he could. Anything I decided to do was strictly up to me. "Do what you got to do, but I'm not asking you to do anything," he underscored.

After about fifteen minutes, the bailiffs escorted us out of the jail, then back down the elevator. They asked Mother if she felt better. "Yes," she said. "That's good," one of them said. They walked Mother, Father, and me outside the Hall of Justice. Mother thanked them, smiling through her tears. They looked at each other, part of the same circle, members in the same secret society. And they were—the society of mothers with sons and daughters. Of mothers who hurt for their children.

Another Clan Sisterhood.

CHAPTER 29

RUB THE HARD-BOILED EGG

Just like when you two were kids in the summertime. Scrambling on your hands and knees to climb up Telegraph Hill to Coit Tower. Slipping and sliding on the rock bar at Aquatic Park, where the baby crabs lived. Falling out of trees in Portsmouth Square. Racing here, dashing there. Wrestling on the sidewalk. Always in playground fights. So of course you two came home with twisted ankles, skinned knees, and black eyes.

I'd clean the injury with warm water and soap. Then I'd boil up an egg. While the egg was still warm, I'd remove the shell. Then I slowly and gently rolled this egg against the injury. Back and forth. Round and round. The white of the egg turned blue as it absorbed the bruise.

When the egg was cold and purplish-blue, I'd toss it away. The egg had absorbed the hurt, the bruise faded away, and your own healing began.

As your mother, whenever my children get hurt in the course of life, I am like this kind of egg. I remain close to you, hover all around you, caring for you, feeding you, and whispering affirmations to you. I absorb your hurts. I remove your bruises.

Richard's conviction was the only time I couldn't even lift a finger when my child got hurt. I cry even now, thirty years later, as we talk about this. I woke up dizzy. Some days, I could not even get up and start my day. Other days, I wouldn't eat. I missed my boy. To see him behind bars. For his life! So young, a good boy. A mistake, the wrong boy.

Father and Bob took care of me then. Father stopped com-

plaining, treated me nice all the time. Said it was Richard's fate, his life, not mine. Don't be so wrapped up that it sickens you. Then, instead of just giving me enough household money, he turned over his entire check to me to spend it all as I pleased. I remember going to the bank to cash the check, so happy to have all the money for the first time in our marriage. I was in the line, and then I couldn't stand it a second longer. I rushed home, closed the bedroom door, and pulled down the shades.

Father helped me see that I needed counseling. He found a Chinese-speaking women's services center in Chinatown. They help battered women, even had a home for them, and helped with just about any kind of problem a woman could have. For one week, they talked to me every day from 9 a.m. to noon. Finally, they said there was nothing physically wrong with me, but that of course the trial had affected me deeply. I needed to take it easy, stay home, and sleep a lot. They recommended certain kinds of foods, happy movies, and lots of visits with friends. But mainly, I was to stay at home. Their doctor prescribed medicine—half a pill a day. It made me sleepy, but helped me to stop thinking about Richard so much, to feel better during the day. I was to keep coming to the center every morning.

But that four-block walk to their center became very difficult. You know how I am. I love the street chatter, calling to my friends, touching the shiny vegetables, smelling the sweet fruits, checking the boxes of dried mushrooms, shrimp, and cuttlefish from China on the sidewalks. But I just couldn't walk it. With every step, I just wanted to turn around and go home. So one counselor came to Ping Yuen every morning. She was so nice, too, talking for several hours over tea and fruits. I always felt better when she left.

You know your father's wonderful that way. Even though we argue a lot about money, he doesn't like to see me unhappy. That's why he gave me his entire check. That's why he found the women's center. He even tried to tip the counselors—money for coffee and pastries—I never saw him do that before or again. They refused so nicely, though.

And that's why he never complained about Bob being my boy-friend, because Bob made me happy. That's a good side of your father, the side that didn't care what anyone thought of how he lived.

It was Bob who watched the children. Reminded them to stay quiet while I slept. He took them out to play and then cooked for all of us, including enough for Father when he returned late at night. Bought me whatever treats I wanted too. Later, when I got better, he drove me anywhere I wanted to go. Dim sum, fresh-baked buns with coffee, movies, and Sizzler. Yes, he took me to Sizzler a lot. I'd be eating my salad—all you can eat too—look up and there'd be all these happy people eating alongside me. Their smiles raised my spirits, made me happy for just a little while longer.

My Clan Sisters came by—Shlaw, Honhn, and the one who babysat Richard when you were kids—I forget her name now. They were telling me, "Mo yeah, mo shloo," that there was nothing wrong. I'd be well soon, go out again to see movies, beat everyone at poker, and so on. They brought white, red, and orange candied fruits, big, sweet oranges, and Sun Wah Kue pies.

So I got better and better. Soon I could go with Bob and the kids to Golden Gate Park. I'd sit on the bench with a sun para-sol—you know that too much sun bothers me—while they played. A picnic lunch of sandwiches, chips, and sodas. I started to feel how happy I was to hear the children playing, the songs on the portable radio we took everywhere. We'd pet the goats and sheep at Chil-dren's Playground; ride the old-fashioned merry-go-round there. We'd climb the old cable car left like a toy in a sandbox and clang its bell like we were climbing up Powell Street hill. We rowed boats around Stow Lake. Life was good. The days were good.

Then I wanted to play cards. Hadn't lost my wits—I could still read a gambler's moves like some people read the newspapers. Then Bob and I went to Reno and had a good time. We went again and again, and always went up on Wednesdays, because that's when they served complimentary corned beef—red, steaming hot, with white potatoes and cabbage. Blackjack! Twenty-one! Became my favorite game. All you had to bet was a dime in those days. Live bands, free breakfast buffet, and free drinks while you played the tables.

After a while, Richard seemed to be okay-okay in jail. That made me very happy, and before long I told the doctor that I didn't need the pills anymore.

Sometimes it rains the right amount and the crops grow large and green. Other times, the sun shines strong for too long and the fields dry up. What can you do? That's the way life is. Just go from there, keep raising the crops as best you can. When I knew I was well again, that's what I did with Richard, made sure he stayed okay-okay. Like the hard-boiled eggs from childhood, I rubbed Richard all over with Toisan ways, Toisan foods, and centuries-old Toisan hopes of better years, marriage, and children. That's what I do with all my boys. Even if inside prison . . . for life.

CHAPTER 30

HEALING RITES

Guilt, failure, shame, anger, hurt, resentment, and betrayal assailed me. Guilt that I had enjoyed Asia that summer while Richard sweltered in the sweatbox of jail—and, consequently, got set up. Failure that I had not worked more closely with his lawyer, had not investigated the situation myself, had not found leads to the real killer.

Shame at Richard's conviction. How do I talk about this with my classmates, like Dale Benveniste from West Los Angeles, Richie Barton from Texas, Arthur Cotugno from Connecticut, or even Caroline Wong from Oakland? "Oh, this Wednesday, I'm going to visit my brother in Tracy. What's he doing there? He's attending a vocational training institute. Just started." Or could I honestly say, "Visiting my brother the convict. In for murder one. One of those Chinatown slayings." And the implausible tagline, "He was framed, though."

I felt resentment at Richard that the tranquility of my life— our family's life—had been destroyed by whatever he had done or had not done but was close enough to have been sucked into and that now we found ourselves clawing the sides of a whirlpool.

Betrayal by a criminal justice system that I trusted. No— more than trusted, that I had faith in, believed in like a religion. Beyond betrayal—I felt the crazy-making need for retribution against the cops, the prosecutor, the judge—all the bastards involved.

"Wake up!" I wanted to scream at my teachers and fellow students in class, in the drafting studio, or as we sat outside in the sun eating lunch. "Why are you all acting so godforsaken normal?"

They could not detect my distress, of course, and I didn't know how to tell them what had happened. Berkeley seemed a dream. Did I even belong here?

And Mother, my busy, energetic mommy, was so vulnerable, so tentative those first few months. She suffered from bouts of melancholy. Downright depression. As she always had done during the ten days of Chinese New Year, she endlessly lip-synched the words of positive affirmations for freedom, success, and family for Richard and forgiveness toward those who had wronged her.

At first, I questioned the value of her incessant prayerlike affirmations. How can any of this help free Richard or get him a new trial, one that is fair? I even questioned how she conducted her rites for Chinese New Year. Chinese New Year wasn't a ten-day festival as she celebrated it, but a fourteen-day celebration, the time between the new moon of New Year's Day and its full ness two weeks later. Chinese families who lived in the suburbs or who came from Hong Kong seemed clearer on what should happen on each day. The first day starts the year right by refraining from the violence of killing, and that's why we eat the vegetarian dish called eight precious ingredients (or jai). But that wasn't ever explained to us, and we never had an exclusively jai day, although she served it every New Year's Eve and during the ever-important opening-year banquet. Then there are specific "birthdays" to express gratitude for the creation of the animal species whose meats are so much a part of our diet—chicken, cow, duck, and sheep—and a day for the horse that transports our goods and our bodies. On the eighth day, the creation of rice is remembered and thanks given. On the ninth day, the vegetables and fruits of our diet are remembered. Then there's a four-day gap before that last day of the celebration—the Lantern Festival. On the night of the full moon, Chinese hang up lit lanterns, as if in solidarity with the full moon, but with the desire of good progeny.

But for Mother, the Chinese New Year equivalents of turtle-doves, colly birds, pipers piping, and lords-a-leaping and our

Western Christmas did not have to appear on specific days or in the correct quantities. So we never expressly thanked specific food groups or hung out lanterns, ever, and now that I knew, Lantern Festival felt like a pretty important miss as far as rites go. Is that why she knows it as a ten-day celebration, because we skipped the Lantern Festival?

But as I carefully watched over her during this brittle time, I realized that Mother had unfailingly celebrated the heartfelt essence of the Chinese New Year celebration, its spiritual power of revitalization. The ancient name for this most important of Chinese celebrations is Spring Festival, the time of early signs that the dead of winter is over, when the first flowers start to poke their sprigs through the cold, plain earth and the tiniest buds start to swell on tree branches, almost as if to test whether spring is really here and that it is safe to blossom and receive the sun and fulfill the cycle of vitality for one more year.

For Mother, this was the meaning of Chinese New Year— resurrection. Her rites were about successful transitions, getting completely free of the past, especially difficulties, and preparing mind, body, and spirit for the new that will always emerge from the dead past. She knew how to get back up and resume after being on the receiving end of one of life's mighty smackdowns. Her way and her rites allowed her to tap into the underlying vitality of life, the precious Ch'i that is everywhere on this earth and is the source of all life as we know it. She put it all into action now, and I had a front-row seat.

Those festive repetitions during my youth had all seemed liked silly old-country mumbo-jumbo, but now I witnessed how they lifted her during this painful time. But there was nothing celebratory about her mutterings now. She was praying desperately, like a Catholic nun white-knuckling her rosary, reciting umpteen thousands of Hail Mary's. Perhaps more accurately, she was like a Buddhist nun clicking off her beads, reciting endless *metta* prayers of loving-kindness toward all beings and forgiveness in an ever-widening circle: from self to family to community, then ultimately including even those who had jailed her son.

To linger on hurt, anger, and regret was self-defeating, so she slowly wrestled to the mat her bitterness, the deadly bitterness that paralyzes vitality. Life without active Ch'i is akin to a living death, to being a zombie, and I could see that Mother would never settle for that.

After a few months, she settled, accepting reality as it was rather than as it should have been. She remained gentle, whereas I was seething. She simply took care of what was in front of her day by day, while I wanted to do something, anything, big enough to fix the mistake.

Just as when I was in Ward 75, Mother pressed us to visit Richard right away, assigning me the task of understanding the rules of how, when, and how often each visitor could go. She kept on top of me to make sure we drove up to see Richard as often as possible—three visits a month for each approved visitor. Then we realized we could create more visitor days for Richard by driving up separately. It seemed that Mother's basic approach—or practice—was to surround Richard with the familiarity of family, a Toisan family, as often as possible. To have us rub off on him. And invariably we were the first to arrive and the last to leave.

Still, I initially resented those prison visits, being searched by guards, being locked up ourselves for the day, feeling the violation again and again. Mother's hellish wail on the last day of the trial had been the dying of a soul. But her phoenixlike activity surprised me and then inspired me to take events within some semblance of stride, to sustain the direction of my own life, and to become the big brother to Richard again.

Then she starting sending Richard money orders for incidentals. Twice a year, she also prepared and mailed a rather large birthday package and then a Christmas box that contained two cartons of cigarettes, Hershey's chocolate bars, Ramen noodle packets, cans of Spam, Chinese oyster sauce, and soy sauce—every treat on the list of permissible items that could be stuffed into their prescribed carton size. Since Richard's birthday was just before Christmas, this task translated into two rather expensive shipments within days of each other.

Finally, three or four times a year, we moved inside the prison for a three-night family visit, staying in cottages built for this purpose. Bob couldn't join us, because he wasn't legally family. But for days he'd help Mother shop for the makings of a three-day Chinese feast. Her sisters gave money. Her brother delivered a couple of pounds of the most delicious shrimp from his chef's job at Fisherman's Wharf.

After our first visit, Mom brought in her own complete set of Delaware cookware, her Chinese plates, bowls, and chopsticks. The rudimentary visitation cottages provided only an incomplete set of white laminate plates and several well-charred pots and pans. The sagging and cracked furnishings seemed to have been rummaged from a bankrupt low-rent rendezvous motel.

But Mother transformed the dark, barren cottage into a Toisan sanctuary, subtly transporting us to our ancestral dining room in Suey Wan, where she herself had been loved in the simplest of settings and nurtured through the horrors of the Japanese occupational depredations. She strengthened Richard's body and, as I could see, his spirit with his favorite foods.

I became more eager to participate in the routine, happily running whatever errands she assigned me despite the tripled demands on my schedule. Our first meal of each visit was an array of dim sum treats from Asia Gardens, then the best dim sum house in Chinatown. Car engine running, illegally doubled-parked and fending off meter maids, Mother made this final purchase before we hit the freeway so Richard could eat the freshest dim sum.

She whipped up endless courses of the fresh, crunchy vegetables, thin-sliced meats, and steamed fish that had given both of us and now John our healthy bodies. These patient, lavish preparations, far beyond satisfying hunger pangs and daily nourishment, created as normal a sense of family as was possible behind twenty-foot-tall electrified fences, a mere thirty feet from an armed guard tower whose klieg light—and gun sights—swept our family cottage all night long.

In the evenings, Richard sipped the herbal soups that had been brewing since early afternoon, the Ch'i soups that had girded both his Ch'i-body and internal fires through the changing seasons.

Within Mother's cocoon, Richard relaxed, found peace in the communal rituals of food preparation, family-style dining, and cleanup as he and Mother engaged in a kind of practiced dance of gentle gestures, softened Toisan words, and unhurried shared tasks.

These were the simple family practices that had been perfected and passed on from generation to generation over a millennium, which even I knew so well from childhood. Despite famine, drought, bandits, twentieth-century warfare with its butterflies of death, and now imprisonment, generations just kept on living this way, grounding themselves against the harsh externalities, healing each other, squeezing vitality out of the good fruits of the earth, our alchemical culinary knowledge transmuting that harvest—however abundant or sparse, however sweet or bitter—into renewed spirit and unmarred hope for a better tomorrow. Ten thousand sorrows followed by ten thousand joys, and sometimes all mixed up in no discernible sequence—this is life, after all.

It became clearer to me that our visits truly renewed Richard. As trapped as he was in this lower level of Dante's Inferno, the glare in Richard's prison-hardened eyes fell away by the second day of each family visit. His taut, cagey body, arms intentionally swinging freely at his side, ready to defend and strike, became relaxed. As he curled into an easy chair after each meal, those same powerful arms and rock-hard fists folded into his lap like a baby. As Richard recharged, the years left his face, as if his body knew he was really part of something greater, something longer in time than a life sentence, something bigger than his infamy as a murderous California convict and his role as the victim of a cynical prosecution. He seemed to remember that he was from a lineage much nobler than his present circumstances. In those simple visitation cottages, I came to see that a prison experience could not only be endured, but also transcended. This too would pass, and he might return to us intact.

When the departure hour inevitably arrived, Richard finished the tasks of cleaning up for the next family while we packed our last bags. The farther we walked from the cottage and toward the visitors' center, the less he acknowledged us. By averting his eyes, I knew he was disconnecting himself from us. As we looked back to wave our final good-byes, Richard's final smile would drop into a stoic line. He turned his back on us a second before the iron door to the outside thundered shut. I could imagine the rest of his cleanup ritual, the slow girding of his mainline exoskeleton. But I felt certain that his inner being had been recharged, reharmonized, and reconnected to us.

Mother, too, put her armor back on, but it was a lighter, flowing suit of energetic, uncomplaining activity and insightful chatting. She'd comment on Richard's face, his health, his attitude, and his job. She'd say that he seemed better this time, or more quiet, or that his cold lingered a bit longer this winter. Like an agronomist, she assessed what she would bring up in the way of nutrients next time to specifically fix this and that physical or attitudinal deficiency. Like a therapist, she considered what she would say to him, which apt words of wisdom to impart, during our next day visit.

From her example, I came to realize that all I should do was what I could do. I was not a Toisan mother, but I was certainly a third-year student at UC Berkeley with knowledge of and growing access to the institutions of power.

Finally, I was able to confide my plight to my two faculty advisors, Professors Ken Simmons and Lars Lerup. I told them I didn't know what to do, that maybe I should take a leave of absence to organize Richard's legal appeals. I thought I might have to work two jobs to pay the lawyers and needed time to organize fund-raisers. A leave often slides too readily into dropping out, so Professor Simmons, an African American who specialized in urban design solutions for the inner city, instead reminded me what the College of Environmental Design (CED) really taught. Like many older African American men who survived the terror of Jim Crow, Professor Simmons dressed low-key, in dark and somber colors, to avoid attracting undue attention. His words, however, were anything but low-key. He stressed that environmental design's underlying philosophy and the core power of its curriculum was to teach us the ability to define the parameters of a problem with all its possibilities and limitations.

"Treat what happened to your family as a design problem and go from there," he told me. He clicked off the CED action litany: Design practical solutions, but within society's constraints—social, cultural, financial, and political. Research, hypothesize, and recheck your findings. Then and only then start formulating your working conclusions. Finally, engage the community in the implementation of the solution. Stay flexible. Just as we have taught you here, in this school, he said. And most of all, stay in school—any distinction between your life and your education is artificial.

Professor Lerup, a tall, lanky Scandinavian with wispy blond hair falling to his shoulders, completely agreed with Professor Simmons. Also, he reminded me that I had successfully finished the rigorous two-year core curriculum, including a mind-boggling year of engineering, and that my last year of study would be a comparative breeze. Like Professor Simmons, Professor Lerup also specialized in designing exciting urban centers full of life, creativity, and commerce. Lars was right—I would have a lot more time and energy during my remaining year at the university. He, too, was adamant that I should not take a leave of absence.

These two men, my faculty advisors, let me know that I still belonged at Berkeley.

I realized that if I had a hard-boiled egg to absorb the injustice of Richard's case, it would be these very tools I had sweated over in our student studios until 2 a.m. over so many nights. But what did designing such a solution really mean? It's one thing to design a building, but how does one design justice and freedom? What they said made sense, but did I have it in me?

One Sunday morning I awoke to all my doubts in a small attic room on the fourth floor of an old grand-dame Victorian mansion in upper Haight-Ashbury. I pushed myself up from the firm mattress, then nestled against the wall. Sipping my coffee, I glanced through the small window overlooking Golden Gate Park, watching the towers of the Golden Gate Bridge snagging strands of fog.

It was my turn to wrestle now. Would I do as well as Mother had? My entire body was sore, as if I had been beaten from head to toe by a professional thug wrecking crew. It was more than the lumpy mattress—the soreness was within me, it was abject helplessness vying with an incendiary rage.

I needed clarity. Clarity, clarity, oh I pray, please descend upon me. What should I do? What can I do?

I knew that I could fake it by pretending this travesty hadn't happened. I'd run for student office, complete my master's degree in urban design, and transition onto the professional success track of America. After all, everyone would understand that it wasn't me in jail. His actions weren't reflective of me. Besides, Richard had personally released me from any brotherly duty to help him.

If Richard's plight were to become an issue in my career, I could turn it around—into a plus, say something enigmatic, a reverse-attitude don't-judge-me-mantra like, "Some of us make it, some of us don't." Yeah, I could turn it into a frigging medal of honor, a testament to my character, focus, and ability to overcome obstacles that defeated others from the exact same background.

Besides, Richard could better himself through correspondence courses, and what's more, I'd tutor him too. Then, upon his release, he could live with me, and I'd save up money for his education or to help him start his own business, maybe a smoke shop like Benny's.

All well and good, except for one thing: I was witness to a frame-up.

This sense of injustice was a separate kind of violation. The wonderful side of assimilation is that it actually instills in you the values of democracy. I believed in America. I believed in our Declaration of Independence and our Constitution; in the right to life, liberty, and the pursuit of happiness; and in equality before the law, due process, and fair trials. I believed that our America, our system, could and would correct this mistake.

Then, I mulled over the evidence. What if Richard had murdered Poole Leong? Just because he said he hadn't didn't mean he was innocent. What was the real reason his alibi witnesses hadn't been called? Was the alibi false, or were they just too easily discreditable as fellow youth-gang members, like in other trials? Or was Richard protecting the real killer? I looped everything through my head time and time again. I believed my brother's assertions in his innocence, and yet at times he was such a stranger. Or did I need to believe in his innocence? The truth was, I hadn't been in Chinatown, and certainly not at the scene of the slaying that night, so perhaps I'd never know the truth.

But I had been at the trial. Witnessed it from opening to closing with my own eyes and heard it all with my own ears. I knew for a fact Richard was railroaded. My instincts screamed that no one goes after a man by using these tactics unless they don't have a case, but someone wanted him to be put away. I had no qualms attempting to rectify that, to get him a second—and fair—trial free of racial bias, dirty tricks, and media sensationalism. That's everyone's right as an American.

Moreover, I had attended one other trial, that of Richard's closest friends, Joe Fong and David Wong. I had witnessed the same thing happening to them, their being framed in the same courtroom by the same prosecutor, with the testimony of the same police intelligence expert, before the same judge, and by the testimony of similarly odious witnesses. This wasn't the first attempt to frame Joe Fong, just the one that succeeded. The district attorney's office had previously tried Joe Fong on another felony charge, but failed only because a white woman remembered selling him a ticket to a movie on the other side of town. The film began minutes before the time of the crime for which Joe Fong was on trial. And there were other cases involving more Chinese American youth, their lawyers and families protesting the same tactics, making the same claims of innocence, frame-ups, and prosecutorial misconduct.

I knew that I could not blithely ride the success train, that I would be living a lie. I could not be a man, and would never be, unless I spoke up and dedicated myself to reversing this. In that moment, I broke down and wept, helplessly and for a long time, keening a sad, miserable lament of the spirit. Unexpectedly and mysteriously, a steeling energy filled my body. My breath evened out. My mind cleared. I couldn't say where that strength and clarity came from—didn't care that day. I was just in the experience, that crystal moment of having no choice but this one way. I had the capacity to do this, only this.

Blessed clarity.

Cursed clarity.

No choice, so start. Just start, said a voice.

And so I started.

In truth, it had started with Mother, as I watched her so carefully, out of concern for her mental balance, in the days and weeks after the conviction. I studied her emotional and mental resurrection and then welcomed her back into my life. Her Toisan feet just kept walking forward despite this season of disaster, these ten thousand daily sorrows. Her Toisan hands kept helping everyone in need, even as the outrages of emotional carnage fell all around her, just as the bombs had struck her war-torn, childhood Toisan.

Her Toisan energy sizzled, emanating from her like the sparks of a powerhouse coil.

Like Mother, I threw myself back into real life. Now there was no longer a rift between campus and Chinatown. My family—three adults and four kids—spent peaceful days visiting with me in Berkeley, walking the campus, picnicking in the nearby hills, and barbecuing on my apartment's balcony. I visited home more often, and Mother cooked my favorite foods.

Unexpectedly assuming the parental role for a while, I not only planned family outings, boosting everyone's spirits and hopes, but also led the way to clearing Richard's reputation and our family name. In coming together, we somehow ducked under the emotional storms bearing down on each of our lives. Oh, the storms raged on, never far away, but the hours were a bit quieter, the days a little less difficult to get through. At times I could even forget what had happened to Richard. Oh, the revels of delicious normality!

Like Mother, I dedicated myself to my work each new day: raising money for Richard's appeal, investigating a changed Chinatown, beating the tom-toms along the Asian American activist network, and somehow finishing my degree. Eventually I applied to law school, hoping that studying the law might help in Richard's appeals.

Like a monk taking vows of a simpler yet more demanding path, I had carefully pared down my life to the essentials. No social life, no intoxicants, no money for the theater, concerts, or movies. I wore the simplest daily attire: white crewneck JC Penney's T-shirts, loose-fitting jeans, desert boots, and a dark blue Sgt. Pepper–style jacket with four pockets. This jacket was not an insouciant sixties Carnaby Street fashion statement. The pockets held my calendar book, notepad, pens, the day's catch of business cards, and a sandwich.

I determined to rise at 6 a.m. every weekday morning, and with the faith of a Saturday-morning Jehovah's Witness, I made my rounds. But for me, every day was a Saturday as I knocked on the doors of lawyers, politicians, activists, and reporters alike—anyone who would give me a few minutes—to persuade them to look into Richard's case and those of other Chinatown youth, read the transcripts if need be, insist on fair trials and not scapegoating and legal lynchings, and help get the real truth out about Chinatown criminality so it could be cleaned up. On weekends, I typed up the week's notes, planned the next week's schedule, clacked away at letters to the editor—any editor would do—and finalized plans for fund-raising dances for Richard's appeals costs.

Because that's what it takes.

CHAPTER 31

TALKING ABOUT BAD THINGS BRINGS THEM BACK

I don't like to talk about those times. The fighting. The killings. The tongs and the police. Richard in jail. All the lawyers and the newspaper stories. It's bad luck to do so.

In Toisan, it was tough enough to get through one year— plenty of bad things in any year. Who had the time or the energy to remember bad things from the past? You talk about it and you feel bad. Then you get mad again and argue with everybody again. Then they get mad at you and, the next thing you know, everybody ends up suffering about something from a long time ago that isn't even happening today. What's the point of that?

In Toisan, we know it's smarter to focus on today, this season, each other, and what we have to do before dinner. That's why during Chinese New Year, we visit each other with fruits and candies, to leave a sweet taste. We apologize, forgive each other, and renew our friendship. No anger. No sadness. No resentment. No debts of any kind. Start the year clean, fresh, and positive.

Did I hate the judge? No. Of course I was shocked at the mean sentence the judge gave Richard—couldn't he see there was no case? So many years in jail for someone so young, a good boy. You know how I cried in the court. But I didn't hate him or the prosecutor or the police. What would hating accomplish? Would it make them better people, more honest and fair? Would it make the witnesses tell the truth? Would it get Richard free?

In written Chinese, the character symbol for a common person's mouth is a single square, like a wide-open mouth trying to say something. But the character symbol for an official has two squares—one on top of the other, connected by a column, and all topped by a large minister's cap with a tassel. This is their superior power, two mouths speaking at you. In Toisan we say, How can one mouth speak back to two mouths?

So it is; there's no point to hating officials. Hate eats you up, drives you crazy, which defeats you, not them. They already forgot about you. That's Toisan philosophy.

As for Father, he said it was Richard's problem, not ours. He said, "Nothing happened, nothing happened." Bob was reflective, said that it was just bad luck that Richard was in the wrong place with the wrong people at the wrong time. But he didn't hate either.

Did I ever feel like getting revenge? No, it's crazy to talk that way and, besides, everyone knows better than to talk to me that way. When a friend starts complaining about someone's criticism, saying who does she think she is and talking about how she's going to do this and that back, I tell her to calm down. I tell her that really it's not such a big deal when you think about it, is it? Then I point out that if she scolded you, there's probably some truth in what she said. She's your friend, so think about it a bit. Then I say, let's just wash all this off, as I'm doing now, and forget it. Life is good.

Did I even feel anger and hate toward the Japanese soldiers during wartime? We were so terrified all the time that we didn't have room for anything else but fear!

But Richard's trial reminded me of China in this way—people with money can get away with bad things and poor people can get put away for nothing. Officials respect you only if you're rich.

I remember how upset you were, how angry—you couldn't stand it because what happened was so wrong. But if I were you, I wouldn't talk about those things in your book. Not the judge, the prosecutor, the police, the witnesses, the news reporters—none of it. You'll give renewed energy to the past. You'll bring those bad things back. Just don't talk about it. No one needs to relive that again.

CHAPTER 32

THE SEASON OF TEN THOUSAND SORROWS

On this I differ from Mother, and so I disobey her warning. I run the risk of her being right, that these memories from our season of ten thousand sorrows may very well rise from the dead past to curse us once again.

This is the American part of me, especially the denial-is-bad Californian sensibility. I tell this tale, however, not as a kind of personal therapy thankfully, I am past that. Nor do I have any desire to refight old cases in the arena of public opinion or to revenge myself on criminal justice officials. But our lives are not the stuff of a quaint, ethnological story, nor are Toisan ways a misty harking back to a romanticized past. For although Toisan ways were not the keys for unlocking the American legal system, they served a more important purpose: They held my family together unbroken through many of America's harshest challenges, and when we finally broke, they mended us.

Nor was Richard's trial our family's first legal encounter, just unexpectedly the worst. We had enjoyed dignified, benign, and fair engagements with the legal system. My father smoothly passed his immigration interrogation during a time of anti-Chinese exclusion legislation. A law firm helped Mother attain her citizenship. A kind judge, proud of her achievement, swore her in as a citizen that day so very long ago. A lawyer helped remove that unfair suspension from my high school record.

I would find people like them, and so I plunged into Richard's case like a workaholic, powered by triple espressos and my hard-earned environmental design skills. The first task was to establish the facts of the Chinatown environment, so changed since my departure three years earlier. The slaying of Barry Fong-Torres had silenced Chinatown's outspoken activists; very few of my old friends would speak freely with me.

So one of my best sources turned out to be Richard himself, now serving his sentence at a state prison named Deuel Vocational Institute (DVI), an hour and a half east of San Francisco.

During my three years away, Chinatown had descended into the nightmare described in Bertolt Brecht's play, *In the Jungle of the Cities*—a grand, random drama of thundering, stark violence between rivals who symbolized contrary views of life. One was morally craven and desired only material things and wealth, and the other was a paragon of astringent idealism, sacrificing everything to protect freedom and personal choice. The drama unfolds against lies, corruption, debasement of the innocent and weak, intentional disinformation, and media manipulation.

With Richard's help, I was able to piece together the unfolding rounds of our own jungle of cities. He and his friends, including a charismatic youth named Joe Fong, had somehow rambled into a pivotal role despite their teenage years. Bilingual, bicultural, outspoken, politically savvy, and advocates of civil rights, Joe Fong, David Wong, Richard Lee, and Raymond Leung exuded natural leadership, forging deep friendships among both American-born Chinese (ABCs) and Fresh-off-the-Boat immigrants (FOBs). They succeeded in bridging the gap between Wah Ching and Leways youth of their age group, a task Il Piccolo's activists had only attempted.

Far from becoming the scapegoat for my high school stridency, Richard and his band used it as a springboard for their own activism, resulting in the appointment of a Chinese American principal—an unimaginable achievement in my high school days.

Within Chinatown, they organized dances, street fairs, picnics, and cultural outings for at-risk youth. In time, they and their followers became loosely known as Yau Li, initially meaning "to have abundance." That was when the tongs began wooing members of Yau Li, just as they had recruited from the Wah Ching factions. They lavished Richard and his friends with banquets; they gave them well-paying jobs as doormen for gambling parlors and made them errand runners for tong leaders.

By the fall of 1971, Yau Li had one foot in the heady idealism of the Chinatown liberal coalition and one foot in the lucrative rackets of the underworld.

Then fights between youths spilled out into the streets. Some Yau Li wandered freely in and out of restaurants and theaters without paying, then disrupted business with their fistfights. Others extorted money from merchants. The new definition of Yau Li became "to have profit," and the elders were not amused.

That was why one tong had issued its infamous bulletin in May 1971. Matters had gotten completely out of hand. Written in Chinese, it warned all remaining lawless youth elements to obey, or "any means necessary" would be used to go after them.

In Chinese dialectics, which are rooted in the nature-based, yin-yang fluidity of Taoism, every position contains the seed of its opposing view. Either the superior position prevails or the organization crumbles under the weight of its own contradiction.

And so Yau Li collapsed one night in September 1971 at its clubhouse, a second-floor walk-up located in a dead-end alley in Chinatown's heart. Richard and his friends argued that elders must not exploit the youth of the community or draw them deeper into crime and that their future was in the larger civil rights struggle for all Asian Americans.

Richard described his shock as the tong-affiliated members disagreed scornfully. Enjoying serious money for the first time, they saw their future with the old-timers. Chinese Americans would never be accepted into the larger white society, they argued. Racketeers provided opportunities and money now—not after years of political activism. Anyone staying in Chinatown must obey the old-timers.

Then the tong-affiliated faction dramatically scratched their names and those of their friends off the Yau Li roster and stormed out. Later that night, at the popular late-night Sai Yon restaurant on Jackson Street just below Grant Avenue, a vicious fistfight broke out. Those who had led the walkout were severely beaten.

Reaction was swift and deadly.

On October 2, 1971, on a busy Saturday afternoon, on Jackson Street and just a few storefronts up from Sai Yon restaurant, three young men shot Raymond Leung in the back and chest. A final shot, the coup de grâce, was fired into Raymond's head.

Weeks later, three young men were kidnapped. Their bodies resurfaced in three spots around the Bay Area during the first week of November. Rice bags covered their blindfolded eyes, gagged mouths, and heads; their hands were hog-tied to their necks; and signs of torture marked their bodies. Two were youths I had once encouraged to stay in high school, but who had apparently joined an independent burglary crew, one not sanctioned by Chinatown's underworld powers-that-be. Clearly the work of professional assassins, the murders' message was clear: The crackdown announced by the tong bulletin had started in earnest.

Richard said that there was no doubt that he, Joe Fong, and David Wong were on that hit list. They avoided death only by avoiding Chinatown; they armed themselves, motivated more by the need for self-defense than intent to war. Surprisingly, they rededicated themselves to a nobler path as the Chung Ching Yee Association, a name that thundered out from the mythic Chinese tale "The Heroes of the Water Margin."

I knew this epic story, which is as integral to Chinese consciousness as *The Odyssey* is to Western consciousness. Legendary martial arts heroes unjustly driven to the "watery margin" of a swamp organized thousands of other exiles into a huge rebel force. Their insurrection swept away a corrupt government and restored the mandate of heaven—that fluid, harmonious, mystical balance between emperor, subjects, and the cosmos—that is so precious to Chinese social conscience.

The heroes' great meeting hall was named Chung Ching Yee, citing the three virtues missing first in the legend and now in the old Chinatown order: Chung—loyalty to each other; Ching—harmony among the brotherhood; and Yee—righteousness in all conduct.

These ideals did not strike me as so very different from the values of Mother's Clan Sisterhood. In their Chung Ching Yee council chamber, these mythic heroes made decisions in an open, equal way akin to speaking-round-and-rounds. They advocated for the common good over personal avarice and for the future of the nation over family aggrandizement—values familiar to Toisan Clans.

But in Richard's world, the entrenched, savvy Chinatown elders and the underworld wing did not construe this cultural invocation as a call back to fiduciary governance, but as a challenge to the death. Chung Ching Yee was a rebel force to be crushed, not a force for good.

So that was the story. Richard was a leader of this audacious, modern-day Chung Ching Yee when he was arrested. These would-be leaders of a brave new youth movement had been struck down, one by one, by the gun or by the sword of criminal justice. As with the protagonists in *In the Jungle of the Cities*, it was unclear who was bad and who was good; what was moral and what was evil; who, if anyone, was winning; and what ideals had been trampled under in the struggle.

What is certain is that the convictions of Richard and his friends changed little in Chinatown. Its underworld continued to rampage as Crazy Six, a former Wah Ching faction leader and now head of a tong's enforcers, warred against the stronger Chinatown tongs from his base in Oakland's Chinatown. Other reorganized factions, old and new racketeering interests, rose and fell against each other. The arc of death soared over the next four years, reaching a mortality toll of over thirty at its zenith before climaxing in the horrendous Golden Dragon Restaurant massacre of Labor Day weekend 1977. That night, three masked men stormed in to slay youthful Hop Sing enforcers who convened there nightly, using the same dining table near the entrance, one with an obstructed view of everyone coming in, as a kind of informal office. These wary thugs reflexively overturned that table, dove to the floor, and survived unscathed. The innocent diners did not react so reflexively: Five were slain and eleven seriously wounded, some disabled for life.

The unfolding of these events increasingly confirmed our contention that Richard's case was larger than Richard. Now sensing the larger story, I focused on prodding the media into action. A few investigative reporters began looking into the Chinatown prosecutions. A May 1973 *San Francisco Chronicle* front-page story supported Joe Fong's claims of innocence. Investigative journalist Paul Avery uncovered evidence of the suppressed confession of the actual gunman, Clifton Wong, who stated that Joe Fong was not even present in the car during the drive-by shooting for which he was convicted. An alibi witness, a Chinese American female, passed a rigorous lie-detector test paid for by the newspaper. Marilyn Baker, a TV reporter with the local PBS station, broadcasted several in-depth interviews with Joe Fong from prison. She also became convinced of his innocence and the likelihood that others had been wrongfully convicted.

But the Office of the District Attorney refused to reopen the Fong case, and then Joe Fong's trial judge, who was also the judge in Richard's case, denied Fong's motion for a new trial.

Our growing ranks of concerned community activists persisted, doing all the things a network of well-meaning poor people with limited influence typically do in a situation like this. Public forums, private meetings, press conferences, legal fund-raisers, fiery letters to officials and news media, vocal public demonstrations, and meetings with the Civil Rights Division of the Justice Department—we tried everything, optimistic that something would work. But we also conscientiously solicited the involvement of family members of the wrongly imprisoned, at least those who could set aside their fears. Unconsciously, in this process of building a community-level consensus, we replicated the safety, confidentiality, and solution-fashioning of a speaking-round-and-round.

Well, something somewhere must have gotten through to someone. Or perhaps folks with greater influence quietly echoed our concerns to the right people. Or perhaps over the years the Department of Justice had carefully developed a network of informants, both honest citizens and criminal insiders who needed a deal. The FBI announced a major investigation into police corruption and gambling in Chinatown, as reported on September 30, 1973, by the *Examiner* in an article entitled "Police Scandal Brews Over Chinatown Graft":

> A major bribery scandal starting with alleged gambling protection "payoffs" by a dozen or more "Chinatown establishments" is about to rock the San Francisco Police Department, the *Examiner* has learned. . . . [A] joint police-FBI strike force investigation conducted over the past several months has zeroed in on four patrolmen and a sergeant presently or formerly assigned to Central Station. . . . Central Station includes all of Chinatown . . . where gambling and prostitution are believed to be widespread. . . . Police officers, at least one in uniform, have appeared under subpoena in a virtual parade before a federal grand jury. . . . At least one of the officers who appeared before the jury during the past week, including a sergeant, are expected to be indicted on bribery charges. . . . The number of police personnel who may be ultimately indicted could climb as the protracted investigation continues.

Confirming that a number of his men were under grand jury subpoena, Chief Scott informed the *Examiner* that

> [t]he multimillion dollar gambling industry in China-town has been the direct cause of a great deal of crime there and in adjacent areas, including burglaries, extortion and even murder. It has led to a climate wherein youth gangs have flourished. . . . There is reason to believe the most recent gang-type assassination in Chinatown . . . was directly linked to extortion within the gambling fraternity.

Finally, a fuller truth was breaking through. Richard and his friends, including the slain Raymond Leung, had not been silenced.

Still, the Chinatown elders who had cunningly survived for more than a century in our American jungle of cities would not be so easily crushed. They could outfox even the FBI. Wai H. Ow, the infamous bagman who routinely paid off the cops, was under subpoena to testify before the grand jury. He could name policemen, dates, and payoff amounts. Several days before he was to appear, the bagman was found dead, hanged by the neck in his own closet. Official conclusion: a suicide, according to police investigators. Along with Mr. Wai H. Ow, the joint police-FBI strike force probe also died.

So much for cleaning up Chinatown and police graft. Meanwhile, our family had its own problems. In early 1974, our appellate counsel, Charles Garry, a renowned civil rights attorney and, as it turned out, the leading expert on minimizing racism through careful juror screening, gave us some bad news: The state court of appeals had rejected Richard's appeal.

Garry agreed with us that the legacy of racial prejudice against Chinese was very much alive and well in the San Francisco of the 1970s. He knew that one hundred years before,

Chinese Americans had successfully invoked the Fourteenth Amendment's equal protection clause in *Yick Wo v. Hopkins*, securing the right to equal enforcement under local regulations, and that this Chinese American case was later successfully cited by NAACP lawyers as legal authority in the landmark 1954 school desegregation case, *Brown v. Board of Education*.

Now, ironically, the US Supreme Court had recently ruled that black defendants in state criminal cases were entitled to have prospective jurors carefully screened for racial prejudice. Perhaps they might extend its applicability to Chinese American defendants? After all, they had seen the connection between *Yick Wo v. Hopkins* and *Brown v. Board of Education*. Garry thus advised that Richard appeal directly to the US Supreme Court.

He strongly recommended that the community send an amicus brief, a friend of the court synopsis outlining the largely unknown history of discrimination against Asian Americans in California, including the internment of Japanese American communities in World War II. It had been a while since *Yick Wo* had been decided, and memories fade, he pointed out. A friend of the court brief from the Asian American community would be more convincing than the assertions of a white law firm.

So once again we started organizing, and soon Richard's supporters—political activists, clergy from the local council of churches, university students, concerned private individuals, and outraged attorneys—raised the funds, compiling a sterling list of concurring organizations and individuals. The Asian Law Caucus, a trio of recently graduated storefront lawyers dedicated to providing legal services to the community, agreed to draft and submit the friend of the court brief to the US Supreme Court. Eugene Tomine led the drafting of the brief in coordination with Dale Minami and under the guidance of a well-reputed appellate lawyer, Dennis Roberts, who formally served as "of counsel."

The American appellate process takes a long time and a lot of money. Through it all, my family kept hope alive by staying in each other's company. Yet, because of my growing public engagement with Richard's campaign and the issues surrounding it, I knew they could be pressured, hurt, perhaps killed.

There is a bit of outlaw derring-do in my family's American sojourn, a willingness to bend the rules when we'd unfairly end up victims otherwise. At the height of the anti-Chinese exclusionary hysteria, my paternal great-grandfather had simply walked across a shallow stretch of riverbed of the Rio Grande into America one summer. His Mexican cotton farm had collapsed due to a worldwide downturn in prices one year. My paternal grandfather, born in America, was by birth a citizen, and his father somehow made sure that that birth was properly recorded, regardless of his own dubious status.

When Father emigrated to join his father, he faced the choice of being stranded at Angel Island for months, perhaps years, for failure to answer the draconian trivia exam about his village, even one whose pathways he knew by heart. Or he could obtain a list of the questions and answers to complement his native knowledge, a list compiled by those who had beaten the tricky exams in order to help others. Father wisely paid, surreptitiously studied in a hidden corner of the ship's deck each day, and then dumped the list into the ocean a few days before reaching San Francisco. He was in and out of Angel Island in record time and employed within days of that.

In her turn, Mother, who did not read or speak American, had memorized phonetics to pass her oral citizenship exam. She passed, was naturalized, and sponsored her family's immigration.

All my forebears had bent the rules of unfair laws or, as Mother did, creatively outstrategized their arbitrary requirements.

And so my time came too. I initiated a subterfuge—to protect my family—in the form of a rumor that my parents had disowned me for my criticism of the police, the judiciary, and the tongs. I said that they thought my work on behalf of Richard's appeals was a waste of money. This was designed to protect them. They, not I, lived within the shooting gallery of Chinatown.

So we met clandestinely as we waited for the US Supreme Court decision. A new trial might also be granted if new information came to light through the efforts, for example, of investigative reporters. But no one was looking into Richard's case.

Then—good news! After reviewing the trial transcripts, Lowell Bergman, an independent investigative reporter, was so shocked that he became interested.[1] Our first break came when Bergman met with the surprise convict witness. This witness told Bergman he had been forced to lie about Richard's confession.

I took the story to the *San Francisco Examiner*, and, after the meeting, William Randolph Hearst III and his editorial team assigned the story to Raul Ramirez, a highly regarded reporter recently recruited from the *Washington Post*. He would work with Bergman.

My parents were pleased. This good news helped us get through the bad news that followed—the US Supreme Court declined to hear Richard's appeal, leaving the *Examiner*'s investigation as our last real hope. In mid-May 1976, the *Examiner* ran its three-part investigative story. The first day's headline read, "Perjured Testimony in Chinatown Trial: Curious conviction in gangland murder."

The series filled in the blanks on the unanswered mysteries of Richard's bizarre trial. The surprise convict witness stated in a signed affidavit that the prosecutor fabricated his testimony; that police induced him to testify under threats of violence and promises of leniency for himself and his pregnant girlfriend and codefendant.

---

[1] Bergman later became famous for resigning from CBS's *60 Minutes* when the program declined to run his interview with tobacco company scientist Jeffrey Weygand, who revealed that Big Tobacco had deceived the public on the dangers of cigarettes. This became the basis for the Al Pacino movie *The Insider*. Bergman currently contributes to the PBS investigative series *Frontline* and the *New York Times*. He teaches at the Graduate School of Journalism at UC Berkeley. In 2004, he won a Pulitzer Prize for a *New York Times* story on worker injuries and fatalities, one of many awards over the years.

May Tom, the sole eyewitness, stated that she was never sure of the killer's identity and that police told her she couldn't go home until she picked out someone from a police photo gallery of gang members. When she couldn't identify Richard at the lineup, she was told instead to pick out the man matching the photo she had previously selected on the night of the murder, one she had had to select in order to go home. Despite expressing her ongoing uncertainty, she testified only after being falsely told that her testimony wasn't that critical, because eleven other witnesses had positively identified Richard Lee as the shooter.

Weyman Tso, who was standing next to the actual gunman, had fled the city immediately after the shooting but later returned. He stated that he saw the killer and that the killer was not Richard Lee.

The prosecutor and the police investigators declined to be interviewed.

Just after the *Examiner* articles, in a highly unusual move, two officers from the state attorney general's office flew out to the federal penitentiary in Terre Haute, Indiana, to meet with the surprise convict witness. They returned with another sworn affidavit. In this one, the witness had now recanted the affidavit relied on by the *Examiner* and reaffirmed his earlier testimony against Richard Lee.

What could explain yet another U-turn? In his survivalist dementia and with his desperate thirst for liberty, had this convict learned to lie instinctively and to say to whomever had power over him or could be of some help whatever testimony they needed? In his ever-shifting state of mind, did the sudden appearance of two state law enforcement officials in business suits waving shiny blue-and-gold badges from California signal to him who it was that really held the power in his personal game of liberty? In contrast, a blue jeans–wearing, long-haired, wire-rimmed, academic-looking freelance journalist like Lowell Bergman suddenly didn't look like he held any ace cards, if he ever did. This convict had expressed concerns that the San Francisco police had a hold on him for unserved time, a hold they could exercise or relinquish, and more importantly that this decision would, of course, be made at a later date, like just before his release from the federal penitentiary. This twice-recanter didn't need a lawyer to understand the threat to his liberty and safety if he were sent back to California. After all, that's all he ever cared about—his own liberty—and what was a third recantation on the same matter, for his changing testimony was truly his only currency.

I didn't know what to make of this surprise convict witness—I was unable to condone or condemn him—for he reminded me of Woody, my best friend in Ward 75, someone so bright and yet so trapped by the streets and likely malformed by generations of the African American experience in our country's history. I could not summon that same sympathy for the prosecutor, the police, and the judge. They knew what kind of person they had banked on to make their case—a compulsive liar facing long prison sentences in both federal and state penitentiaries.

In the wake of the *Examiner* series, the California Supreme Court unexpectedly ordered the recalcitrant local judiciary to hear Richard's motion for a new trial. Relatives and supporters raised enough money to fly out witnesses from Oregon and Indiana and to pay some attorney's fees. We believed that if a new trial was ordered and a jury truly composed of Richard's peers and free of bias were impanelled, a just verdict could be reached. We could live with that verdict then, even if, as unlikely as it seemed, it might concur with the first verdict.

The case ended up back before Richard's trial judge, who would not recuse himself. Pessimistically, our lawyers presented the new evidence uncovered by the *Examiner*. Predictably, after several full days of testimony, he ruled against Richard—there would be no new and fair trial. This ruling was, effectively, the death knell for Richard's legal campaign.

Shortly after that ruling, the assistant district attorney and the two investigating homicide inspectors filed a lawsuit and later won a $4.56 million libel verdict against the *Examiner* and its reporters in a trial heard before another old-line San Francisco judge. This libel case judge was perceived as being so anti-reporter that one participant was moved to an act of guerrilla theater—the placement of a paper toilet seat cover on the judge's chair. But in 1986, the California Supreme Court unanimously upheld the legality of the *Examiner*'s reporting and quashed the $4.56 million award. In the court's opinion, the reporters raised well-founded questions about the trial and conducted a careful, detailed investigation over eighteen months. They concluded that no libel had been committed.[2]

By the first week of June 1978, with the denial of his motion for a new trial, Richard had reached the end of the line legally. There was no further appeal. I was devastated, but Richard had a somewhat different attitude. At the end of the *Examiner* series, Ramirez quoted Richard as saying:

> The way I see it, they put me here according to their law of the land. I can't fight it because they've got me in a situation where if you fight it, they'll just get you more, lock you up, charge you. . . . I have resigned myself right now to being here. . . . They've got my body in here. Physically, they've got me but my mind is still free. As long as my mind can still function freely and think what I want to think and feel what I want to feel, it's OK. I'll make it.

[2] Readers interested in some salient facts of both Richard's prosecution and the reporter's investigation may wish to review this rather insightful, unanimous opinion of the California Supreme Court. The opinion factually examines the context of the police force, the Chinatown community, local politics, and organized crime in the questionable prosecutions of Richard Lee and other Chinatown youths during the early 1970s. It delineates, at some length, the application of the First Amendment protections to the investigative reporting process and news stories alleging misdeeds by police or prosecutors. This opinion may be found in major law libraries or on the Web under the case name and citation *Frank McCoy v. Hearst Corporation*, 42 Cal. 3d 835; 231 Cal.Rptr. 518; 727 P.2d 711 [Nov. 1986].

In all the years of working on Richard's case, I had cut off parts of myself to just make it through another day. I did it to help Richard, of course. Now I was completely devastated. Yet here he was, not focused on the ups and downs of his own case, but solely on his internal journey. He was inside, I was outside, yet he possessed a clearer grasp of reality, was stronger in spirit and freer than I was. He was neither cynical nor embittered. Sounded like a blessed saint to boot.

How did he do it? It was Mother's Toisan ways. She had wrapped Richard in those ways, and, so protected, he lived immanently, free of the fray of frustrating legal outcomes, the daily hell of prison, and interrupted personal ambitions. I was hurting because I was attached to another reality, a reality of the outer victory of legal and public vindication—one that I had bet my life, my energy, money, and career on.

Mother had warned that officialdom's "two mouths" would out-shout the "one mouth" of little people like us. Turned out that she was right.

What had I failed to understand?

It would be Richard's example, his words in that last article of the series, that would help me to understand, to reconnect to all things Toisan, and to fully see that Mother was a transmitter of its tried-and-true wisdom, as versed and trained as any spiritual teacher of any tradition.

CHAPTER 33

MOTHERING ALL
THE CHILDREN

You see, you must understand one thing about children. A child is basically good and will stay good. You must watch over the child, watch every little thing.

Now, some people would say Le Wai was a bad boy, a thief, that I should have scolded him and never let him into my house again. But to me, he was just a boy being a boy. Yes, he turned out okay.

Le Wai was the first son of the Vietnamese boat-people family who moved in next door—1977, something like that. A single mother with two young boys. Le Wai was eleven and the other one—I can't remember his name—was about eight. They were Chinese Vietnamese. Cantonese speakers. I don't know what happened to the husband, just that he was dead. Their mother worked, and so I watched her boys for her after school. The younger one was mentally damaged. He'd play like a normal boy and suddenly his eyes would float off to the ceiling. He'd start waving his fingers around like a dancer and then singsong talk in a strange language that made no sense. But I'd call his name, offer some candy, and after a while he would return to us. Someone must have hurt him, maybe a pirate when they left Vietnam. They wouldn't talk about it.

They fled the Communists after their war, just like my own family. Many Chinese Vietnamese boat people came to Chinatown.

Aiiyahh—lots of suffering. I think they lived in a camp in Samoa or someplace like that, waiting for their visas to the United States.

I helped them to settle down. You know, enrolled the children in school, took them to the playgrounds, applied for medical coverage, and rode the buses with them until they knew the routes. I introduced them to the best places in Chinatown to shop. Vegetables, meat, and fish. I walked them downtown to Macy's, Emporium, and all the other stores.

They lived next door, the three of them in a small studio, and so Le Wai came over all the time. He liked my apartment—always clean and so much more room. Just made himself at home right after school and on weekends. Laid on the sofa and rested. Watched TV. Did his homework. Played with John and read books together, and with Ada, David, and Victor too. I cooked extra food for Le Wai and his brother all the time, because their mother worked late. We were all like one family.

Le Wai shopped for me, just like you and Richard when you were little. He always wanted to do some chore for me. Well mannered and really smart. Le Wai studied hard, earned good grades, just like you. Sometimes I helped him with Chinese-school homework.

Do you remember Richard's coin collection? Indian Head nickels, Lady Liberty dimes, old quarters, and so on? And silver dollars—real silver through and through, souvenirs from my winnings in Reno. Well, Le Wai stole from Richard's coin collection. Sometimes Le Wai played alone in your old bedroom and then left quickly, like he had done something he shouldn't have. I started checking, and always a few more coins were missing. But I never accused him. They had suffered so much and were so poor. He just wanted to be a boy. Eat potato chips. Drink Coca-Colas. Buy comic books. So how could I call him a thief? I just pretended it never happened.

After a while, they moved away. The mother's sister was doing well, and they moved near San Jose, into a Little Saigon. New immigrants don't seem to stay long in Chinatown anymore. They move out the first chance they get. Well, later Le Wai went on to college and got a good job. For years, he visited me every Chinese New Year's and brought gifts. Bags of tangerines. Dried coconut candy, plums, red watermelon seeds. Whole roasted duck. Crackling skin barbecue pork. So many Chinese New Year goodies. And red envelopes with lots of money, so much more than he ever took from Richard's coin collection.

Now, if I had treated him like a bad boy, scolded him, told all the neighbors, banished him from our home, and made him feel like he was really bad, you think that would have helped him? Of course not. Le Wai was too good in far too many other ways. Just like any other kid, his mouth watered for treats. He took only a little bit of money, after all. You must understand children. A child is basically good and will stay good. But you must watch over the child every day, every little thing. That's the way to raise a child.

That's why I tell you so many times that in the village, Toisanese mothers stay close to their children all day long. Even if my mother was working in the fields during spring planting or fall harvest, she made sure to eat lunch with us and check in on us several times before dinner. That's the only way to make sure children turn out well.

CHAPTER 34

INSIDE MOVES

There is a 1974 Associated Press wire photo of a sixteen-year-old youth, Chi-ko Wong, a Chinese American from Los Angeles. Chi-ko's place in California history is that he was the first teenager to be tried and convicted as an adult in the state of California. He's starkly framed against the side of what must be a very tall door, as if pausing between two worlds. Behind him is a guard, which we know only because we see a corner of one side of his head. But perhaps the oddest, most starkly troubling element is Chi-ko's own choirboy face—"baby-faced" is the Associated Press reporter's description. Chi-ko himself is skinny and rendered optically thinner by his child-size Sunday school jacket and shirt. His wrists are so tightly manacled to a metal chain around his waist that his elbows involuntarily bend backward. He's facing his mother, whose own face is hidden by the knuckles of her right fist, which perhaps hides her tears too. Then it sinks in that this is a child, and he's going into an adult prison . . . for life.

Chi-ko was the poster child, a graphic announcement that California had officially given up on the idea that all youths could or should be rehabilitated. His mother's facelessness only reinforces the universality of the message "Mothers watch your babies; this could be you."

This turn in American jurisprudence had picked up steam with the decision to charge Richard, Joe Fong, and David Wong as adults. They were youths barely out of high school and eligible for youth authority incarceration when arrested. In those years, young men up to the age of twenty who were first-time offenders were more typically sent to Youth Authority facilities. This was so, even for serious offenses like murder.

But Richard and I never got to discuss such weighty policy issues during our earlier visits. In fact, it took months of visits before Richard would even describe to me his first days inside Deuel Vocational Institute (DVI) state prison. Why should he? After all, I was a stranger to him, familiar only because of our childhood closeness, but unknown after years of mutual independence. I had left for university, but perhaps in his eyes I had left Chinatown too and left him to finish a fight I started. Finally, I had left for what he called my "vacation" and, despite his consent and his lawyer's concurrence, had left him in jail to be set up. I hadn't exactly watched his back these past few years—so how worthy was I of him?

All I could do now was to show up, visiting Richard as often as I was allowed to under the guidelines. First to arrive and last to leave. Always with enough money, despite my stringent student budget, to stuff coins into the machines for overpriced, stale sandwiches, chips, candy bars, and soft drinks. I booked the dates, processed all the paperwork for family visits, and then got everyone there and everything in through the tight security check.

At first, our topics tended to be legal—the progress of the Garry law firm appeal, the new evidence in Joe Fong's case, Bergman's remarkable interview with the recanting convict witness, the *Examiner* investigation, and the steady emergence of his case as a cause célèbre. The family was the other safe topic: an outing to Marine World/Africa USA, a picnic on Mount Tamalpais with its bird's-eye views of the entire Bay Area, or that rare, warm day at Santa Cruz beach.

I don't know when the turning point clicked in, when we went around the bend of our estrangement, but Richard started to share details about his life within DVI. He actually never really narrated it, but rather dropped hints, telling clues that I deciphered over my long drives home and over many visits and could arrange into a sketch of life inside.

One day, he said that inmates called DVI the Gladiator School, because of the violent race gangs that ran the prison. Richard was the first and for a time only Chinese American in DVI. An outcast among outlaws, he may as well have come from Jupiter.

Those first few days, he had warily made his way, always glancing from side to side or looking over his shoulder, his arms and clenched fists swinging free, ready to block a prison-made blade, to lash out in return. But, to his growing surprise, he discovered that his "beef," the very conviction for first-degree murder—however wrongful—and his "rep" as the assassin-on-command of a mythologized, cold-blooded crime boss scared off the prison predators who reflexively preyed on young first-timers.

Soon enough, Joe Fong and his codefendant David Wong joined him, and their equally impressive beefs—convictions stemming from one of the earliest drive-by shootings in California—and the media-inflamed crime-family legend kept the treacherous gangs a respectful distance from this legendary triumvirate.

Richard said DVI inmates ranged in age from eighteen to thirty years old. Gangs ran the prison, and DVI was Nuestra Familia turf. The Mexican Mafia was their bitter rival, and any Mexican Mafia member assigned to DVI would be dead within a week. The white supremacist Aryan Brotherhood wielded power over white inmates, and the small Black Guerrilla Family, heirs to George Jackson's revolutionary prison legacy, commanded limited sway over African American prisoners too disorganized to be a dominant force despite their superior numbers. Each gang ran a share of commonplace rackets—drugs, prison-brewed alcohol, cigarettes, male prostitution, smuggled-in knives and prison-made weapons called shanks, and, finally, violence for hire.

I couldn't believe what he was telling me. Nor could I comprehend how anyone could survive here with his dignity intact, his body unmarred by violence, or his sanity unscarred. Frightened, I became doubly motivated to secure his release somehow. Yet the increasing number of Chinese American inmates sent to DVI managed to survive with bodies intact and a modicum of dignity.

One summer, Richard expressed his frustration at the inmates' habitual "summer gladiator games." As California's Central Valley blazed with long days of unclouded sun in July and August, these young, overheated, testosterone-laden gangs actually looked forward to ritualistic gladiator battles in the arena of the prison courtyard. On the appointed date, at an hour mysteriously known to every inmate, weapons magically appeared out of thin air. Jagged shanks, clubs embedded with nails and razors, forks wrapped around fists with their tines turned out like claws, and smuggled-in kitchen knives slashed the air, skin, tendons, bones, and vital organs as shrieking inmates fell upon each other, wave after wave.

Within minutes, old scores were settled as territory and rackets changed hands. The guards would somehow regain control and then lock down the prison for weeks. Richard's ire arose, because even as a noncombatant, he too was locked down, with his cell now a sweatbox in the unrelenting heat.

At once frightened for Richard and fascinated by this insider's anthropological report, I slowly felt some relief. Somehow Richard and his friends protected their own small but safe corner. That much was clear from the nature of his complaint that day, one of inconvenience only. During lockdowns, I could hear in the background the unabated din of hundreds of inmates yelling their insanity and rage, like the devil's version of speaking in tongues. Richard was oblivious, relieved to be in the air-conditioned visiting room. On those days, I stretched out our visits as long as possible, lingering despite the guard's signal that we needed to give the table up for other visitors.

Richard was talking to me now—sharing, even if it was in tough-guy, clipped, neutral terms—about the daily fears, dangers, and triumphs of his life. I was getting to know him as I had not known him since our drifting apart. He was my brother again, someone I loved, and once again in my life.

During another visit, Richard casually mentioned that he personally had forged a mutual protection alliance with Native American inmates, who were fewer in number than even Chinese Americans. Numbering approximately thirty, the Asian/Native alliance respectfully announced their intention to stay out of prison rackets and warfare and simply "to do the time" in peace. They shrewdly pointed out that, despite their limited numbers, they were large enough to relentlessly and brutally retaliate against anyone or any group who might harm any one of them. "We may go down, but so will the fools who mess with us."

That was the only break that came young Chi-ko Wong's way in 1974. He ended up at the Gladiator School—if that can be described as good fortune—where Richard placed him under his personal protection and that of their new Asian/Native alliance. In any other prison, with his childlike look and size, Chi-ko would have been victimized in the most horrid ways.

I was impressed—blown away that in this lower circle of Dante's Inferno, in this compacted dark hole of human misery and rage, Richard had wrought an alliance. Not Joe or David, but Richard himself worked out the flexible solution, one worthy of Toisan pragmatism. Not a gang, but a mutual-protection society. It seemed remarkable, this alliance between Native Americans and Chinese Americans, until I realized that cross-cultural alliance building was nothing new to Richard—he had breached the divide between ABCs and FOBs.

But the most interesting topic was Richard's take on time. For the typical workaholic—as I was during this period—there is never enough time. In my quixotic campaign on behalf of Richard, I careened through my day, crossing the Bay Bridge three and four times some days to meet with growing numbers of supporters, lawyers, and reporters. I got up earlier, drove faster, and stayed up later so that I could create more minutes here, a quarter hour there.

But when Richard talked about time, he talked about it like it was dense, massive, and immovable. Too much of it to begin with. He talked about "*dooo*ing" time as if it were a pool of mud he pushed through all day long. As if he were wearing away a giant boulder with the palms of his hands. If an inmate at the next visitor's table complained that he wasn't doing so well, Richard intoned, "You just got to know how to *dooo* the time. You just got to *dooo* the time."

If only I could have swapped my vanishing minutes for his superfluous hours and moved up his release date.

Later, when it became clear that his appeals would take years, I imagined his body calcifying within the walls, then freezing like a prehistoric bee perfectly preserved in amber. In a photo of us at the time, I'm smiling easily, lithe in a tight disco shirt seamlessly tucked into form-fitting white, flare-bottom jeans, long hair blowing off to the side as I lean gently against his shoulder. But Richard stands solid like a Stonehenge column, nondescript in basic prison blues; his arms extend stiffly like pistons by his sides. Dismayingly, Richard was actually losing fluidity, the careless, dancing, hand-flinging, skip-walking, okay-to-change-your-mind pirouette of the free. He moved more deliberately now, his turns slow like the rotation of an expanse of stone fence, as his eyes monitored every square inch of his surroundings for danger before fully committing to the turn.

So I moved at the speed of life of two people, nonsensically believing I could gather up a store of life equity that I'd transfer to him in our visits. I filled him up with stories of the interesting people I was meeting, like Harvey Milk, the gay organizer, and Margo St. James, the former hooker turned union organizer. I pestered him with my personal insights into the lives of Charles Garry and Mayor George Moscone and a meeting we had with the governor's chief of staff. I inserted him into the newest dance spots—the I-Beam, the Mind Shaft, and the City with its ceiling-high jukebox DJ booth—and described the latest dance craze. I detailed the décor of this or that new inexpensive restaurant or how Sai Yon's Duck Broth Yee Foo Wonton Soup was slipping in quality. I regaled him with stories of new girlfriends, what hot tubs felt like, and that strange mystical cowboy movie, *El Topo*, by the Chilean avant-garde, surrealist director Alejandro Jodorowsky, an erratic narrative of violence, resurrection, and strange allies all wrapped in Catholic symbolism and signifying a profundity that eluded the audience (which somehow befitted our situation). I drew him into the fun of our annual Lake Tahoe family vacation—which cousin learned to swim this year, how it differed from last year—hoping it would feel like he had been with us. On and on I would blather, like a desperate rescuer.

I even grew my hair outrageously long, because Richard couldn't. A full yard, falling to below my waist, way past the chic urban hippie's midback trim. Like the biblical Samson, I felt power in the fierce defiance of my unclipped locks. Later I discovered that ancient martial arts heroes grew their hair long, way below the waist.

Richard always listened respectfully to my "One Thousand and One Tales of San Franciscan Nights." He just kept reminding me that all he could do was "to dooo the time." But from time to time, an ephemeral smile disclosed his pleasure at a good story or showed that his spirits rose at the growing numbers of his supporters. I learned to spot, then listen for, these songs from his soul.

Was I trying to make up for not being there for him during the summer before his trial? There's truth in that too, but there must have been a moment when the scales evened up, when that debt—never articulated and perhaps only my burden—was completely discharged, including interest and administrative fees. Then, too, I realized that silence was a convict trait and learned not to overreact to it as a sign of trouble or of his losing all connection with the outside.

I relaxed more into Richard's silences as my storytelling mania eased off. I was there. He was there. He was safe. I was safe. That's what mattered now.

After the *Examiner*'s investigative series ran, Richard quietly dropped another piece of information. He had been assigned to an escalating series of favorable day jobs. This latest one, managing the guards' canteen, actually took him outside of the prison, away from the daily madness. It was against policy to trust a lifer so early into his sentence outside the fence. He'd bolt for freedom—who wouldn't when facing a choice of decades behind bars or the blue sky? Richard speculated that the guards wanted to "do right by me."

One vertebra at a time, I uncurled upright against the hard back of the visitor's chair, blinking rapidly, taking slow breaths as I sought to reconcile this with my attitude. Like the members of many other visitor families, I lumped the prison guards into the corrupt system that had put Richard away; they were the ones enforcing his odious imprisonment. Besides, most of the guards seemed dour to me, none particularly alert, fitting the stereotype of bureaucratic lifers whose physical fitness waned and waistlines broadened the closer they got to retirement.

But over time, I discerned that this nonchalant watchfulness was at the heart of their work. Watch and watch some more, day after day, whether anyone thought they noticed or not.

I did not doubt the stories of prison guards who routinely manipulated prison gangs, favored one faction over another, or abusively beat inmates, and then spitefully added more prison time for resisting. Richard himself complained of several particularly mean-spirited guards.

But at DVI, what I observed was that mostly they watched, interpreted, and meted out punishments and benefits based on what they saw. I came to conclude that most guards had heard it all, seen it all, and dealt with it all. In ways I initially loathed granting, I came to realize that many of the prison guards possessed a levelheaded wisdom about inmates—who could or couldn't do the time well—and about their families.

Well, something about our family must have touched their hardened hearts. Something about Richard must have affected their view of him. Perhaps it was the way he protected Chi-ko Wong or the way he forged the alliance with the Native Americans. Perhaps it was our clockwork regular visits and our penchant for being the first in line to sign up for our lavish family stay-overs. Perhaps all this and the *Examiner* made an impression. They couldn't grant Richard a new trial, but they would "do right" by him in other ways.

As hard as we worked on the outside to win his freedom, Richard had diligently and quietly worked from the inside to push past the walls of his imprisonment. He was taking care of himself in this strange reality for which nothing had prepared him. Just like Father when he came to America and like Mother too.

Richard wasn't just *doooing* the time anymore; he was transmuting it, creating freedom.

CHAPTER 35

DEAD STOP

We visited you more after you moved back to San Francisco for law school—to help Richard, you said. But not just for Richard, but so you could help other people too. I was proud of you, a poor boy smart enough to become a lawyer. I'm sure many rich kids couldn't do that.

After the Golden Dragon, everything was really tense in Chinatown. Everyone was angry, looking for someone to blame, to get back at. Grant Avenue emptied out as soon as night fell. Not just tourists, but the white customers who had kept Chinatown restaurants busy at night, until 3 a.m. and 4 a.m. on weekends. Kum Hon, Sai Yon, Woey Loey Guey, Jackson Café, and the Golden Dragon—all empty after dark now, the waiters just standing around now. Hundreds of thousands of dollars in lost business every month, said the Chinese newspapers.

With you speaking out against the Six Companies, police corruption, and how the tongs used young Chinese like tissue paper, I was worried they would blame you too, just like they blamed Richard. Someone might even kill you, I feared. You were back in the city—it would be easier than Berkeley! Then I heard rumors, and one day one of my Clan Sisters who ran a gambling parlor—the only woman in Chinatown to run a gambling parlor—came to me. She was close to the tong bosses. She talked in a general way, nothing specific. She said that times were dangerous, that it was a good time for critics of Chinatown to stop.

That's why I came by that day to visit you. It was in the afternoon, after school. Your father was working, so Bob drove all of us,

John, Ada, David, and Victor. We surprised you, since we didn't call first. We joined you on the floor, on those seagull print pillows, some pink and some blue, around the low Japanese table. You had some law books on the table and the earthenware Chinese liquor jug you drank water out of. Tap water, you said that you liked tap water. You asked if we wanted to stay for dinner.

"No need. I came by to talk to you about something very important. We will leave after that," I said.

You waited for me to speak. I asked you to stop. Stop everything you're doing involving Chinatown. Just stop.

At first you refused.

I said to stop working on Richard's case. You have done everything you could. No one could have done more for his brother. The court system doesn't care. We lost at every turn. You have sacrificed enough. Time to finish law school and find a job. Then pay off your school loans and make a living. Get married, have children.

When Richard is released, we will help him then. He's doing okay-okay now. Good boy. Nobody is harming him. Maybe it's better he's where he can't be killed.

I said to stop working with the street kids in the youth agency, that you've done enough for them too. Time for new people to do their part.

I said to stop criticizing the police, the gamblers, and the tongs. Chinatown is not going to change because of one person.

I said I have already lost one son to prison. I didn't want to lose you too.

Then you were quiet for a long time.

Then you said that my reasons made sense. You would stop. You would call everyone today and say the family had asked you to stop. That you could not refuse us.

CHAPTER 36

BLUES SPIRAL

Acquiescing to Mother's request wasn't natural. The afternoon visit had taken me by surprise. The kids looked at me with so much love in their eyes. Emotionally, Ada, David, and Victor were as much my kid brothers and sister as our own little John. I had long ago accepted Bob as a member of our family. They would really be devastated if . . . anyway, their love stopped me in my place. I could listen now, as I turned off the cruise control of my manic drive.

Mother spoke from a place of courage, clearheadedness, and respect for me as an individual. She spoke, as always, with love. Richard had the right to appeal the trial judge's denial of a new trial ad nauseum, but a favorable outcome was unlikely. Similarly, the compelling legal campaigns for other questionably incarcerated Chinatown youths had petered out. Expecting redress from the courts was a quixotic fantasy.

Mother's intervention was uncannily timely. I was feeling the futility, the fatigue, and the insanity of trying to turn around the San Francisco judiciary. Our family's scarce financial resources were depleted, and in squaring off against the dwindling legal options, we could not in good faith solicit more from our steadfast supporters. Soon I would be devoting months to preparing for the California bar examination, the toughest law-license exam in the nation. After that, I had to start repaying my student loans, a great portion of which had gone to cover Richard's appeals. The congenital perversity of Chinatown machinations was a dragon too savage to reason with, impossible to subjugate.

That was why I replied yes so readily that afternoon. In my

heart, I knew it was over, and in my spirit, I knew that nothing would change. On my own, I couldn't bring myself to quit. But in the presence of the kids and Bob, my word to Mother was like a sacred vow, one I could stick to.

Any relief I felt from this decision rapidly spiraled down into a new misery. I felt like a complete failure. We had lost. So much energy expended, day after day, year after year. So many people involved—priests, ministers, union leaders, undergraduates, politicians, community service directors, lawyers, and my classmates. So much money raised and gobbled up by the legal system—all a waste. They had gotten away with it. Richard, Joe Fong, and others were still in jail—and there wasn't anything we could do about it.

As for Chinatown? The FBI strike force caught only small fish, and the big fish swam away to play another day. The small fish were two lower-ranking policemen who pleaded guilty and then went mum about everyone else. One of them was a Chinatown old-timer, the beat cop who used to jangle doorknobs on Kearny Street when Richard and I were kids and who took time to play with us and gave us money for ice cream and chips. Our entire neighborhood knew him as Danny the Wop. If anyone in the police force could have named names, he was the one. But apparently he decided to stick to the old-timer code of silence: Don't rat on your friends and keep your trap shut.

Chinatown stayed aflame in the wake of the Golden Dragon massacre. Vengeance was in the air. Was I still a target even as I called it quits?

I focused on finishing my final year at Hastings law school— I was nowhere near my 3.9 grade point average of UC Berkeley. I spent most of my free time with Jacqueline, a modern dance performer with a ballet background and my live-in partner of two years, and her daughter, Caroline.

With the free-and-easy seventies disco lifestyle, how had I ended up with my own family? Very simply, Jacqueline and I had fallen in love. Still, so many men drew the line at becoming Daddy—and shockingly, many single mothers with children assented, shunting their children aside whenever the man graced her with his appearance. My friends skeptically wondered at my willingness to play the daddy young Caroline had never had, what with attending law school full-time, working on Richard's appeals, and co-organizing a controversial youth center. I was surprised too, but the decision had come so easily. I saw Caroline as a young, vivacious girl who had never had a daddy, who craved family. After all, there were no orphans in my mother's village, so how could there be in my life?

Like many dancers, Jacqueline worked a paying job, photographing tourists at San Francisco's finest hotel rooftop lounges. Many evenings, I ended up serving as den father to Caroline and a surprising number of twelve- and thirteen-year-old daughters (all white like Caroline), the sole offspring of single mothers, lending an ear to their teenage dramas of boyfriends, misunderstandings with other girls, homework, and peer pressure about sex and drugs. Yet this cobbled-together family was a tonic, the one place where I could drop the mental and emotional loads of the rest of my life.

But even this oasis was no longer off-limits. Strange unidentified men called our home and grilled Caroline and Jacqueline mercilessly about our living arrangement before we decided to hang up on such calls. That was extremely upsetting but still small potatoes compared to the media maelstrom following the Golden Dragon massacre, as my name surfaced more than once. This was the way the media logic worked: Richard was at DVI with Joe Fong. The executive director of the youth agency I helped to co-organize was a regular visitor of Joe Fong. Therefore, I was a member of the Joe Fong Gang. In the TV news-rating wars, Chinatown slayings were a long-running hit, precursors of today's reality TV drama series, and they had notably elevated drive-by shootings into the popular consciousness. New and surprising plot twists and turns developed week after week, with an ever-changing cast of characters as old players were killed. Each fresh murder spiked TV news ratings for days. It was pretty clear that breaking a Chinatown story first took precedence over reporting the story with accuracy and limiting damage to individuals.

One local network television affiliate was particularly unrestrained. Their stories openly connected me to the Golden Dragon massacre, an event I had no involvement in, no connection with, and no knowledge of, before or after, outside of what was generally reported in the news. Words hurt, but bullets killed, and their inflammatory newscasts virtually painted a bull's-eye on me with the subtitle "Shoot This Man." It wasn't hard to predict what would come next. The *Chronicle* would parrot the lead. Then Chinatown papers would reprint their articles as gospel truth. That last step was tantamount to my death warrant. Yeah, I was running scared for the first time in my life.

It took the intercession of James Brosnahan, a senior partner of a large downtown law firm and at that time the president of the San Francisco Bar Association, for the news directors of this number-one-in-the-ratings newscast to agree to establish some facts to support their assertions of my involvement before flinging my name into the public consciousness. Overnight, my name disappeared from the airwaves.

Was my life truly in danger? Yes, and that became clear one weeknight when I picked up Jacqueline at her workplace and drove us back home. During the half-block walk from my parked car to our Seventeenth Street flat in the Castro district, I noticed a late-model car full of young Chinese men parked across the street and facing our doorway. Their engine was running, although the car was legally parked against the curb. Several of them had longish hair, the kind of stylish *Superfly* hairstyles favored by many of the tong enforcers. Only tong enforcers could afford cherried out, souped-up muscle cars like Pontiac Trans Ams, Oldsmobile 442s, and Ford Mustangs.

In 1978, the Castro district was a pluralistic neighborhood of white Russians, Swedes, Italians, bohemians, hippies, and the first wave of gays moving in from all over America. Chinese Americans did not frequent the neighborhood. Moreover, our street was infrequently traveled, since it appeared to be little more than a driveway splitting off from the confusing intersection of Market and Castro streets. The presence of young Chinese men was always out of the ordinary and was glaringly so at this late weeknight hour.

I warned Jacqueline to move quickly away from me and into the house. I slowed my pace so that if they leapt out of the car firing at me, she would at least be out of the line of fire. The young men stared directly at me. Their car's interior light came on as they opened their doors, possibly readying themselves to spring out. "This is it, it's over," I thought.

But, weary from work, Jacqueline did not quicken her pace, and in the shadowy light of Seventeenth Street, it may have been hard to tell who I was. Or perhaps it was seeing me with a tall, attractive, elegant, blonde Caucasian woman that psychologically threw them off their game. Easy enough to kill Chinese Americans, and their instincts were honed to do that. But to kill a white person, even accidentally, was taboo. Easy enough to vanish within Chinatown, with its warren of busy streets that they knew intimately. But the Castro was an alien landscape. So they hesitated just long enough for us to get into the house safely.

I triple-locked the doors and rushed Jacqueline and Caroline to the back of the long apartment, advising them that if they heard any shooting, they should dash down the back stairs. At the insistence of friends, I had purchased a shotgun when I returned to San Francisco. While I abhor violence, a shotgun is a home defense weapon. Still, I had never fired it, believing the sight of one was sufficiently dissuasive. I took it down from the closet shelf where I had secreted it from Caroline, loaded a birdshot shell in the right barrel for a warning shot and a double-O shell in the left to take care of business. "I may go down, but I'm going to take some fools with me," I mumbled, echoing the slogan of Richard's Asian/Native American alliance. I returned to the front living room with the shotgun in one hand and a box of double-O shells in the other. Shutting off the lights, I crouched by a bay window, pushed it up slightly so I could stick the barrel out, cocked both barrels, and placed my finger on the two triggers.

Their car was still directly across the street, engine running. The young men, eyes squinting, peered toward my windows. They seemed to be debating. I stuck the shotgun barrel out the window, aimed it at them, and moved it around to make it gleam in the light of the overhead street lamp. They evidently saw the shotgun's shine, for the doors slammed loudly, the headlights flared up, and they rocketed up the steep Seventeenth Street grade. I slept that night on the living room sofa, the loaded shotgun next to me.

But Death's stalking did not end as even my dreams augured its inevitable appearance. One night, I had the most graphic nightmare of my life, so real that upon awakening I was unable to distinguish it from reality. In the dream, I was corralled by a group of young Chinese gunmen who fired point-blank into my body, their bullets tearing into me as I crumpled to the ground. My lungs gasped for air. I blacked out. My spirit left my body and watched from above as one young man bent over to discharge the coup de grâce—a bullet into my brain.

Then, just as suddenly, I was in the midst of a mysterious, metaphysical struggle. I was refusing to die. I slowly willed myself to come back to life. This wasn't about making deals with God, promising to live a new and different way if He would cut me this last piece of slack. No, this was a stubborn refusal to die, to be ignobly killed. I fought to live the rest of my life, and suddenly, like a film rolling backward, the steps of my slaying reversed themselves. When I was upright again, my breath returned, the holes in my body mended, and soon I was whole. The assassins had vanished too.

Bolting upright in bed, I was chilled, a rock of fear in my stomach, convinced that I had cheated death.

Had the encounter with the young Chinese men discombobulated me so much that their thwarted plans found their way into my dreams? Or was some deep place in me warning that the danger was still great, that death was on the rampage, and that only my deep love of life would keep me alive?

I didn't know during those dangerous days that this was the beginning of the end of an entire era for me, a macabre dance of death with an ending that went beyond Richard's case and Chinatown. Death, as it turned out, was indeed filling her dance card for a gruesome dance marathon.

On November 18, 1978, my Café Flores irregulars began hearing rumors about a mass suicide in Jonestown, Guyana, where more than one thousand members of San Francisco's utopian community, the People's Temple, had emigrated en masse. The news initially reported a mind-numbing hundred deaths by mass suicide and then quickly leapfrogged to an incomprehensible nine hundred–plus victims. There were rumors that Jonestown gunmen had murdered Bay Area congressman Leo Ryan and three journalists. Then this too was confirmed.

I remembered my dream. Death was indeed dancing and harvesting. But we were far from last call.

On November 27, 1978, a little more than a week after Jonestown, former city supervisor and ex–police officer Dan White assassinated Supervisor Harvey Milk and Mayor George Moscone. Supervisor Dianne Feinstein, later a California US senator, may also have been on his hit list but was out of her office that day.

Harvey, as we called Milk, had openly supported Richard's campaign for a new trial. Best known as an advocate for gay rights, Harvey was unlike many in the white gay community—he considered the gay rights struggle to be part of the overall fight against bigotry. That was how we met, as members of Citizens for

Justice, a coalition of African Americans, Chicanos, Asian Americans, gays, and women seeking to transform the city's criminal justice system.

At twenty-eight, I was their peer, in my own San Francisco–wide version of the Il Piccolo's band of activists. In our modern way, we were knitting a new "village" of sorts, united by our common experience of discrimination and our faith in change. In a sardonic nod to our mutual criminalization by San Francisco's finest, we coined an unofficial name, "Criminals for Justice." All in the group were equal, and no one was dominant. We spoke in round-and-round fashion as we began to piece together the patterns of police brutality, including the policy of transferring known "mad dogs"—sadistic police who beat people senseless—from district to district instead of firing them. We developed solutions to curb them and, ultimately, to change the police culture. Harvey was more than a celebrity: He was our friend, an indispensable voice in our circle.

In my already fragile state, Jonestown and the assassinations signified that it was time to move in another direction. The decade came to a personal close for me when singer Joan Baez summoned us to a healing concert, a novel idea for the times, at dusk on Christmas Eve 1978. Thousands flocked to Civic Center Plaza across from City Hall, the site of the assassinations. Joanie sang song after soothing song and together we sang "Amazing Grace" and held our candles high, signifying that our inner fires had not been extinguished by tragedy, but burned strong still. And then we drifted off into the night.

My own inner fire, though, didn't hold up. From that Christmas Eve until well into the Chinese New Year of 1979, my burnout spread throughout my mind and body like an illness. From Chinatown's civil rights summer of 1968 until its end, the decade had fed me, but ultimately it took more out of me than it provided. I could not imagine myself physically waking up to another day as an activist.

To be sure, both Chinatown and San Francisco were changing for the better.

But Richard continued to sit wrongfully in jail. All those larger changes, and my role in them, had the satisfaction of a Pyrrhic victory—they were great for society, but in the areas where my work was most personal, we had lost.

Or so I thought.

PART V

RENEWAL

(1979–1983)

CHAPTER 37

RAGE UNDER
A MOTHER'S GAZE

In those first few years in prison, Richard was angry and so distracted and confused that he barely followed our conversations. I suffered, oh how I suffered.

We couldn't really talk except during family stay-overs. Richard really enjoyed those—he was more himself then. He enjoyed chopping vegetables with me, slicing meat, and watching me cook. He always washed the dishes, more than he ever did at home. It was like he was making up to me in some way.

Those were the times when we talked—chopping, cooking, and cleaning up. I told him that what was done, was done. Whatever his mistakes were that put him into prison, they were the past. He had to look to the future when he got out. "You are young; your future is waiting for you when you come out," I said over and over.

Richard told me how violent the prison was. Every day some kind of fight. Every day someone hospitalized or killed. And so I drilled into him at every family visit: "Stay out of the fighting! Don't let anyone make you angry! Don't do anything bad, so they can't keep you in prison a day longer!" You know how I am, how I say the same things over and over to my children. Stay out of trouble! Just get through your day, day by day! Just stay out of the trouble!

Richard always said, "That's exactly what I'm doing, Mom. That's exactly what I'm doing."

Richard enjoyed playing with little John. John didn't even know he was inside a prison. Richard was gentle and patient, teaching

John this and that, like a big brother should. He was never strict with John. Richard even brought books into the stay-overs to teach John reading. I think he got those books from his friends inside, like from David Wong.

After a while, Richard was more at ease. He wasn't angry all the time. Not so confused. Just kind of relaxed, like he was used to everything now. Accepted what had happened. He was cooking for the guards then. After work, he spent time with David and Chi-ko, panfrying nighttime snacks of Ramen noodles, with Spam instead of Chinese barbecue pork, American vegetables from his job instead of bok choy, and oyster sauce from his Christmas package.

About that time, we went back one last time to that same stupid old judge, and he turned Richard down. Even after the newspaper stories!

Of course, I wish we could have won. Richard was still young. He could easily start his life all over again. He had stayed out of trouble in prison. Still a good boy, everybody could see that.

I had taken some pills during the first two years of Richard's jail time. Just a half a pill a day. Made me sleepy, dreamy, so I didn't think about Richard in jail. Still, after each family visit, I was sad for a week, thinking this and thinking that.

Then I noticed Richard was doing better in prison. First, he seemed strong, healthy, with an inner peace. Then the guards started treating him like they knew he was innocent, giving him special jobs outside the prison fence, cooking for them, many different tasks. But anyway, the main thing was Richard was okay-okay now. That was the most important thing to me.

That's when I told the doctor I was getting better. I stopped the pills.

Years later, they transferred Richard to a redwood forest camp. There was no fence, only tall trees, and the air was so fresh, you felt better breathing it. After a few months, Richard's face turned so much softer. He whistled when he walked. He greeted us with great big smiles. He hugged me for long times now. He would even drive off to a town for a couple of hours during our stay-overs. "Pick up supplies for the camp," he said. He took long walks with Father, John, and you, deep into the woods. As long as he got back by dinner, no one seemed to mind. I was never concerned that Richard would escape. He promised me he would be a good boy, and he was.

As for me, I enjoyed cooking Richard's favorite dishes—pan-fried Hong Kong–style sam see (triple meats) chow mein, with slices of pork, chicken, and beef combined with crunchy sprouts, sliced celery, and black mushrooms; homemade wonton soup with baby bok choy and thin-sliced oyster sauce beef; and whatever other dishes he wanted for dinner. Guards dropped in to eat, especially Sergeant Carpenter, who was so nice to us.

It was there that Richard and I made plans about his life back outside. I told him to look forward to marriage and kids. Getting a job and making money. What could be more wonderful than raising his own children? Richard agreed, said that was what he was going to do. He promised that when he got out, he was no longer going to get involved with foolishness. He was going to stay away from Chinatown.

I was happy again. There was going to be a happy ending to all this. My boy Richard was unharmed, in good health. His mind was fine, and he was young enough to start all over.

You know me, I kept saying these words over and over every time I saw him. You used to call it "bugging." But I tell you, that's what a mother must do. Oh, children hear you with their ears, but not all the way through into their stomach. That's how I get through to all my boys. I said to Richard over and over: family, marriage, children. Work and friends. All waiting for you when you come out. That's how I got through, all the way to Richard's stomach.

CHAPTER 38

ANGELS OF LIGHT AND SLAM DANCERS

I did not attend my law school graduation. My absence was an unobserved act of personal protest against the fact that, three years later, with a law degree in my hand, Richard was no closer to justice or freedom than he had been on the Saturday morning I sweated over the Law School Aptitude Test.

I was burned out, and, as it turned out, the adverse media coverage had curtailed once-accessible job options. Friends in government didn't relish taking on the political risk that later revelations about me, even speculative ones, might harm their careers. As for hanging out my own shingle, who would hire a lawyer who had pissed off the entire San Francisco judiciary and police?

I was down to two choices: Move to another city or into a new field free of local influences. I decided upon the latter, and with Hastings's core of international law courses in my résumé, plus my Chinese language skills, I searched for a job in international law and transactions. Bank of America took me on.

Standing on the lurching, overcrowded #8 Market Street bus on my way to my first day of work, I almost didn't make it. The downtown-bound bus crawled by a prophetlike man waving a large cardboard sign that read "Wage Slaves, Free Yourselves." Was the universe signaling me that this was a wrong turn? I had cut my long hair into a corporate style held in place with gel. I wore a fresh blue blazer with pressed gray slacks, a starched white shirt, and a Windsor-knotted red, white, and blue striped tie. Part of me suddenly wanted to exit and dump this costume. But no, I had made my choice, and I would stick to it stoically.

I worked enthusiastically that first year, even serving in the coveted position of chief assistant to an international bankwide task force of senior officers from every major division, including my hoped-for assignment, World Banking Division. I also bit my tongue so often at my colleagues' racist and sexist jokes that a groove must have formed on it. As a new hire, I had to pick my battles, and changing their mentality was a fight I could not even start. The burnout, thankfully, subsided; but during the second year, a funk slowly replaced it and then grew into a depression, all from my failure to free Richard.

Unlike my mother, I was not skilled in deflecting negative states of mind. I didn't know to whisper prayerful mantras of positive affirmations. Instead, a workaholic, I had buried my feelings in an overdrive of activity. The demands of Richard's case, college and law school, grassroots electoral politics, a youth agency, and my life with Jacqueline and her daughter had left me with no time to feel. Now, in my late twenties, free of even family demands since Jacqueline and I had parted ways, I settled into an undemanding nine-to-five job with lots more free time, and long-suppressed feelings lashed themselves into the unbattened-down spaces of my life. I was drowning in my own underground river of ten thousand sorrows.

I was perilously unaware of the corrosive effect of stored grief and trauma. A process called healing needed to take place. To everyone else, I must have looked great in my three-piece suits. My job sounded wonderful, and—look—there was my spanking-new law license on the wall. But inside I was sinking into a malaise where I often stopped caring about anything—romance, work, friends, causes, and then even my family. Live or die; at least death delivers finality's repose, I felt at times.

The only time I could admit this descent was when riding my Triumph motorcycle. It was an impulse buy. I needed some kind of triumph, even if only a brand name. The beauty of the bike—its clean lines, dusky red and blinding chrome, and its double pipes with weblike heat deflectors—offset my misanthropic self-loathing. The roar of its 650 cc engines and its sudden bursts and responsiveness re-endowed me with a sense of mastery over life. It sounds bullshit trite, but the bike and I truly became one that year. My legs existed only to carry and clamp my upper body onto that Triumph so I could begin living.

Riding became a daily choice between life and death. "Easy enough to mask suicide as an 'accident,' " I cynically considered as I ripped around the hostile San Francisco streets, racing against the vanishing point between packed lanes, popping my clutch into ephemeral openings like a drowning man chasing his own oxygen bubbles. I instinctively downshifted back from oblivious drivers a nanosecond before they merged into where I had just been. I shot through red lights during rush hour, roaring past wall-sized delivery trucks and startled pedestrians, jackrabbiting on and off the sidewalk as if it were another traffic lane. The crazier the moves, the deadlier the risks, the more alive I felt and the less I wanted to die. It finally dawned on me that I was consistently choosing to live.

The Triumph may have brought me back to life, but my healing began when I joined the Angels of Light Theater Company. Unconsciously searching for a new community, perhaps a Clan of some kind, I discovered that the Angels of Light captured the essential compassion of Mother's Toisan village.

On the surface, the Angels were like the bohemians in the movie musical *Moulin Rouge*, living for the flames of romance and the magic of theater. They were "gender benders" whose personas switched daily between male, female, and androgyne, and they dressed to the nines either way or in some clever cross-sexual farrago, betraying their genders only with their own voices. Mainly composed of gays, lesbians, and bisexuals, a few, like me, were strictly heterosexual. But with the Angels, sexual orientation didn't matter in the slightest, for at heart an Angel of Light was polymorphously sexual, alive in a constant state of revelry and lust for every person, detail, taste, and moment. Their company became like fresh air reviving my dying embers.

Their stage productions came into being through a series of unpaid sessions not unlike a speaking-round-and-round. Members freely contributed their own plot ideas, characters, songs, dances, and special effects; and other members took those suggestions and refined them, until, at the end, they had consensus on a script, the music, the choreography, and the sets.

Their resourcefulness inspired me, since I also was depleted of resources, patching together my new life. Every Angel's costume was created on a shoestring—items from secondhand clothing stores and other people's castoffs, all sewn together using one simple Singer machine. The majestic, mesmerizing, twelve- to fourteen-foot-high prosceniums and ever-changing scenery were constructed of discarded cardboard boxes held together by duct tape and propped up by scavenged two-by-fours. In my backstage role, I came to know the cardboard backsides of these lovingly painted and glittery panoramas of illusion—Scott Tissues, Post Grape Nuts Cereal, Tide, Colgate—that I lovingly reset performance after performance, night after night.

They split each weekend's profit regardless of star status. Just like Mother's village—share and share alike. At a mere five dollars, the ticket price was intentionally and outrageously low for the early 1970s. No one was ever turned away for lack of funds, and single mothers with children were admitted free, leading them to return weekend after weekend.

Mother was pleased that I had found such fine new friends. So one Chinese New Year, the core Angels trooped over to Chinatown for a special vegetarian Chinese New Year dinner at Mother's. They marveled at the celebratory colors of the shiny tangerines glistening with green leaves, the garish red and gold wall posters of millennia-old affirmations, and the red buds of spreading quince blossoms next to the family altar, as awed as if they had stumbled upon a secret civilization. They bowed to our ancestors, smoking incense sticks in hand. But most of all, these offspring of middle- and upper-class America loved the simple, utilitarian homeliness of Mother's housing project apartment, able to decode what many could not, an interior design language of ancient authenticity.

They gasped at each new dish—black mushrooms over mustard greens; Buddhist Lo Han jai; deep-fried mushroom puffs with crunchy celery in light soy sauce; tofu squares with lotus roots, bamboo shoots, and cashew nuts; and many more Toisanese treats—crunching away and gushing gratitude to Mother throughout the dinner. Mother and the Angels took to each other like long-lost kin.

In gratitude, they invited Mother and the kids as special guests to their greatest, most popular production, *Holy Cow!*, a spiritual immersion disguised as a musical. Many Angels had journeyed to India and steeped themselves in tales of the mythological pantheon of Hindu deities. Returning as adepts of Indian music, they composed an original score of traditional Hindi music fused with jazz, new wave, and Western classical music. Others, now masters of intricate Indian dances, wove their graceful, enchanting dancing into the drama.

Seated front and center, Mother, Bob, and the kids were thunderstruck, despite their lack of comprehension of most of the dialogue. In the play, the maharajah's evil advisor opened by announcing his presence with gunpowder explosions mere feet away from my family, who screamed with delight as stage lighting transformed the plumes of smoke into red, green, and gold columns that ascended fifty feet to the ceiling of the converted canning factory that was Theater Artaud. A glittering Chinese-style dragon swirled out and then broke apart into a chorus line of tap-dancing demons. The enchantress, the sinuous Robin, undulated in her yellow, skintight full-body leotard, a cobra closing in on her prey, hissing and softly singing her mesmerizing melody to the music of a solo instrumentalist.

After that night's final standing ovation, still dressed in their costumes, the core Angels filed out to greet Mother, paying homage to her own very special presence.

Watching *Holy Cow!* night after night from my vantage point as a backstage hand, I felt the play's magic wash away the sludge in my spirit, rejuvenate my innocence, and remind me of life's ten thousand joys. The story's ultimate triumph of good over evil, always and forever, resurrected my hope for Richard's freedom.

But the greatest Angel gift was their presence as fellow travelers into my shadow side. Each one of them not only openly lived their shadow, but imbued their *Holy Cow!* characters with it, expressing it fully onstage. Life's ugliness was normal, and they had full faith that always, always, the light side and good would prevail. Feeling safe to do so, I soon unleashed my shadow to run into the night with this parallel troupe, recast as the Demons of Darkness. I let loose my stored-up rage and unreleased frustration, transforming into a seething, don't-give-a-fuck, motorcycle-riding punk rock nightclubber, a full-on expression of my duct-taped, pine board–propped, cardboard-patched, dark side private persona.

I slam danced weekend after weekend. Slamming was therapy. Feel it. Live it. Express it. Get rid of it. I leaned against ceiling-high speakers, craving the booming rapid-fire bass and jarring harsh guitar runs that blasted through my body. Then I jumped onto the floor to slam again and again, way past last call, and then roared off to all-night parties. Like a wild pack of wolves, we ran until dawn. That year, the twenty-ninth of my life, I bled free the deepest-seated, evilest portion of my depression. When my nihilism disappeared, I sold my motorcycle for a sensible Honda Civic hatchback. I stopped slamming and joined a gym.

That was when my career at Bank of America took off. I was happy again. My parents and Bob were proud, dropping in to visit me in my high-rise, bay-view office. In the evenings, I tutored John, and on some weekends, he and the kid cousins slept over.

As chief legal officer and a vice president for one of Bank of America's international subsidiaries, I discovered that my multicultural personality helped me succeed in countries where my American colleagues had hit an impasse. My counterparts—whether Saudi Arabian, Yemeni, French, German, English, Venezuelan, Chilean, Argentinean, Singaporean, Japanese, or Chinese—detected my openness to them and my sincere interest in their culture.

I went against the faultfinding grain of my legal training, respectfully probing into the human reasons why a historically good customer would default. In doing so, I inadvertently created speaking-round-and-rounds. Once the other party recognized that I wasn't out to get him, but instead was seeking to work things out, he and his lawyer started to parcel out the important facts, express their most urgent concerns. We could then take turns suggesting solutions and fashion one together.

As it turned out, most defaults were necessitated by unanticipated business exigencies. Our financially troubled clients had treated our traveler's checks as a temporary loan until they got back on their feet. Just as my mother did not see little Le Wai, the coin-taker, as a thief, but understood his basic human goodness and his little-boy need, so did I search for the human necessity implicit in each situation. Just as Mother's village sought to work things out because of their we-are-all-in-this-together-like-it-or-not sensibility, I saw these hardworking businessmen as invaluable members of our global business community. In their gratitude, they always paid us back and ended up delivering ongoing profit to the bank—just like Le Wai had returned to Mother all the coins he had filched and much more, year after year.

The power of my improvised speaking-round-and-round was not hampered by differences in language. It seemed that if I could create the right atmosphere—a kind of vibration or spell of resolution—the process worked out in its own way. In one meeting in Paraguay, held entirely in Spanish—a language I did not understand—I was somehow able to interject timely comments in American, advancing the speaking to its resolution stage. Afterward, the other side remarked, incredulously, that I had followed along like a native speaker.

In Saudi Arabia, before a specially impaneled ministry of the Saudi Arabian Monetary Authority, I replicated the same process and reached an equally fair resolution, despite differences in language and the application of the mysterious Islamic Sharia legal system. I had uncovered the Sharia concept of the *Amana*—a concept not dissimilar to the Toisanese concept of a community trust, which depends upon trusting one another's word, honesty, and cooperation for communal survival. I reminded the ministers of the spirit of their Amana, which had its roots in an earlier, communally dependent time, when honor was honed by the barren, baking, and waterless desert of Saudi Arabia. I proved that the bank had honored its side of the Amana in all our dealings and relayed that we expected no less in return. They deliberated briefly and recognized our debt as a priority trust claim, positioning our debt ahead of even fully secured creditors. My own Toisanese Amana was rooted in the uncertain dictates of a different climate, but they could feel that I understood it deeply, as deeply as they did.

Yet, in cases of unapologetic downright fraud, I came down hard. A former governor of Zulia, the biggest state in Venezuela and its oil state, in his role as CEO of a major savings and loan, defrauded us of hundreds of thousands of dollars worth of Bank of America traveler's checks. His family then indulged themselves in a wild spending spree—with our traveler's checks—throughout the Caribbean and Europe while common Venezuelans suffered from downward spiraling cycles of currency devaluation. After a friendly, unproductive visit at his Maracaibo City headquarters, the defrauder informed my attorney that he personally would see to it that I would be shot if I ever set foot on Venezuelan soil again. After all, he mentioned casually to our attorney, the price of a hit was a mere thousand dollars in US funds. Presumably, he would pay the gunman with our stolen traveler's checks.

How could this gentleman have known that his arrogant corruption would steel me and that his death threat would rekindle in me a ruthlessness forged in Chinatown battles? I brought down the law as hard as it can be brought against an arrogant, corrupt, wealthy, elitist crook—one who robbed by the pen and then shielded himself behind his privilege and power. Early one morning, coordinating a number of attorneys retained in several countries, we simultaneously attached and froze all his bank accounts outside of Venezuela. Within a week, the "gentleman" paid in full.

University and law school had qualified me for a career in international banking, so my family's belief in the value of a college education was vindicated. But, fundamentally, my way of doing business was a reflection of Mother's character and the Toisanese way of living with others. In approaching any problem, I instinctively sought a common solution, engaging in a tai chi dance of harmonious balance in my relationships with all people, a skill my mother, by her example, had instilled in me. I applied the speaking-round-and-round of her Clan Sisterhood, assuming that people were honest, even if human enough to succumb to desperation.

One perk of my success was that I could peruse the morning newspapers over my first cup of office coffee while the sun rose slowly over the bay and warmed my quarters. One morning, a small article about a motorcycle fatality caught my eye. The previous afternoon, a young man had raced his Ninja motorcycle at speeds of up to 50 mph down the lurching obstacle course of Mission Street. Weaving in and out of traffic, he had roared down the narrow space next to parked cars. When he ran his final red light, he was struck broadside by a truck. The biker was DOA.

Once upon a time, that could have been me.

CHAPTER 39

QUILT

I've lived in the projects for over forty years now, you know. I never wanted to leave Chinatown. Your father, though, saw a chance to buy some flats in North Beach in the 1950s or 1960s—only fifteen thousand dollars way back then. Worth millions now, I am sure, with lots of rental income.

The newer immigrants think of Chinatown as a place for poor people. Leave as soon as you make some money, especially if you live in the Ping Yuen housing projects, is the new attitude. My brother Wah and my sister Tien bought a house together in the Sunset district. My sister Yoong has her apartment building on California Street. "First sister in America and still living in Chinatown, in a housing project, yet!" they say to me.

I say, "Where would you be if my husband and I hadn't sacrificed so much to get you here?" I know a lot of sisters who didn't care about their relatives stuck in China. They were having such a good time, they forgot about their family! Didn't even write letters! I didn't have to work so hard to send money home—and suffer when your father argued about every penny. I didn't have to make up stories to confuse him and sometimes take a beating. I didn't have to be so nice to Mr. Wong and Mr. Lee so they would like my sisters, thinking they must be like me, you know. Sometimes I get a little angry at their ingratitude. And they disrespect your father too. Your father and I had it the toughest, and but for us, my family would still be stuck in Hong Kong, in that overcrowded, crime-infested slum named So Uk Choon, with the squat toilet room that is also the shower and kitchen sink.

But thankfully there're a lot of us who don't feel we got stuck in Chinatown, especially those who came in the 1950s. Chinatown is our community, and everything we want is here. It's also pretty safe now, after the muggings and robberies of the 1980s. Especially with the new gates and guards that we won in our rent strike in 1980. My husband was one of the tenant leaders. You remember that, don't you? You had just become a lawyer, working for Bank of America. You advised the president of the tenants' union.

The Chong kids from Kearny Street—Jerry and Sonney—live in nice parts of Sacramento. Big shots now, I hear. Their sister, Maxine, has her own house in San Francisco. Yet, Mrs. Chong refused to move in with any one of them, even though she lives alone since her husband passed. She likes bumping into her friends, talking with the shop owners. And the old Wongs who lived across from us at Kearny Street—they never moved out either.

The best place is not always what looks good on the outside or where the most successful want to be, but a place where you feel good walking, where your friends are, where you can easily get everything you need to be happy. A place where life is.

Maybe Americans move so much because they want the new feeling. Yeah, I know—the new feeling is necessary. That's why I change the furniture every few years—new sofa, new stove, new table. I go to Levitz store—they always have good prices for solid furniture, and they deliver for free too. William just took me to Ikea—ooh yahh!—lots of good sofas, chairs, and kitchenware. Very cheap too! And the housing authority repaints the entire apartment every few years. Yeah, that's how I get the new feeling, like I'm in a new home, but without moving.

Besides, moving all the time makes you feel lost. Staying in one good place for a long time makes you happier, your family stronger, and a better life for everyone. Maybe in China our Clan stayed in one place for so long because we didn't have a choice. But it turned out for the better, to have a place you know you can always return to, be welcomed and remembered. To speak a language that is yours and to recognize each other by that tongue wherever you go. And if we bump into each other somewhere else in the world, to know we'll help one another out, sometimes a little bit, sometimes a lot.

That's the way it was back there. Poor, but always happy. Always busy, dawn to dusk. Always using your head, figuring out the next best way of doing the same old thing. I remember the rice paddies—so shiny and quiet in the morning. And the green vegetables—so beautiful when they grew, their leaves and blossoms spreading full. Makes me feel so good to remember those days. So much joy.

Richard in jail was my toughest time in America. William's friends helped out a lot, and I thought for a while that maybe we could even out the power, that perhaps common people could right wrong decisions in America. Maybe we might have, maybe we almost won. But as it turned out for Richard, all those friends weren't enough.

That's why I spent all my time thinking about our visits with Richard, planning our food, and sending the gift packages. I don't know much about officials, but I know about people, how to nurture them when they're unhappy or in trouble. That's the way it was in the village—attending to each other, keeping one another happy, no matter what. Richard's okay-okay now.

Maybe I stayed in Chinatown so long for this same reason, to recreate a way of life that I had left behind in China. Maybe I stayed in Chinatown because I don't know any better. But I cannot imagine living anywhere else, any other way.

CHAPTER 40

A PRIVATE VICTORY

I was not the only one wrestling with a shadow side.

During a 1983 visit, Richard casually dropped an amazing admission. I had driven up on a Sunday morning after a waterskiing party weekend at a friend's lakeside cabin on Clear Lake. Due to my slightly hungover state of mind and the long drive, the visit stayed low-key. Richard seemed somber himself, even mildly distracted. We spoke little, but we did not need to articulate our connection with each other. We were not only brothers, but also fellow warriors who had fought well in an unexpected war. Although we had lost and one of us was a prisoner, we had survived. Sitting across the picnic table, we leaned our backs against the wall, our legs stretched out along the length of the benches. Richard lit up a cigarette from time to time.

Then, as if talking about nothing, he recounted an incident at DVI from some years back. An inmate had violated Richard's honor. Under the rules of prison society, Richard had to retaliate or invite further victimization from one prison gang or another. Richard went so far as to hone a shank. He prepared to do "what a man has got to do."

Then a countervailing impulse surfaced. Richard felt the presence of all his supporters. One by one, he recited their names, those who believed in his innocence and those who knew he deserved a new and fair trial. He remembered those kind strangers who had actually visited him in prison. One by one, he recalled their faces, their words, and the sunlight that day.

He reflected on our family's years of sticking by him. Of

Mother cooking him feasts during family visits, mailing him money orders, and faithfully sending birthday and Christmas packages every year. Her unceasing and never-changing mantras of advice: "Stay out of trouble. Stay away from the violence. Don't do anything bad that will keep you in prison a day longer." And he remembered his promise to her: "That is what I'm doing, Mom."

He remembered Father's dismay, suffering, and shame at his own powerlessness. He thought of our little John and of how good it could be to be a big brother. He thought of me and the fact that I had set aside my own ambitions to champion his case.

A deep appreciation and an understanding that he had not been forgotten welled within him. Although he lived in the sticky, toxic, and lethal web of the Gladiator School, he could refuse to abide by all their rules. He slowly recovered the memory of his origins, that he was the son of brave Toisan refugees and immigrants who somehow persevered through all the unkindness, difficulties, and insults to provide him with a decent home, food, clothing, and time to study.

Any retributive action, however justified by the dictates of prison culture, would hurt the reputations of many kind strangers. Richard clutched at his membership in the community of San Francisco, especially of Chinatown, a home he would return to one day. In spite of everything, Toisan Chinese had forged a viable community—he still belonged to it. There his parents still lived, people spoke his first language, restaurants still served his favorite foods the old-fashioned way, and familiar streets waited for him to walk them once again in his freedom. So he would make peace with Chinatown too. His soul wrestled in this way for many days and many nights.

Richard slowly released himself from the wicked spell of the fatalistic prison code. He put down the shank once and for all. In peaceful ways, he worked things out. The grudge was settled, and the gangs left him alone.

I listened to Richard, but whether because of my own torpor or Richard's casual way of speaking, I did not register the significance of his words during the actual visit. It wasn't until I was about an hour into my four-hour drive home that the import of what Richard had said struck me fully.

Exactly like a lightning bolt.

Like the Cantonese martial arts heroes of our childhood Hong Kong movies and true to the ideals of the mythic Water Margin heroes—the vows of Chung Ching Yee, the fraternal values of loyalty, harmony, and righteousness—Richard had made a moral choice under the direst circumstances.

I quickly realized that Richard had reclaimed his own best self. As my wheels squealed around the tight curves of a rushing river that ran alongside the highway, a metaphor came to me of how well Richard had pressed through the treacherous whitewater of this internal moral passage, snatching the victory of staying human from its impossibly high drops and deepest whirlpools. I realized that the victory one seeks is not always the victory one needs. It could have felt so glorious to have won in court, and certainly it was a victory I had yearned to taste. But at that moment, I overflowed with the joy of this private, unglamorous, internal victory. I knew this was immensely truer and longer lasting.

We lost the legal case, but not Richard. Richard had triumphed.

In contrast, I thought of another DVI inmate, another highly publicized Chinatown frame-up from that era—someone who actually won his appellate battle against equally impossible odds by having two murder convictions reversed (the second one a prison slaying). But that inmate had been on his own too early and had apparently not had the same nurturing from childhood as Richard. Certainly there was no mother recreating a timeless family hearth in family visits, whispering affirmative mantras in his ear, reminding him to avoid trouble, and reassuring him that he was young enough still to make money, marry, and raise children. When released, that other young man eventually returned to a life of crime, became addicted to drugs, and was eventually incarcerated again.

That Richard wasn't similarly overcome—not even by that clear but mysterious provocation that led him to prepare to kill another—was a telltale and instructive distinction. That said a lot about how Mother had not only nourished him with Toisanese food, but also fortified his core Toisanese character with her repetitive affirmations.

At the moment of that realization, I recalled a similar moral decision of my own. Sometime in 1974, I collaborated with several others to organize a youth service agency that focused on hardcore street youth and younger youths at risk who had been turned away by other agencies. My role included counseling young adults who were capable of deadly violence, including a young man named Gerald.

Gerald stood apart from most of the youth we served. In his early twenties, he dressed stylishly, often in an expensive white linen suit. A twenty-two-carat gold chain and expensive jade amulet dangled over his taut, Bruce Lee build. "Provides protection against death," he explained. Once, Gerald dazzled us with a close-to-the-body, swirling, double-knife attack demonstration, efficiently stabbing at all the major organs of the body. Equally striking was that he refused use of the traditional twin knives, insisting instead on two common twelve-inch kitchen knives.

One day, Gerald confided his true identity to me. He was a highly trained killer and member of a secret criminal society based in New York's Chinatown. He had graduated from their deadly training academy, named *Hung Men* (Red Door). Hung Men's campus was discreetly nestled among the large private estates of upstate New York.

In Chinese organized crime, hung—the color red—symbolizes its dark side, the blood of violent death, not the invigorating lifeblood that marks Chinese New Year. *Hung Men* translated culturally into something like "the Gateway into the Arts of

Blood Violence." At Hung Men, Gerald had learned to clean, reassemble, and fire numerous handguns, submachine guns, and rifles. He was drilled until he could maximize the terror potential of each gun during a robbery or, alternatively, swiftly assassinate his target. He learned the craft of torturing people for information by striking at different parts of the body with his fists or with clubs, chains, metal pipes, blackjacks, or brass knuckles. He mastered his twelve-inch kitchen knives set at Hung Men.

After his training, Gerald worked as an enforcer and then as a commando-style armed robber. In the early 1970s, he was promoted to a heroin courier—he described to me the six-hour Toronto-to-Manhattan pipeline. In the morning, he'd fly to Toronto's Chinatown to pick up a well-wrapped packet of heroin. In the afternoon, he delivered this to his bosses in New York's Chinatown. The next morning, a courier walked the packet across Canal Street to Mafia contacts in Little Italy. By the morning of the third day, the heroin was cut and coursing through the arms of addicts in Harlem, the Lower East Side, and Brooklyn.

Gerald fled Manhattan's Chinatown because he had botched a job—or, as I speculated, robbed one of his own bosses. I knew Gerald hadn't originally come to us to turn his life around, although, as we discovered long after he left the agency, he did turn it around. But it was not our policy to turn away anyone who behaved within the four walls of the center and didn't otherwise deliver trouble to our doors.

It was Gerald's perverse way of expressing gratitude for whatever respite we provided him that prompted him to offer to assassinate Richard's trial judge. Perhaps he was also testing me to see if I was "for real," unlike so many other adults in his young life. Would I really walk this talk of peace, of working through the system, and actually refuse the easy way out? In truth, if a Gerald had made that same offer a year earlier, I am not sure that I could have refused. In the Bay Area of the 1970s, deadly violence against authority was not unthinkable. Nor did I lack malice toward that judge. If a ten-ton truck had hit him, I wouldn't have been heartbroken about it.

I had only to say yes, and our family would taste revenge. But like Richard, I passed my test, for I turned Gerald down.

By then, I knew that violence never resolved differences, but only caused more violence. The power of Mother's seasonal Chinese New Year practice of releasing the wrongs of the past year and forgiving those who have harmed you, thereby making room to let in the New Year's offerings, finally penetrated my skeptical Western upbringing. On that long afternoon drive home from my visit with Richard, it slowly dawned on me that, like Richard, I had not lost either—I had won. Our family had truly won, for we had our humanity.

In our localized version of an epic, archetypal struggle, the Lee family had won the deep, enduring victory. And Mother led the way during this most intimate of battles, these most private of victories. For over a millennium, like so many Toisan Chinese before us, we had sourced a sustenance that carried us through life's ten thousand sorrows. That power, as I discovered one special day in a small, humble village square, was the power of Toisan Chinese culture. The source was our relationship with our land; but for me, my mother was simultaneously the embodiment and holder of this legacy. It was she who transmitted it to me by living as completely as possible the Eighth Promise, the promise to live the compassionate path of her Toisanese lineage. By her example, Mother taught me the gift of forgiveness, that to hold on to hate and revenge damaged one and blocked the wonderful providence that patiently waits to enter our lives. Through our own ten thousand sorrows, Mother helped us to find our way back to the ten thousand joys. In this way, Mother fulfilled her Eighth Promise, the silent promise she had made to Grandmother Chun so many decades ago.

THE PRESENT

A MILLENNIAL CHINESE NEW YEAR IN TOISAN

That first visit to Toisan in 1983 turned out to be the keystone of a reintegration of self, the first physical experience of the land of my ancestors. Almost two decades later, I felt the urge to go again.

So in 2000, as a gift to myself, I decided to celebrate my fiftieth birthday, on January 16, in Toisan. I invited Mother to come and also to celebrate Chinese New Year there, as the first of the lunar calendar started around mid-January. It would also be the first year of the new millennium, and Suey Wan itself would be a thousand years old. My fiftieth birthday as compared to Suey Wan's one thousandth birthday. But in the Toisanese way, we don't celebrate individual birthdays, but rather a collective Clan birthday once a year, traditionally the seventh day of the Chinese New Year festival period. The reason is that we all always survive together or perish together, not individually. As the village makes it through another year, every villager simply adds one more year to his or her own life on that same collective birthday. So in 2000, I simultaneously turned fifty years old and, in a way, also one thousand years old.

It was not only my mother's and my first time traveling together to China, but my first Chinese New Year in China and my mother's first Chinese New Year season there since she had left in 1949. Traditionally, Chinese New Year is celebrated at home, and since America has been our home for half a century, Mother initially refused to leave until we had our New Year's dinners. But after reflection, she fashioned a flexible solution—an early, preemptive, but still heartfelt Chinese New Year's dinner, mere hours before our midnight flight.

We landed in Hong Kong at sunrise on Chinese New Year's Eve. A comfortable powerboat ferried us through the green waters, banks, and hills of the Pearl River delta to Toisan. The local bus dropped us off at our simple but clean hotel, located smack-dab in the middle of Hoisin's historic district. In 1983, my first time here, the historic district was the whole of Hoisin. In less than two decades, its population had soared from 30,000 to more than 300,000. Concentric circles of new residences, high-rises, and factories spiraled out for miles from the historic Hoisin district to form what was now a boomtown that manufactured fashionable athletic shoes, home entertainment systems, and brand-name clothes and housewares sold at Macy's, Target, and Wal-Mart.

I was grateful that someone had had the foresight to preserve this charming neighborhood of seventeenth- and eighteenth-century Western and Chinese buildings, with its captivating winding streets intended not for use by automobiles, but by pedestrians and horse-drawn wagons. Perhaps the magistrate-husband of Mother's adopted sister Kow Woon had established the special zoning before leaving for Canada? My nightly promenades through its quiet streets were unexpectedly reminiscent of my magical midnight sauntering through other historic districts, like the town of Aix-en-Provence in the south of France and the city of Oaxaca in southern Mexico.

That first night, Mother telephoned her Clan Sisters, and before long, our room was full of happy young women in their twenties and thirties. They lavished attention on Mother. And their infectious joy visibly transformed Mother into a younger woman herself, despite the jet lag and her years. Just another young girl yukking it up at a pajama party.

I could only share a hotel room with Mother for the first few nights, for her Clan Sisters dropped in continuously, at all hours. Then at 11:00 p.m. each and every night, the assembled Sisters descended to a restaurant conveniently located on the third floor of the hotel for its final seating, the *sell yeah* (traditional late-night cuisine).

This ornate, large restaurant belonged to a Clan Sister from Mother's own village. It specialized in completely fresh ingredients, cuisine a la Toisan, and thus was hugely popular throughout all three daily sittings. Dim sum started at 7 a.m. and ran until noon. Banquet-style dining began at 5 p.m., winding down around 9 p.m. And the late-night snack packed them in from 11 p.m. until the food ran out. We ate there a lot, in the mornings and then every evening at 11 p.m. The Sisterhood routinely monopolized tables at these late sell yeah snacks, gabbing for hours before returning to the room to continue their *ji-ji-jah-jah*ing.

There Mother held court until sleepy-eyed Sisters started to peel away home. One or two Clan Sisters always slept over, turning our room into a slumber party. They casually ducked under my mother's covers, some nestled into armchairs while dangling their pajama-clad legs over the armrest, and everyone drank hot tea and nibbled on dried fruits. They were blissfully oblivious to my male presence. One night, one of the Sisters even innocently tucked herself in next to me for her stay-over. Then and there, I decided it was high time to move into my own room if I were going to get any sleep or privacy for my writing.

I had expected the Clan Sisters to be Mother's age, but they were mostly in their twenties and thirties. These younger Clan Sisters treated Mother with the greatest reverence. Belying their youth, they behaved like they had known her for decades, sincerely delighting in her company. My mother, like her mother before her, had the reputation of being uniquely compassionate, one of a kind and first-class. Mother had quietly inherited her mother's mantle as the revered grand elder of this Clan Sisterhood.

During the day, the younger Sisters escorted Mother everywhere, affectionately holding her hands as we strolled through the old town, slicing through the thicker crowds of Chinese New Year. They protectively cradled her arms as we crossed streets filled with the chaotic traffic of bicycles, motorbikes, pedicabs, and autos that miraculously never hit anyone. The Sisters made dental appointments and restaurant reservations for her. They tracked the best prices and then bargained on her behalf. They arranged for cars to take us through the countryside to our ancestral village, all at their own expense.

One morning, Vee Son drove us out to Suey Wan for the traditional expression of gratitude to all our ancestors. The ritual recognized our connection to them, those who had worked hard and lived well so that we could be born into a loving family and a safe village. Kow Woon's fiery friend Hung, now retired from his postman job, opened up the doors. As the protector of the spirits of the house, he had the only set of keys. Vee Son set off a four-foot-long double line of red firecrackers before the entrance. Its ear-splitting bursts cleared the home of dead energy and unwanted spirits. Presumably, they also awakened the good spirits of the house to welcome us.

The house was musty from being shuttered. Hung's spirit fire–tending duties did not include cleaning or, for that matter, protecting the house from the elements. Water had leaked onto the upper floor. But as the sunlight streamed in and the breezes swirled through the rooms, the house seemed to refresh itself, to come alive once again as a home. With a few swipes of a wet cloth, we easily cleared the dust from the ancestral shrine and the dining table. Old plates, rice bowls, and chopsticks appeared from cupboards. We burned incense, and Mother and I bowed three times before our family hearth in acknowledgment of our connection to this village. We offered to our forebears chopped white boiled chicken; barbecued pork; libations of wine, water, and soda; and tangerines with stem and leaves still attached. Then, in that practical Toisan way, we took the food off the altar and made a Chinese New Year's meal of it.

Later, an endless procession of Chuns came by to welcome Mother, genuinely pleased to see her in her home once again.

After cleaning up some old rough-hewn shelves, I noticed something that I had somehow missed during my first visit in 1983. There, on the highest shelf of the family altar, discreetly tucked against the wall, was a simple, tiny statuette of Kuan Yin, the feminine Buddha of compassion. Mother confirmed that she had sat there for decades, even during my first visit in 1983. How had I missed her?

Like the Holy Mother Mary in Christianity, Kuan Yin aids the desperate and heals those in great pain. In Buddhist lore, Kuan Yin broke with the male patriarchs of the early Buddhist religion over their doctrinal viewpoint that only a man could attain enlightenment. Originally an androgyne, Kuan Yin transmuted herself fully into a woman, vowing that she would attain enlightenment in a woman's body—or not at all.

She attained her enlightenment and then, like the Buddha, recited the Bodhisattva vow that she would not leave this earthly plane until all beings were free of suffering and until each one in turn had attained their own enlightenment. She vowed to help all who called upon her in their suffering. Kuan Yin had always fueled our ancestral spirit fires. I knew that now. Remarkably, no other statues were displayed on our family shrine despite the hundreds of religious figurines from the colorful ecumenical Chinese pantheon of Buddhism, Taoism, Confucianism, and Sino-Christianity that are found in so many homes.

I reflected upon Grandmother Chun. I had not known her well. She lived only a few years in America before she passed. Low-key, loving, undemanding, and considerate, she always smiled, even as her grandbabies spilled goopy soups onto her lap. My strongest memory is of her sitting serenely in her armchair, wearing her traditional black cap with a jade amulet, as her grandchildren crawled all over her lap, shoulders, and arms, as if she were a climbing structure. She then resembled those porcelain statues found in so many Chinese homes, the cherubic, robed Buddha with children hanging all over him. I still knew so little about her, and so I began to ask.

Wherever I inquired about Grandmother Chun, backs straightened, voices leaped up a couple of octaves, and hands began to gesticulate wildly as the speakers sang her praises. It was like witnessing the start of a Holy Spirit possession.

"Oh, she was just the kindest woman. Never an unkind word. Never raised her voice. She was good to everybody. She helped everyone. You know, she took Kow Woon in and raised her as one of her own daughters."

"And your mother is just like her—a very good person."

To the villagers, the matrilineal compassion of the Eighth Promise had passed to Mother. The transmission was subtle—a quiet, living force. Yet this force had proved to be reliable, nurturing, and powerful in my life—and this is my true inheritance.

I arranged to spend a night in my mother's house. My next-door Auntie invited me to select my favorite vegetables from her garden patch. Along with the steaming plates of fresh organic vegetables, she served a hot soup, rice, and a young chicken slaughtered that afternoon for me. She left me with a thermos of hot water for instant coffee in the morning. I felt as precious as one of her sons.

Lying awake in the dark for hours, I reflected upon my one thousand years of forebears. I started feeling their presence, currents of energy that seemed strong, old, and yet very much alive. Presence after presence swirled and rolled in and out of that house. Eventually, I thought of Mother's father. He was a gambling man before the Japanese invasion. But he left for Burma during those destitute war years to work and send money home. One day, a Japanese Zero dropped a bomb directly on his busy laundry, killing him and all his workers. I wondered at his determination to stifle his wasteful habit and at his courageous journey to such a dangerous place to support his family. An inexorable and mighty love of family must have straightened him out to live up to his role as a vital link in its continuity. And although he died before I was born, I was grateful for his sacrifice. I also recognized that this grandfather was the source of Mother's canny gambling skill, which made the difference between whether or not we had new clothes, notebooks, and ballpoint pens for the school year.

I then thought of Mother's elder brother, a gentle scholar and beloved teacher of children, who died while under investigation by the victorious Communists. I felt his sensitive terror and his ultimate anxious desperation. I then felt his presence, in the very house from which he had jumped or, more likely, been pushed to his death, as if he had seated himself in the chair next to me. I became frightened in the presence of that gloomy spirit.

Then, when I remembered that I was in a house of the loving, protective presence of Kuan Yin, that Grandmother Chun herself was Kuan Yin personified, joy and well-being swept over me. I nestled in deeper under the dense cotton comforter and fell into a deep, satisfying sleep.

In the mid-1990s, after leaving a highly lucrative partnership, a relationship, and a materially opulent lifestyle in the old-wealth town of Hillsborough, south of San Francisco, I started meditating and formally studying Buddhism. I found that many of the ethical guidelines of Buddhism's fundamental eight-point path to living right—always speaking kindly, refraining from hurtful speech, acting from good intentions, considering the impact of your actions, applying the right effort and focus in your actions, and finding a way of making a living that did not hurt others—already had been modeled by Mother. Cogently, she long ago forgave the ones who had hurt her the most: the Japanese pilots and soldiers, the Communist investigators, the trial judge, the assistant district attorney, the police expert, May Tom the manipulated eyewitness, and the lying jailhouse snitch.

I learned that in Tibetan Buddhism, the most advanced students practice a metaphysical healing technique known as *tonglin*. Tonglin involves taking into one's body the physical disease, mental illness, or emotional suffering of another. That person is then healed, but the healer now holds the negativity and risks being sickened in turn. These skilled practitioners are able to transform this negativity into positive energy and put it back out into the world in its positive form. My mother, her mother before her, and the many matriarchs before them had all practiced tonglin. Tonglin was the same as the egg Mother rubbed on us to remove our pain. I understood now that her steady, silent mantra was her practice of transmuting those deep sufferings into positive energy.

In Toisan, tonglin and other well-known Buddhist practices of loving-kindness and forgiveness were implicit in daily village life. Yet at the Buddhist retreats I attended, these teachings were presented as something newly discovered and in a way that felt separate from our daily American lives. I realized that this was because my teachers were in the first major generation of American Buddhists—it would be some time before these teachings would be indistinguishable from their lifestyles. In contrast, Mother and our village have been living this way for countless generations, and through centuries of life's ten thousand joys and ten thousand sorrows, it had become second nature. Our Clan was incapable of extrapolating them as "teachings," separable from the rest of life. Kuan Yin's presence on my family's altar now seemed inevitable, so natural as to be unremarkable to anyone else but me.

So once again, I had tapped into the source of the energy I had encountered on my first visit here in 1983—the mother-root underneath the surface—alive, wise, and mysterious, constantly streaming her vitality to me through a hidden mesh of energy channels. She contained the presence of all my ancestors, the memory of all their stories, and the lessons of their triumphs and tragedies—the sum of their ten thousand joys and ten thousand sorrows. I was but one more shoot running off from this ancient, fecund, gargantuan mother plant. The most beautiful flowering of this Toisan mother-root is the compassion of Kuan Yin. I accepted that I contain all that is Toisan: the collective wisdom, the strength, and above all the compassion of all my ancestors. Like my mother and her mother before her, I have the potential to blossom into this full flower of compassion, season after season.

In 1983, I was not yet ready for this teaching. In 2001, at the age of fifty, I was finally prepared to see Kuan Yin's quiet, beaming face, her power in the heart of my family's life.

I was home. I was finally home.

We flew back to the United States a few days later, and I returned to my home in Berkeley, California. Here, in this land called America that was so strange to my mother when she arrived in 1950, I am, as usual, completely at ease. Curled up on an antique American mahogany bed under a warm goose-down comforter and covered by an American quilt, I sleep as deeply as I did on that recent night in our ancestral home. Months before the New Year's trip to the village with Mother, I had placed a small statuette of Kuan Yin on my fireplace mantel, presciently replicating the one on my family's ancestral hearth. Well, I am finally equally at home in America and in Toisan.

The power of Kuan Yin had been a millennium-long matrilineal transmission: through Grandmother Chun, directly to my mother, and then passed on to me. So I have come to recognize my mother as more than a good soul and an admirable woman. In truth, she has been and remains my greatest wisdom teacher.

I promised my mother and my Clan many things before I left. I completed them, one by one. Even though my husband could be difficult, he really was my partner. Without him, I could not have fulfilled the promises.

I fulfilled my first promise, to raise my children to be Chinese so they could one day return to their ancestral village. All my sons speak Chinese and are comfortable with Chinese ways. John and Richard speak mostly Cantonese, but William speaks the best Toisanese as well as some Cantonese and a little Mandarin. But my sons will not be returning to China. They are Americans; America is our home.

I fulfilled my second promise to my two sisters, to find suitable Chinese American husbands for them so they could come over. I've matched other Clan Sisters with husbands, and many of them live in America now.

I fulfilled my third promise and became an American citizen so I could sponsor the immigration of my mother, my brother, and his family over to America.

As for my fourth promise, to keep alive in my children the dream of a democratic Nationalist China, the dream of Sun Yat-sen—well, we observed every October 10 (the Nationalist Party Independence Day), welcomed Nationalist Party dignitaries of Taiwan whenever they came through Chinatown, sang the Nationalist anthem, and saluted the Nationalist flag at banquets. But according to my Clan Sisters who stayed and from what I have seen, the Communists did a pretty good job of making China safe and strong.

As for my fifth promise, to keep my children connected to the village, I faithfully wrote letters home and sent back baby and school pictures, and they're mounted in my old house. Since the 1990s, I've gone back regularly, mostly with John and once with William. Richard hasn't been back yet—too busy raising his two daughters. I hope one day soon Richard will make the time too.

The sixth promise was to keep the Clan Sisterhood traditions alive in America. When I first got here, I organized women from other villages, and together we helped make the soups for mothers and babies during birth time and organized the red egg parties. Over the years, our Toisan Sisterhood got larger, as more Toisanese women migrated over. We talked over family problems, just like in the old days. We lent each other money and babysat each other's children. We discussed items in the Chinese newspapers that affected our lives and voiced our concerns to the family associations when we could. We helped new Sisters get settled, attended family association events together, went to every restaurant's grand opening, and found good sales downtown. Many have passed on now, but we still get together to gossip over coffee and rolls, four-dollar lunch specials at Uncle's Restaurant, and dim sum. When someone new comes over from China, we still introduce them to everyone, let them know we're here to help them.

I fulfilled my seventh promise, to cook the energy soups for my family. I still make them for my sons. That's why they're so healthy. Everyone says they look ten or fifteen years younger than their age. William wants to learn how to make them. Easy to make, I say. Be sure to simmer any soup for at least three hours. I've been giving him herbs to practice with.

But most of all, my biggest promise—the Eighth Promise— was to raise my children the way my mother raised me, to teach them the Toisan ways. I've stuck with them through the worst times. Just raising them by myself was hard enough—they don't know how much work being a mother is. But when they got into trouble, oh, that was really hard. William in the hospital by himself. Later fighting the high school principal. Richard in jail for thirteen years from 1972 to 1985. John running here, running there like a sleepy, *lost chicken in the night. I've sat up late into the night until they each came home. I've been with them every step of the way. I've taught them to be nice to everyone, to help people they meet along the way, to not hold on to grudges or resentment at wrongdoing. That's the best way, cooperate and work together for the future.*

This doesn't mean you should be taken advantage of or that you shouldn't stand up for yourself. But you must try to work problems out in everyone's best interest whenever you can. My sons had to learn to let go of bad things. They know now that bad feelings can trap you by keeping you angry, so that you desire revenge and end up doing something to someone that makes them do something back to you. They know that life is too wonderful to waste this way. That's what we Toisanese believe, that letting go of the bad prepares a place to allow in the many joys in life: new friends, new travels, new fortunes, the next delicious restaurant, healthy and happy grandchildren, a nice, sunny drive over the mountains to Reno, and maybe win at Twenty-One Blackjack—the ten thousand joys just around the corner.

If I died and a supreme being granted me a choice to come back to this world or to stay in heaven, what would I decide? Oh, I'd come back—no question about it.

And oh, yes, of course, I would ask to live in America!

AN AMERICAN PROMISE

One recent winter afternoon, my mother paid me the highest compliment. "You cook just like a lady," she said in American. I was puzzled. It was a cold day for a visit, and so I had made her a simple cabbage soup. But, she said, this is a Ch'i soup. True, I had taken the time to use local ingredients, organic and freshly plucked from the soil: a head of Santa Rosa cabbage, several garden-grown carrots and tomatoes, a fat red onion, and two cloves of garlic with a chunk of home-baked, free-range turkey added to sweeten the soup. After I brought the soup to a boil, I had simmered it for three hours in the time-honored Toisan way of building the Ch'i fire. In that critical gourmand way of Toisanese Clan Sisters, Mother remarked on the comforting feeling of the soup's fire clearing her chest. She chuckled at its sweetness, its nutritiousness, asking whether I had used pork to give it such a wonderful body or herbs to make the fire.

No, I had not.

The secret to the Ch'i recipe was not exotic ingredients or ancient technique—the secret was one I had learned from my mother, the secret of the Eighth Promise. The most precious ingredient is compassion, that singular appreciation for each person, that ability to see the *Nue*—the child in each one—and thus, the desire to make them completely comfortable. I have no children. I am an American, not a citizen of China. But with this soup I make a promise to my own mother, an American Promise, to keep alive the ways of the Toisan even as I, like my father, continue to find my way on American soil.

For Toisan once was only a place, but now it is a state of being, an interior sensibility of home, no matter where I may reside in this world.